Should I Stay or Go?

Should I Stay or Go?

How Controlled Separation (CS) Can Save Your Marriage

Lee Raffel, M.S.W.

Foreword by Jean Houston, Ph.D.

CB
CONTEMPORARY BOOKS

Library of Congress Cataloging-in-Publication Data

Raffel, Lee.
    Should I stay or go? : how controlled separation (CS) can save your
marriage / Lee Raffel : foreword by Jean Houston.
       p.   cm.
    Includes bibliographical references and index.
    ISBN 0-8092-2997-8
      1. Marriage—Psychological aspects.   2. Marriage counseling.
3. Separated people.   4. Divorce counseling.   I. Title.
HQ734.R14   1998
306.81—dc21   98-16841
                                                     CIP

Cover design by Mary Lockwood
Cover image copyright © 1997 PhotoDisc, Inc.
Interior design by Scott Rattray
Interior illustration by Christian Collins

Published by Contemporary Books
A division of NTC/Contemporary Publishing Group, Inc.
4255 West Touhy Avenue, Lincolnwood (Chicago), Illinois 60646-1975 U.S.A.
Printed in the United States of America
International Standard Book Number: 0-8092-2997-8
98   99   00   01   02   03   mv   6   5   4   3   2   1

In memory of my son,
Donald Irving Bern,
for his ever-present guiding light;
and to Mark,
my devoted husband and best friend;
and to my daughters,
Holly and Laurel, and Mark's daughters, Cherie and Dawn.
Your loving presence has enriched my life.

Contents

Part III
Operating Instructions

Foreword

LEE RAFFEL IS the best friend of anyone caught in the throes of marital conflict. In this stirring and provocative yet pragmatic book, she has written a masterpiece of hope, a luminous guide through and beyond the quagmires of troubled marriage.

Should I Stay or Go? fills the neglected gap in the literature of marital relationships, dealing as it does with that tenuous, ambiguous area of marital separation. In a time of so much change and uncertainty, when eons-old expectations are crashing before and within our lives, nothing is more useful than a wise and compassionate guide to lead us to new ways of being in marriage and divorce. Every page of this important work is filled with innovative paths and potent suggestions that respond to the desperation that couples may feel in their marriage. Lee pulls no punches, has seen it all and then some, and offers trailblazing structures and doable guidelines that enrich the couple while encompassing most of the issues that inevitably arise.

I have had the joy and blessing of knowing Lee and her husband, Mark, since 1982 when they attended my seminar on "The Possible Human" at the Oasis Center in Chicago. Here was the possible couple—bright, merry, and very, very happy with life, with each other, and with all whom they met. They had a passion for ideas equal to the passion they felt for each other. And those who encountered them felt quickened in the meeting. Subsequently they both became serious students of my work and our friendship developed. Over the years, I have seen Lee and Mark continue to thrive as they did their "human homework" of personal and mutual growth and sought the essence of their own and each other's being.

Together they became artists of the possible, true partners in human excellence.

As can be gathered from the sprightly writing of this book, Lee is diamond-faceted. At my seminars I have seen her demonstrate the cakewalk on demand, become a brilliant stand-up comedian and mistress of ceremonies, and perform a powerful and poignant dance of life when her beloved son died. Then there was Lee the hardy and Homeric traveler as she sailed the isles of Greece, sending me poems and essays about this epic journey with its many trials and triumphs. Through all this and more, Lee's engaging smile, easy tears, enviable purpose, and practical self shone with the luster of one who never bores God!

The new millennium brings challenges unique to the experience of humankind. As divorce and its dilemmas batter both family and society, we have a deep need of those who bring relief and common sense to couples and children suffering the consequences of chaotic family life.

Lee has put it all together with keen insights about intimate relationships that clearly make this a must-read book for partners who have lost their way. This expertly conceived and much needed volume offers us possibilities for living in the light of wholesome, respectful, ever-evolving creative relationships.

Jean Houston

Preface

It is with heartfelt appreciation that I pay homage to my mentor and friend, Jean Houston (*A Passion for the Possible*), with whom I have trained for over 16 years. As I began to grasp and integrate her interpretation of the word *void*, with all its interweavings of complexity—order and chaos—I became convinced it is possible to move into the worst of the marital void to extract the good, the best life has to offer.

Dr. Houston's enlightened understanding of human growth and development in many cultures and many times and her extraordinary comprehension of whole systems transformation and self-transformation have opened vistas of personal and professional insights—a spiritual gifting.

It was years of frustration, of feeling helpless in not being able to instruct and guide my client-couples through their tempestuous ambivalence and futile separations, that prompted me to search for a better solution.

With Dr. Houston's inspiring words resounding in my head like a mantra, "Hold to the vision and you can make the impossible possible," I found a way—the Controlled Separation (CS), replete with 12 guidelines—for couples on the cusp to risk journeying into their abyss. In so doing, many troubled partners found an oasis in the middle of their marital desert and reaped seemingly impossible rewards. It was the restoration of their integrity, once given the explicit time to search their souls, that made it possible for these mates to make a sane marriage-versus-divorce decision.

When I initially began my research for this book, I expected to find a host of references on the creative implementation of a pragmatic separation. Much to my surprise, I found only four obscure professional articles, one unpublished paper, and two clinical commentaries, all by enlightened professionals who were ahead of their time.

Professor Donald K. Granvold writes, "For the marital and family therapist there is but an embryonic body of knowledge upon which to draw in implementing a marital separation and counseling the couple while separated."[1]

I owe a debt of gratitude to the following professionals who have validated my concept of the CS method:

Marjorie Kawin Toomin, who breathed vitality and life into what she referred to as a "fourth alternative: a moderately structured, time-limited period of separation with counseling."[2]

The team of Bernard L. Greene, Ronald R. Lee, and Noel Lustig, who sanctioned "transient structured distance" as a worthy option rather than staying miserably stuck.[3]

Donald K. Granvold and Roxanne Tarrant, who spoke of a structured marital separation, elaborating on the possibilities and benefits of making personal changes in the course of making a decision.[4] In a follow-up article, Granvold presented a simplified version of a structured separation contract.[5]

Richard B. Stuart, who reviewed the advantages of such a strategy for ambivalent couples;[6] likewise, David G. Rice and Joy K. Rice indicated that this method could give partners a sense of choice about the direction of their lives.[7]

Overall, I perceive the vestiges of marriage, separation, and divorce with all their disparate parts embodied within a whole system—a gestalt—of interconnected life transitions and changes.

To bring my understanding of marital separation to you with its many faces, profiles, voices, hats, and spats is a fulfilling mission. I hope this book will open the door to many new awakenings, the resolution of your marital impasse, and the realization of your own personal transformation, hopes, and dreams.

Part I
Breaking the Marital Impasse

1

Couples on the Cusp

Being Stuck

IT'S NOT A question of the zip being gone from your marriage. You can't stand your marriage. The thought of being stuck in this relationship for the rest of your life is more than you can bear, but the thought of an ugly divorce is even worse. You feel trapped.

Sleep brings dreams of being chased, as though you are running and getting nowhere. You're paralyzed. Your wishes feel much like your dreams—intangible but loaded with possibilities. Can your marriage be saved, can you right the wrongs, can you escape the fracas and save face?

"I wish I knew if our marriage was worth saving."

"I wish my spouse would agree to counseling."

"I wish I could separate for a while—maybe that would do me some good."

"I wish my children could be spared this trauma."

"I wish I weren't so undecided—this is the pits."

"I wish I could feel free again without having to go through an ugly divorce."

"I wish I knew what was normal so I wouldn't feel so crazy."
"I wish I knew whether to stay or to go."
"I wish I didn't have to face this question at all."

If you find yourself wishing for an end to this indecision, you are in good company. Judging from current divorce rates, half of all first marriages terminate in divorce and 60 percent of second marriages fail. The recently married—five years or less—fare the worst. They have a whopping 67 percent divorce rate.[1] When you keep in mind that many additional couples separate one or more times, it is evident that at one time or another a vast number of spouses question the validity and reliability of their partnerships.

"Should I stay or go?" is not a tidy topic. So momentous a decision affects every aspect of your life: children, family, friends, house, money, job, religious teachings, and values. Your life is "on hold." Your doubts are loaded with unfinished business and toxic waste—you are swamped with guilt, revenge, remorse, regrets. Disillusioned, you feel powerless and out of control. The enormity of it all tears your insides apart.

My Story

I am reminded of my own mother, who died of a broken heart rather than get a divorce. She trained me well. For 26 years I, too, saw no way to open the door to divorce, although I secretly ached to be released from the oppressive bondage of my own bad marriage.

I began to fantasize about romance and a healthier relationship, but the question "Should I stay or go?" could not even be formulated in my mind, much less spoken aloud. So I lived with a nameless, shadowy discontent.

I turned the other cheek and looked the other way. Played hide-and-seek with my feelings. Cried a lot when I was mad and laughed a lot to push the sadness away. My "stay put" script worked fairly well for many years: be grateful for what you have in life and don't complain about what you don't have.

It took a crisis of catastrophic proportions before a new direction was made clear to me. And it has taken a good second marriage for me to gain sufficient insights to be able to help others. I'll be sharing more of my story in the chapters ahead, as well as the stories of numerous couples who have come to me for professional marriage counseling over the past 25 years.

Distractions Don't Work

If you are struggling with these same issues, you know that distractions don't work. You try to put the whole issue aside by diverting your attention to other matters—cleaning the garage, caretaking your elderly parent, improving your golf game, going on a diet. For a time, immersing yourself in talk radio or soap operas fools you into believing that if things are so much worse for other families, your situation isn't so bad after all.

Any distraction offers a good reason not to think, much less come up with an answer. It is easier to go on hoping that your ambivalence and confusion will somehow resolve themselves in time.

But you are tricked. It doesn't happen that way. The question "Should I stay or go?" hangs suspended. You vacillate. You fret. You hurt. You're scared.

Maybe you are still living with your spouse; maybe you are separated. You might have already experienced a trial separation—once, or twice—but it didn't work. Maybe you are in a second or third marriage and dread what feels like another "failure."

Perhaps you have consulted a divorce lawyer but can't bring yourself to file the papers. Or maybe you've filed, but nothing is final . . . not yet. There is always the chance of something happening to make reconciliation possible. And the question keeps coming back, the dilemma keeps growing. You are at an impasse. Stuck. On the cusp.

Trying Hard and Fearing Failure

On your wedding day you made a commitment—a sacred promise to yourself and your mate to stay together no matter what. Now you aren't sure you can—or should—keep that commitment. Or you may be absolutely sure of your commitment to the marriage but not at all sure what your spouse wants. Whether this is your first marriage or not, the fear of failure makes your decision even harder. It seems there are no options between the finality of divorce and the living hell of an unhappy marriage.

You vowed it would never happen to you. But it has. You don't want to keep punishing yourself or your spouse. True, you are hurting, but you simply aren't ready to fight the legal battles and experience the whole disruption that answering the question "stay or go?" demands of you.

If you've been keeping all your feelings to yourself, your mate notices that you are "not acting like yourself." You lie and say, "I'm really OK." But you know you aren't. Your spouse knows it, too.

If you are a very private person, you probably haven't talked about your problems—with anyone. No one knows what's going on in your household, and you are proud of being able to keep it that way. You wouldn't dream of hanging your dirty laundry on the line for all the world to see. Even if you were to talk to someone, you are sure no one else could know your anguish and understand your pain. Your troubles remain inside, where uncertainty and worry are eating you alive.

Talking to family or friends raises other problems. You get such conflicting advice.

- "Get rid of her . . . she's no good. Never thought you two were meant for each other. I left and it's the best thing I've ever done."

- "Don't be silly. He pays the bills, you have such lovely children, and you just bought that beautiful home. What happened? Why are you thinking this way?"

You tried to placate your mate but that didn't work. You tried confrontation but you are arguing more now than ever—or not talking at all. Both of you are miserable. You tried marriage therapy, individual counseling, or both, and nothing changed. Or maybe your mate refused professional help.

Talking to a minister or counselor gets you more advice—or no advice at all—as the ball is thrown back to you: "What do you really want to do?"

If you knew that, you wouldn't be seeking outside counsel.

You tell yourself you should have the answer and mentally punish yourself because you don't. More pain.

Normalizing Your Crisis

As a marriage and family therapist, I often hear people in marital crisis say, "I feel so stupid. I don't know why I can't figure this whole thing out."

Being indecisive doesn't feel normal. You see yourself as inadequate, and that heaps humiliation on top of all the other angst.

Let me assure you that what you are going through in your situation is normal. Most people have an extremely hard time with such decisions. The stress component is immense. Even if you possess very effective decision-making skills and use them successfully in business, they may not work well in this highly personal, everything's-at-stake crisis. You are too close to the situation, too emotionally involved. You probably don't even have all the information you need to consider all your options.

Safety or Risk?

This is no time for gambling, for making a decision by a toss of the coin. Too much is at stake. This could be the most important decision of your life. You don't want to make a snap decision, yet nothing is preparing you to make a sane decision.

So you stay caught on the cusp. But doing nothing is also a choice—one that imprisons you in the purgatory of uncertainty.

Since 1972, when I began working with couples, I have seen the devastation spouses have caused in vain attempts to reach a workable decision. I've seen how spouses sometimes beat one another up—psychologically as well as physically—seeking revenge, seemingly hell-bent on a collision course that leads them to even more disasters.

I've witnessed the futility of trial separations and observed the havoc caused when mates vacillate and change their minds from one week to the next. They teeter. They waffle. They do the on-again, off-again waltz. Decisions, when ultimately made, are based on whim, conjecture, inadequate communication, or lack of vital information. As bitterness, rudeness, and crudeness prevail, the marriage deteriorates, and couples and children become worse off than ever. These marriages are "in the pits," and the pits keep getting dug deeper.

Yearning for More

We live in a fluid world of beginnings and endings, of twisted lives, of condemnation, penitence, and rebirth. We struggle to keep pace with the shifting shape of complex institutions such as the family. Marriage isn't what it used to be in the "good old days." Today, mothers abandon their children and fathers are left to rear the kids, embittered mates find the single life as torturous as if they had never left it, spouses remarry again and again and never learn any lessons from their mistakes, and others are transfixed in their marital union but still wage war with self and each other. All tell us of lives in turmoil and transition.

My Therapeutic Philosophy

When I wear my marriage therapist hat, my goal is to do more than just "save" the coupling. I see myself inspiring mates to achieve a genuinely good, functioning relationship that makes each party proud. If I were not in a second marriage that enables and encourages me to go about my tasks with joy, with high energy, in a loving and stimulating environment, I wouldn't be writing this book at all. Creating a good marriage with my second husband, Mark, achieving a partnership of equals, replete with all the ups and downs that life sends our way, has convinced me that you can do it, too, if you and your mate give yourselves half a chance.

However, I am equally convinced that when a couple's differences are irreconcilable and divorce is inevitable, I can put on my divorce therapist hat and assist the parties in finding viable ways to mediate and mend their relationship sufficiently to achieve a good divorce. And this means the parties not only save themselves, but they also spare their children and loved ones needless anguish.

I believe partners are not failures because their marriages have failed. From my vantage point, divorce can be as liberating for one person as a revitalized marriage can be for another.

A Breakthrough Solution

Let us say that you know you do not want to abandon your partnership but would rather repair your coupling. Let us say your spouse is sitting on the fence, and both of you are waiting to see what happens next. Or you want to separate without making matters worse, without becoming bitter enemies. How is it possible to profit through a transition?

In the early years of my professional life, I grew restless watching my clients make mincemeat of their coupling, particularly when they were ensnared in a wretched trial separation that was taking them nowhere. It wasn't easy to watch spouses lose their dignity, sorely disrupt their children's lives, and destroy the last salvageable shreds of their relationships.

As these hapless mates experimented with trial separation, I would often suggest they establish a reasonable time frame, say four to six months. But without a bonafide plan to offer, my counsel, inevitably, was all too easy to ignore. From my vantage point, this was no time to be trifling with solutions, yet that is exactly what was happening. Here were my clients, sitting on the fence, not knowing where their separation was going. The couple's chaos was exacerbating their calamity, and indecision about whether to stay or go was making them physically and emotionally ill.

Then, in the mid-eighties, one desperate couple, Jill and Jim, challenged me to "do something." Each partner was stuck and feeling out of control. Their previous trial separations had failed, and their relationship was deteriorating. Jill wanted to separate, Jim was worrying about a possible divorce, but neither party would sit still for marital therapy. As they pleaded for some kind of help, I took their challenge literally.

In a flash of insight I visualized a bold experiment: a separation, but with a radical difference, not at all like a trial separation. This one would require a structure with guidelines spelled out to reduce much of the guesswork. This structured separation would help each partner gain a fresh perspective on his and her marital impasse. Here was a means for Jill and Jim to take charge and regain control of themselves and their lives.

I wanted this method to be substantial enough to entice the couple, capture their imagination, and get them energetically involved in working together as a team instead of pulling apart.

This proactive plan I called a Controlled Separation (CS). In brief it is defined as a couple-guided or therapist-guided, time-limited separation, replete with 12 guidelines, structured for the purpose of constructively breaking the marital impasse and allowing for a sane decision whether to stay or go.

The 12 Basic CS Guidelines

The CS Guidelines help you eliminate the stumbling blocks inherent in marital separation. These pragmatic points show couples on the cusp how to liberate themselves humanely from their stuckness and reestablish order in their daily lives. The structure in brief includes the following items:

1. Time limits—set a time frame of one to six months.

2. Legal counsel—neither partner files for divorce during the specified time frame.

3. Moving out—decide which party goes, which one stays.

4. Division of home furnishings—possessions should be fairly distributed.

5. Finances—terms are to be just.

6. Children—their welfare is primary.

7. Couple's continuing relationship—determine whether and when to see each other.

8. Dating others—this needs to be spelled out.

9. Confidentiality—decide what is said and to whom.

10. Teamwork and homework—this is a joint venture.

11. CS Contract—this should preferably be written.

12. Renegotiation—provide for adjustment to the contract.

When you and your mate come to an agreement on these 12 basic issues, you will have negotiated a workable separation that enables you to break your marital impasse and make a sane marriage-versus-divorce decision.

CS: A Call for Action

The CS acts as a catalyst—a call for action that puts the focus on your concern for your troubled marriage. As one woman said of her 25-year union, "I must confess we live in the same house, but the wall between us feels like we are already separated. It's time we do something about this."

The CS Guidelines generate a renewal of energy that has lain dormant, possibly for years. As mates join together to address their stalemate, they begin the process of productively breaking their marital impasse. Partners now have the advantage of seeing a vast array of options that were out of sight before, and herein lies the possibility of healing gaping wounds.

A Plea for Prevention

In working with separated, divorced, or remarried parties, I often hear people comment:

- "My husband and I just needed a little direction . . . we were so lost, it was pathetic."

- "I'm sure we could have done something like a CS so we wouldn't have botched our separation like we did."

- "Oh, I wish I had known about a CS and your other solutions to fix our relationship."

- "Where were you when I needed you the most? Our divorce tore our family apart."

I assume that you, like my clients, are not going to be satisfied with superficial solutions. Although your concerns are many, I am aware that two basic issues of prevention are the bottom line for couples on the cusp:

1. If your marriage survives, you do not want to keep making the same relationship mistakes over and over again.

2. If your marriage dissolves, you do not want to be involved in an "ugly" divorce.

CS: A Paradox

The CS is a paradox: a single solution that enables partners to achieve one of two diametrically opposed outcomes. This method paves the way for couples on the cusp to break their marital impasse with their dignity intact. As you band together rather than pull apart, the CS gives you an opportunity to escape the adversarial trap and join forces to become advocates for one another. In this way your marital impasse can become a lesson in renewal rather than a lesson in futility.

The Wisdom of CS

The CS is a multifaceted plan that promptly opens the door to frank discussions that set the stage for sane decision making. The following admissions get you moving:

1. Admit your relationship has reached a crisis and is teetering on the brink of disintegration.

2. Agree to slow down the decision-making process and concede that certain issues of contention have gotten out of hand.

3. Acknowledge that neither party can rescue the marital relationship single-handedly.

4. Agree that more can be achieved if you and your mate band together as advocates—as a team—to resolve your marital stalemate.

Like a breath of fresh air, your CS presents you with a valid means for slowing down the decision-making process. It allows you to take time to reflect on the nature of your marital stalemate without having the menacing threat of divorce hanging over your head.

If you thought your marriage was all but "dead in the water," the CS gives you a chance to recover your voice of reason and get closure on your marital standoff with fewer regrets.

I've witnessed many couples in the most undoable relationships stay with the CS, tap into their own inner resources, and make wise choices. You and your spouse have the same opportunity to learn how to negotiate as teammates on equal terms. As you reclaim your sanity, you make satisfactory decisions that leave you feeling whole.

Whether you revitalize your marriage as sweethearts or make yours a friendly divorce, the CS provides a reasonable plan whereby you put your life back in order and regain control. I believe such momentous possibilities are something to shout about!

How to Use This Book

My intent is to take you on a journey that includes a comprehensive overview of the intricate dimensions of marital separation, from its inception—which may be only a fleeting thought—to physical separation in all its complexities.

Keep an open mind. The very act of reading will give you time to think. Whether you are sharing this book with your spouse or reading alone—perhaps without your mate's knowledge—you should be able to assess your marital predicament more confidently and accurately, thus enabling you to act with greater conviction.

This book is complete with operating instructions, checklists, charts, and directives that point the way to achieving positive results. Even if you decide not to take any action at this time, you'll find new information here to enlighten your perspective and lighten your load.

Show and Tell

Although the CS is the cornerstone of this book, it is the "show and tell," the couples' tales and vignettes, that best reveals the inner workings of the CS. The tales are the "show" illustrating how many different couples in crisis resolved their impasses. Here we see how these mates learned to deal with conflicts relating to intimacy, parenting, money, abuse, affairs, identity crises, secrets, betrayals, rage, blame, revenge, communication, compassion, and forgiving.

The "tell" is my explanation of how couples in transition matured and transformed their lives. For the most part, these results came as a welcome relief for them and for me.

Several new concepts are introduced in the chapters that follow: "imaginitis," "bedroom antics," "double-duty anger," "couple advocacy," "active waiting," "passive waiting," "elusive intimacy," and "invested intimacy." These ideas can enhance your understanding of the central issues that couples on the cusp are apt to face.

The tales and vignettes are taken from my case files; names and identifying details have been changed to safeguard the couples' identities.

Collaboration with Client-Couples

This book could not have been written without the collaboration of my client-couples, who shared their heartaches and headaches and their hopes and dreams of coping with the "stay or go" dilemma. We shared ideas, we hugged for encouragement, and we prayed together. For their accomplishments and my own professional growth, I am forever grateful. Without my client-couples' input this book could not have come to fruition.

Your Options

There are several ways for you to use the methods described in this book. You can make this either a "do-it-ourselves" or a therapist-guided journey of discovery. If you and your partner are ready to work together as advocates, you will discover what pitfalls to avoid and learn many techniques for enhancing your relationship and improving your communication skills.

Let's Begin

The bus is ready and you have your travel guide in hand. As you and your partner become more familiar with the route, you will each learn to recognize how and when you reach a new crossroads. Rather than being unsure of which way to turn, you'll be better able to anticipate which paths are less treacherous than others. As you eliminate much of the guesswork, you will be prepared to reach your own best destination sensibly and with greater insight.

Whether your destination preserves your marriage or reveals a different path, the nagging questions and painful indecision will be gone, and you will have saved your sanity. You will know that both you and your spouse did your best. That knowledge saves you from agonizing over whether things might have turned out differently if you had tried just one more time.

There are no easy answers, but there is an answer that's right for you.

2

$\mathcal{Y}$our Travel Guide to Becoming Advocates

How to Interpret CS

THE IDEA OF marital separation—living apart—looms as an evil force, boding the unimaginable worst for many married folks. When I mention Controlled Separation (CS) to clients, at least one-third of them misinterpret and don't even want to know what I'm talking about.

Some mates assume separation means divorce, and they jump to the conclusion they should give up on their marriage altogether. Some upbraid me for intimating they hadn't tried hard enough to save their relationship. And a few totally misunderstand and think I'm suggesting we talk about divorce.

Paradoxically, these strong reactions are just what I am seeking by introducing the CS Guidelines, *a powerful impetus for partners to rethink their options and get one another moving*. By a twist of irony, these same partners will usually settle down when I offer them an alternative way to salvage their marital wreckage. People like the idea of saving face.

The Controlled Separation Journey

Generally, partners approach their CS journey with a built-in understanding that this is their last-ditch effort to make or break their marriage. Physical separation is necessary for the CS plan to be effective, whether it be within the home or in separate dwellings. Once removed from your familiar environment, you have space and time to clear your head. As you become familiar with the CS Guidelines, you settle down, get organized, and start thinking about where you are going and what you and your partner want to accomplish.

CS Guidelines Fill a Void

In 1986, Diane Vaughan noted the need for separation guidelines in her book, *Uncoupling: How Relationships Come Apart*:

> Disentangling a shared life into two separate ones is no easy trick. Few guidelines exist as to how to do it, and decisions must be made immediately.[1]

The field of marriage and family therapy, like the general population, has worked hard to keep pace with the swelling impact of divorce on people's lives over the past three decades. However, for therapists who work with couples on the cusp, there has been an acute shortage of options for the partner who is inclined to separate but not to divorce.

Ironically, to this day the vast body of literature on marriage and divorce has yet to focus specifically on the arena of marital separation as a *distinct entity*. Inasmuch as information on a guided marital separation has never been broadcast to the public at large, it is safe to say the CS Guidelines that follow should go some distance to fill this void.

Exploring the CS Guidelines

1. Time limits
2. Legal counsel
3. Moving out
4. Division of home furnishings
5. Finances
6. Children
7. Couple's continuing relationship
8. Dating others
9. Confidentiality
10. Teamwork and homework
11. Contract
12. Renegotiation

Time Limits

Your first step is to establish how long you will be separated. From my experience, one to six months works well. Or you may decide on three months with an option to renew. Another alternative is a month-to-month arrangement, subject to review and/or renewal at the close of each month.

If there are no time limits, you are in a state of limbo that perpetuates anxiety instead of diffuses it. Without knowing from one minute to the next where you stand, or what tricks your spouse may be up to, your suspicion is sure to mount. As fear of divorce rises, the tendency is to give up and say, "I can't stand this kind of stress; it's not worth it."

Legal Counsel

Both partners agree not to file for divorce during the life of their CS Contract. This pledge safeguards your separation so it has time to work without the threat of divorce controlling the outcome. Freed from such power plays and insidious hounding, each of you is able to think better and perform more effectively.

Should you want to learn more about your legal rights, you can consult with a family law attorney at any time during your CS. This might be a joint or individual undertaking, as the option is left to your discretion.

Moving Out

Who moves out and who stays is usually a self-selecting process. Those who take their CS seriously will communicate directly:

SHE: "I'm the one who wants this separation, so I'll move out."

HE: "I don't want to upset the children any more than necessary, so you stay with the kids and I'll leave."

SHE: "Living in the country like we do, I think I'm best suited to stay here and take care of the chores."

HE: "I have a lot of leads; it won't be hard to find my own place."

Whether one partner sets up temporary housekeeping, moves in with a friend or relative, rents by the month, or signs a longer lease will depend on your particular financial circumstances.

The in-house separation has some unique parameters to consider. A discussion of this alternative is found in Chapter 9.

Division of Home Furnishings

Division of household furnishings is a practical matter that reflects what one spouse needs to make a second residence livable. It also takes into account what the other mate is willing to give up to make this possible.

Dividing the pots and pans is not meant to be a prelude to divorce but merely a convenience in a temporary arrangement. But partners teetering on the brink of divorce may see the bartering and bargaining as a preview to a more permanent living arrangement. However, until you decide your marital future beyond a shadow of a doubt, I urge you to keep an open mind and heart.

The worldly goods each of you gives or takes are not nearly as important as your attitude, which sets the stage for effecting a good separation.

Finances

A frank discussion of your financial picture is to both parties' advantage. In terms of sound money management, be informed of joint funds and savings, as well as debts. Review your expenses and determine who pays which bills. Be clear about the use of checking, savings, and charge accounts. Car, mortgage, utilities, child care, schooling, and other expenses should also be included.

A written budget can be a great assist. This is no time for either excessive frivolities or extreme sacrifices. Astute money management will hold you in good stead.

Remember, this is separation, not divorce. It is not necessary to catastrophize the situation. Realistically, dual households incur additional expenses. However, the easiest way to handle your finances is to make as few changes as possible. *The more you manage your monies in your usual way, the better off you are.*

Children

Expect your children to react, and comfort them by giving them adequate time to ask questions and express their feelings. As you and your spouse express your own feelings of sorrow and regret, the children are spared as much grief and worry as possible under the circumstances.

- Make every effort to keep the children in their present home, rather than move them.

- Work out an equitable schedule of joint child care.

- Arrange weekly or semimonthly family outings so that parent-child interaction is changed as little as possible.

Many parents fret about what, when, and how to tell their youngsters about their pending separation. You will find in Chapter 11 an in-depth discussion and specific guidance to simplify your explanation to your children.

Couple's Continuing Relationship

When a marriage is in shambles, how much contact is enough but not too much? It is best to have some time together, but not so much that you step on one another's toes. Such arrangements need to be made explicit if the CS is to be a constructive instrument for change. In designing your agreement, you will be considering three vital issues of relationship boundaries: privacy, dating each other, and the extent of sexual intimacy.

Privacy. Your CS is designed to allow each of you a chance to heal your hurts. Crowding or invading one another's private abode is a no-no. Thus, it behooves you both to spell out your expectations and ensure that you get the time and space you need.

Telephone contact can be as often as daily or as infrequent as once or twice a week. Regular phoning is usually required when children are involved.

Specify when or if you are welcome to visit one another's residence, business, or job site and under what conditions. Agree to what extent you will help one another with special chores: mowing the lawn, shoveling snow, putting in storm windows, or any other fixer-uppers.

Be aware that all these basics, which are daily taken for granted, rarely are taken into account when parties are engrossed in an unstructured trial separation. Once you and your spouse are settled in your separate routines, then regularly scheduled phoning and dating should give you adequate time for being forthright and putting your best foot forward, rather than hedging and hinting at the worst possible scenario.

Dating. You and your spouse need to set aside discrete time to be alone with each other. Dating gives you a unique opportunity to find out how much you mean to one another.

Confirm how often you will date—once or twice a week is fairly standard. More than that, particularly during the first month, can feel "clingy." Pressure for togetherness defeats the purpose of your separation and jeopardizes what you are trying to accomplish.

It might be advisable to defer dating for two or three weeks to give you and your mate sufficient time to get resettled and be alone.

Dating arrangements require special handling. Be clear about frequency, time, and locale. Any ambiguity can easily be misinterpreted. Preferably, spend your dating time away from either party's home if possible. This gives you a chance to put aside talk about broken plumbing or carpooling.

Your dating experience resembles "courting time." Take nature walks, engage in sports together, or make short day trips for sheer relaxation. Find out if the attraction you originally had for one another can be rekindled.

Couples who diligently honor these recommendations will find out soon enough whether that special spark is still there.

Sexual Intimacy. You cannot take sexual arrangements for granted or assume you will or won't have sexual contact. To erase the likelihood of misunderstandings, spell out what kind and how much touching and closeness you can handle. This includes an open discussion about whether you agree or do not agree to engage in sexual intercourse. When you are in accord, negotiations flow seamlessly.

If you are at loggerheads—one has conditions about sexual contact and the other spouse disagrees—do not fight it. In such circumstances, the party who wants the least sexual intimacy is in charge. You know you can't *force* the matter. Thus, I urge you to accept these conditions. Perhaps the very lack of sexual closeness is a telling reason why you both decided on a CS.

In my practice, I have had only two instances in which couples made a fuss about these matters. In Chapter 5 you meet Sam (Samantha), who insisted that every possible display of intimacy be written in their contract. As for sexual intercourse—well, that's the rest of their story. Another couple held firm to their right to privacy and refused to even discuss the issue with me. And I immediately backed off.

Above all, you and your spouse must be clear about how much or how little sexual contact you will have. This ensures that neither partner is pressured by unwanted hugs, kisses, and whatever follows after that. If the two of you are troubled by this touchy issue, therapeutic assistance is advisable.

Dating Others

The decision to date others can be an "ouch" in your CS negotiations or it can be readily resolved. Again, if you and your partner agree—be it yes or no—there will be no conflict. If you disagree, the mate who wants to date others gets the "go" signal, despite the spouse's objections.

It may surprise you, as it did me, that many parties are so scarred they scarcely react to their spouse's interest in dating others. Having been bruised by their mates' sexual indiscretions, these parties just want to get on with the CS and determine whether there is any good reason to stay.

When secret affairs and sexual incompatibility come to the fore, many severely conflicted couples wisely seek therapeutic support. The critical dimensions of sexual excesses are described in Chapter 13.

Confidentiality

What is said and to whom needs to be specified. Partners need to show respect for each other by agreeing to use discretion in deciding whom to tell and what to say about their CS. To ensure privacy and minimize negative feedback from family and close friends yet maintain the support of loved ones, the following statement works wonders: *"We are separated and working things out together [with a therapist, if that is the case]. That's as much as I can say right now."*

Seldom is it necessary to provide any more details unless you wish to share your troubles with a trusted confidant.

When you adhere to these words of caution, you stand to gain the following benefits:

- You discourage others from taking sides.

- You avoid much unproductive gossip.

- You don't receive opposing opinions and unwanted advice.

- You cushion your emotional reserves.

Although disparaging remarks and negative influences cannot always be prevented, saying less about your CS, rather than more, does not discourage your ardent supporters but does secure your right to privacy.

Teamwork and Homework

To establish a framework of neutrality, if yours is a couple-guided CS, I ask you to *temporarily refrain from discussing the whys and where-*

fores that led to the breakdown of your relationship, for at least one month. Halt your fault finding. Efforts to deal with your relationship will be more productive if you give yourselves a reasonable time to get resettled—after all 12 guidelines have been negotiated.

Look at the term of your separation as a team project. When you have attained more objectivity, you can start to reshape your coupling by talking about your separation experience. Share with your partner by describing what is currently happening and how you are feeling. Nothing is to be gained by rehashing old complaints or twisting the knife in old wounds. This is unproductive and solves nothing.

The same holds true if your CS is therapist-guided. After-therapy hours are no time for fault finding or grilling one another: "Why did you say this and why didn't you do that?" This will inevitably reinforce an adversarial standoff.

To shift your focus to a more enlightened perspective, your counselor is likely to give you homework assignments that can improve team interaction and cooperation. This kind of assist has much merit.

CS Contract

Wrap up your contract in writing, although some of my client couples state their simplest agreements verbally. Completion usually requires two to four meetings. Take all the time you need so that you can comfortably abide by the rules you have established.

Provisions for Renegotiation of Contract

It is worth mentioning that rarely can all the details of your contract be anticipated at the time you initially plan your separation. Tie down any loose ends in your contract if any of the arrangements aren't working out satisfactorily. Agree to meet again for the purpose of making necessary adjustments.

Conversely, if changes are made by one partner without discussing or taking the other party into account, then the contract is sabotaged and it is back to the drawing board again. A variety of hints and instructions for completing your contract are found in Chapter 4. Refer to the following sample CS Contract as your guide.

Sample CS Contract

1. Time Limits: I agree to a _____ month separation commencing _____ (date).

2. Legal Counsel: I will/will not contact an attorney in order to become informed. I agree not to make any efforts to file for divorce during the life of this contract.

3. Living Arrangements: _____ will move out on _____ (date).

4. Dividing Home Furnishings: I agree to cooperatively divide household goods to ensure maximum comfort in our separate living quarters.

5. Finances: I agree to make as few changes in our finances as possible.

6. Child Care: I agree to flexible and cooperative child-care arrangements. I agree to give 24 hours' advance notice for special events.

7. Couple's Interpersonal Relationship:

    a. Telephone: I will phone my spouse _____ times weekly for the purpose of _____. I will telephone children _____ times weekly.

    b. Entering Spouse's Residence: _____

    c. Household Repairs: _____

    d. Family Outings: _____

    e. Holidays: _____

    f. Dating Spouse: _____

8. Dating Others: I do/do not intend to date others.

9. Confidentiality: Parents and friends: I agree to limit explanation of the details of this contract to discourage unnecessary gossip. I also agree to refrain from maligning my spouse and will not encourage others to take sides.

10. Counseling: I agree to counseling or mediation if either party is unable to negotiate any of the given terms of this contract in an amicable manner.

11. Contract: no changes will be made in this contract unless both partners agree to the terms.

12. Termination of Contract: I agree to inform my spouse verbally or in writing of my intention to terminate this contract.

Signed:_____

_____

Date: _____

CS Guidelines: A Potent Motivator

The CS Guidelines serve a mission by calling attention to your faltering relationship. If you have talked until you are blue in the face, if you can't seem to pry your spouse off the couch or awaken your Rip Van Winkle, you won't have long to wait once your mate has the guidelines in hand. They seem to have magical powers and be a potent motivator to get you and your partner moving forward.

There are seven options open to you:

1. Use the Guidelines for a do-it-yourselves separation.

2. Agree to a therapist-guided CS when communication is at a standstill.

3. Reject the Guidelines in favor of strengthening your relationship with couple therapy, individual therapy, or a combination of these methods.

4. Reject the Guidelines and attempt to restabilize the marriage independent of therapeutic support.

5. Opt for a transitional separation in anticipation of a divorce. Guidelines and operating instructions for a good divorce are included in Chapter 19.

6. Ignore the Guidelines and plunge willy-nilly into an unstructured trial separation (TS).

7. Discuss the Guidelines with your partner, put the CS option on hold for a specific length of time—say three to four weeks—and allow your ideas to germinate.

The guidelines ensure you get a yes or no answer to some of the most pressing issues affecting your deadlock. No more "dragging the feet." I have never seen a case of indifference. At this juncture, any reaction, positive or negative, could be better than none at all.

Next, let's follow the tale of Jill and Jim to see how the CS Guidelines originally took shape. As this distraught couple became actively involved in their CS, they learned how to become cooperative teammates and salvage their worn-out marriage.

3

Controlled Separation: A Breakthrough Solution

Jill and Jim: The Country Club Couple

"I've come to the end of my rope. I'm through with him forever!" Jill exploded.

"I had to leave her, Lee! What else could I do?" Jim implored.

Jill's and Jim's words kept ringing in my ears. It all started when I received a frantic call one morning from Jill, who was hoping for an appointment the same day. "Jim walked out on me last night . . . didn't say a word. So unfair of him. He got in touch today, but I'm so mad I don't even want to talk to him. How rotten can he get?" Jill was in the grip of a marital crisis.

Before me sat a stunning woman of 45, ash-blond hair, mother of two sons in college. Eyes on fire, Jill choked back her tears. "Jim says the affair is over now, but it's all I can think about . . . can't help it. I trusted him. I trusted her . . . we were close friends. It's eating at me—driving me crazy."

Jill vented bitterness over Jim's rejection. She thought she had done her part, been a caring wife, homemaker, and mother. Her husband's needs had always come first, her career incidental to Jim's. Jill seemed to brace herself before blurting out, "Maybe I've been drinking too much. I've not been myself . . . hard to think straight. Guess I'll have to cut back."

I thought it wise to see her husband. Sometimes the mate is just waiting for the partner's invitation; at other times it is a futile effort. Jill agreed to ask him.

Jim, a handsome, graying man of 50, came to my office the next day alone. "I told Jill I was sorry. The affair's been over for six months, but she won't let it go. As I see it, we argue more after partying. It's late, we're tired, and Jill wants to talk about 'us.' Bad timing . . . scared I'll say things I'll regret in the morning."

I heard a sigh. "I've tried to make it up to her; then she returns the gifts I buy. Now Jill's so mad she's refusing sex." Jim did not take lightly to being put off like that. Separation looked like his last resort.

It was the fourth day since the blowup, and Jim still had not returned to Jill. The pair had spoken briefly, but Jim was vague and noncommittal about his separation plans. The suspense was wearing Jill down. Discouraged, she said, "I feel like an old shoe. Jim's taken me for granted for years, and would you know, he still flirts with every pretty skirt around."

Our contact was minimal, Jill twice, Jim once, and then to my surprise neither partner rescheduled. After waiting a month, I made a follow-up phone call. Jill was all bubbly and thanked me for calling. "Jim's been home four weeks; he was gone only five days."

"How is it going for you?" I asked. Jill was brief. "Oh, we're doing just fine." Then I inquired, "Are you considering further therapy?" and just as easily she replied, "No, we won't be needing any more counseling. But thank you for calling."

Frankly, so pat a reply took me aback. How could she be so sure of herself when I had such a strong hunch this case was far from closed? I couldn't believe their unresolved issues would not resurface sooner or later. It was evident the couple was not ready to resolve their deeper relationship conflicts—not yet.

Sickness Prevails

Three years later my prediction came true. This time Jim called in a panic, wanting to see me as soon as possible. Jill followed suit a few days later. This second go-around was essentially the same marital crisis except for one difference. Not only were the mates preoccupied with their falling-apart marriage, but also each partner was plagued with ill health.

Jim had rushed to the doctor with severe chest pains, fearing a heart attack or stroke. The doctor said it was acute stress. Jill had been hospitalized three days with a severe bout of abdominal pain and was anxiously waiting for test results, fearing a malignancy.

Communication had ground to a halt with incessant arguing. Both partners were frantic.

Jim spoke to me alone. "I'd like to stay and work things out, but if it's divorce Jill wants, I'll go. I'm so confused, I don't know what to do."

Jill told me privately, "Jim's crowding me for sex. All we do is fight . . . nothing I say matters anymore. He's hard to live with. We used to have fun together, but not anymore. I wish he would go away and leave me alone!"

All this was magnified by still another worry. Jill's mother was scheduled for cancer surgery the following week.

Option: Couple Therapy

It was time to bring the couple together, to see them eyeball each other, and to assess what the fireworks were all about. When they arrived, Jill looked peaked and Jim seemed preoccupied. Both were so irritable they could barely look at one another.

All but jumping off her chair, Jill took the lead. "I'm worn out. I don't think I can sit around waiting for marriage counseling to help. We've got too much working against us."

Jim chimed in, his voice huskier than usual. "We're out of control here. I can't think straight anymore . . . can't even concentrate on my job. The heat at home is getting to me. We need help fast. What can you do for us, Lee?"

To make sure I got the point, Jill bluntly added, "I can't live like this. I need some space. Lee, you gotta do something!"

The Country Club Life

Jill and Jim had much in common. They wanted action and answers fast—like their lives, a whirlwind crowded with careers, travel, tennis, the country club, partying, booze. Gossip ran rampant in their social circle. Pals were involved in one another's comings and goings. Privacy was a privilege all but unknown to either partner.

Each was prone to blame and complain. When she wanted to talk, he was too busy. When he was ready, she would shut down. It was push-pull but not in unison. Her behavior had Jim confused. His behavior had her frustrated. Then there were other times when each would act as if nothing were the matter. But their nerves were so frazzled that any complaint was cause for more blame. As Jim phrased it, "There is no reaching her." Smarting, Jill put it like this: "He has no idea how much he has hurt me all these years."

Other Trial Separations

According to Jim, twice Jill had impulsively separated. A disappointing first anniversary had set her off, and she spent a night at a nearby hotel "to cool down." Eleven years later she had become despondent, threatened suicide, and then took refuge with her widowed mother. Jim was fuzzy about the details, recalling she had left after an "ungodly fight." He had been afraid for Jill and for himself. Was he to blame? He didn't know, nor did he remember what had gotten her so riled up. A week later she returned to the marital nest, contrite and apologetic. They picked up the pieces—for better or for worse.

In the aftermath of an unstructured trial separation, be it once or multiple times, spouses easily remember the worst of their apart time but avoid thinking about the total experience. Thus, they are cheated, denying themselves an opportunity to gain insight into what made their trial separation(s) so unproductive. Partners who are bent on setting the whole experience aside take small, if any, profit from such brief escapes. Jill and Jim were no different.

My mind was racing. Their case file had become a repository for stacks of letters exchanged: impassioned self-justifications, yearnings to be heard, appeals for compassion, and pleas that the other might change enough to resolve their unhappy coupling. They had endured a stormy marriage too long. They expected answers fast.

Quickly, I went to the heart of their situation with one pressing question that all couples on the cusp need to confront: "Does either of you want a divorce?" Jill's and Jim's unanimous "No" was convincing. Both were privy to the goings-on in their social circle of ugly separations and divorces. They wanted no part of that.

A Last-Ditch Effort

I took this to be the couple's final try at salvaging their marriage, and surely it was my last chance to "divine" an option with enough pizzazz and drama to grab their imagination. Looking at the bottom line, I summarized their situation:

1. Each spouse wanted to control the other.

2. Each spouse personally felt out of control.

3. Each was in a hurry-up mode—impatient.

4. Each put up resistance to marital therapy.

5. Jill wanted space.

6. Jim was sitting on the fence.

What option did I have that would break their crisis? What could I offer that would slow the pace, get one spouse off the fence, and give the other space? This posed a hefty challenge.

Introducing a Controlled Separation

It was at this juncture that I began to sketch my ideas about a separation that conceivably could be negotiated with the three of us working in tandem. The couple pulling together looked a lot more productive than their attempting one more fruitless separation.

I explained why I called my innovative plan a Controlled Separation. "It would appear you have each felt out of control. Let's see if you can put your lives back together again and regain the control you've lost." I envisioned order restored instead of their disorderly fussing and fuming. For reassurance I added, "I'll work closely with you. Let's think positive."

I didn't want to overwhelm them with too much. But I had so much to explain. "Your CS Contract will be tailor-made. You tell me what you want; then, we'll work through the stumbling blocks as a team." Rambling on, I spoke of meeting on a weekly basis for continuity, to make things happen systematically. Were they game to try?

Sensibly, Jill wanted to know who would be the one to move out. Her question addressed the first hurdle to be met. Now the ball was in the couple's court. Quite soberly Jim volunteered, "I'll go," without missing a beat. I was so astonished my mouth probably dropped open.

Each partner consented to a six-month separation. A sensible estimate. From my perspective the couple would need this block of time to determine their ultimate marital course.

Having agreed that neither mate would file for a divorce as long as the separation was in effect, Jim announced he thought it best to talk to an attorney "just to be on the safe side." Jill asked if she could join him, and Jim was amenable. And I concurred.

Next I asked the couple to stop analyzing what went wrong with their marriage and limit all discussion of their conflicts to our therapy sessions. Jill glared at Jim, and he avoided her glance, with his eyes fixed on his shoes. Neither party had any objection to this essential rule, and I asked them to look directly at one another as they gave their assent.

With that settled, Jill perked up a bit and said, "Good, at least this will cut out the arguing—I need a little peace before Jim moves out. Besides, I have my mother's surgery coming up . . . a lot to think about."

Looking ahead, Jim sensed trouble. Astutely he observed, "There's a lot more to figure out, like when we get together and all that stuff—but I guess we can do that later. Yeah, we'll go for it. What do we have to lose?"

When people are stuck in a marriage going nowhere, even an option with no track record can be worth a try. They had the bare bones of a plan, which in time would be expanded to include all 12 Guidelines. They also had to negotiate finances, communication, children, and family, but that could come later.

Now the couple was involved in something constructive. Their first four agreements gave this impatient pair assignments to focus on. Action-oriented folks, they had been much too antsy to sit around and wait for something to happen. They had done that for too many miserable years. Their motivation to move forward was impressive.

Preliminary Planning

Jim said he would start looking for a place to live immediately, although he was concerned about when to move, given his mother-in-law's surgery. He muttered under his breath, "Perhaps Jill will need me."

Originally, Jill had planned for her mother to recuperate at the couple's home, but with the marriage so unsettled, she began to think she'd be taking on more stress than she could handle. Instead she arranged for her mother to do her mending at her sister's home.

Then came the inevitable question: "Lee, how do you think the CS will work out?" Every couple has this tense moment on the eve of so important a voyage with so unpredictable a destination. Spouses wish I could tell their future. Facing the implication of whether it will be marriage or divorce becomes a disconcerting reality. The answer I gave Jill and Jim has now become my standard reply: "Let's take a wait-and-see approach. Trust me; you will know in time."

Though the launching of their separation had gone smoothly, I didn't delude myself that sailing through such treacherous waters would be a simple matter. Time would tell.

Contract Negotiations Move Forward

There was good news: the doctor had given Jill a clean bill of health, and her mother's postoperative recovery was going fairly well. Jill was relieved to put these worries behind her and move on.

Meanwhile, Jim had rented an apartment for six months and was busy getting his new place in order. In his doing so, I noticed he was no longer complaining about his physical symptoms. A change in focus can do that for a person.

In the early stages of negotiating their CS Contract, the couple concentrated on making sure Jim's apartment would be livable so their children would be comfortable spending time with their dad.

Jim wanted to buy a new bed, but Jill suggested he use the hide-a-bed and take the drop-leaf table in the den. Each party spoke in a conversational voice as he and she discussed which lamps, sheets, and kitchen utensils Jill could spare.

Finances were privately arranged, to which I was not made privy. The grace displayed by these recently embattled spouses was remarkable to witness.

The mates took their responsibilities seriously. So far it was easy. What came next was not.

The First Three Months

Jim moved out. This illustrious day was their official CS starting date. Living apart, however, was no panacea. Nothing had changed in the way they related—both parties managed to irritate one another time and again.

We were meeting weekly as agreed. Jill was discouraged with Jim hanging around, phoning daily, arriving unannounced, being nosy, and generally invading her space. To his face she called him "an insufferable pest!" Jill wanted less, not more, of him.

Jim was livid. Glaring at Jill he shouted, "It's not fair!" How could his wife be so rude, cutting him short, slamming down the phone, making herself "unavailable"? He wasn't too keen on this "damned separation." Eyeing me, not Jill, he went on doggedly protesting, "I've got a right to talk with . . . to see my wife!"

Couple's Continuing Relationship

Inevitably, each mate had a different perspective on what these terms should be. They had different needs, and assuredly each felt "I am right."

Fortunately, the partners wanted to prove to one another they could temper their emotions; thus, it took a minimum of input on my part and a little haggling between themselves to make sure "all was fair." The following five relationship rules were negotiated:

1. Jim was "allowed" two social telephone calls weekly. (He wanted more.)

2. Jill "permitted" her spouse one date per week without sex. (Jim turned on the charm to get that much.)

3. Jim agreed to stay away from the house unless invited by Jill. (He was resigned by this time.)

4. Jill insisted Jim make his own arrangements with their sons. She refused to be a go-between. (He grudgingly agreed.)

5. Jim agreed to help his wife in the event of a household emergency. (He was glad to be needed.)

I believed that if I pointed them in the direction of a constructive journey, surely they could figure out the rest. I was confident that if they got stuck in their negotiations, I would be there to "coach."

Flexibility and Exceptions to the Rule

I have always considered flexibility essential in bargaining. In the design of any contract, exceptions to the rules are inevitable. Rule number five is a case in point. Although Jill insisted that Jim stay away from the house, she still wanted to ensure he would come in case of an emergency.

Even this apparent contradiction, which met an important need for security on Jill's part, was able to work because it was made part of the negotiation process and their CS Contract agreement.

Dating Others

I've learned that it is unwise to make assumptions when it comes to the issue of dating others. In reality, little in a couple's relationship can be assumed, unless specifically spelled out. Prior to confirming the Contract agreement, Jim needed to see me to discuss the other women in his life. Evidently he had a lady friend or two he was interested in dating.

So there would be no misunderstanding, I introduced the matter of dating others at our next joint session. Jim, already prepared, was quick to grab the option. Jill neither wanted the option for herself nor protested Jim's having it, apparently not caring what he did at that point.

I said nothing. Over time I have found that the matter of dating others can be a red-hot issue for some mates, but others are remarkably casual about it. There is no taking this or any of the other separation issues for granted.

Gossip: A No-No

Jill was seething. She launched her attack in my office about a month after the CS began. Squarely facing Jim, she began. "I've heard what you said about me at the club. You had no right! You fixed it so you look like the sweetheart. How could you!" Humiliated that "his story" had not matched hers, she hated being the butt of malicious gossip.

I was prepared for a big harangue, but instead the partners calmly took charge. After listening to one another's side of this sore subject, Jim solemnly promised to say no more to mutual friends. He was learning that gossip can do much harm. As I put it, "Gossip is a no-no." The subject was dropped.

The CS Contract helps couples define the meaning of gossip. The mates decide whom to tell, what to say, and when to inform others about their CS. Once again, we were writing the guidelines on the spot.

Control Issues Are a Delicate Matter

The couple continued to astound me. They needed my direction, but they didn't need to be spoon-fed. We had been meeting weekly, moving along at a brisk pace, and I anticipated this schedule would be maintained. But they had other ideas—suddenly they wanted to wait a month for their next appointment. So much for my control. This was their CS, not mine. I was bound to honor their wishes.

At the close of the third month, Jill said she felt "pressure free." The couple were "dating" weekly, Jim had given up being a "pest," and they were more relaxed with one another.

Jim became the needy one. By habit, he had enjoyed sharing the marital dirt with pals. But having stopped all that, he was desperate to talk. Several experiences with "girlfriends" had left him scarred and scared. He was ready to make amends. "If I ever get back with Jill, this 'dallying about' is a thing of the past."

By this time, there was less growling and grumbling between the partners. They had stopped criticizing, threatening, dissecting, and divining who was right or wrong. No wonder they felt freer.

The Final Three Months: Transition and Transformation

By the beginning of the fourth month, both Jill and Jim said they wanted to make theirs a good marriage.

Jill said, "I really had a hard time when Jim started his sweet talk with me. I always figured, well . . . what does he want now?"

Jim added, "At first Jill got real sarcastic and kept putting me off like she used to do."

Jill chimed in, "Well, I've always had a hard time trusting him. But this time Jim isn't faultfinding and accusing me of being the cause of our troubles. He's admitting he's not perfect. He's apologized for hurting me and seems more interested in me and how I feel."

Jim wrapped up the session saying, "I keep telling Jill how much I love her, but now I know it's my actions that count more than my words. I've got a quick temper sometimes, and I snap and get nasty. I've got to curb that."

I noted that the partners' attitudes had become more positive. They never deviated from their Contract. They were persistent in rooting out nonconstructive communication. It was evident neither wanted the marriage to fail.

At the same time, both mates realized the importance of sharpening their relationship skills, all of which earmarked their readiness for the second phase of the CS: Relationship Skills Training. This phase takes on the appearance of conventional marital therapy. It turns the hope of restructuring a marriage into a reality.

Relationship Skills Training

There were major sources of conflict the couple had yet to face. Jill listed three:

1. Jim's repeated depressed moods and irritability

2. Jim's thoughtlessness and deprecating remarks, which she took as discounting her worthiness

3. Jim's defensiveness, which made her feel distanced and unloved

Jim likewise had three major sources of discontent:

1. Jill's propensity to withhold sex when she was angry

2. Jill's inclination to repeatedly resurrect past hurts

3. Jill's habit of clamming up and making herself unavailable when she was angry

By this time the couple understood that a satisfying relationship could not be achieved until the whys and wherefores of these six issues were resolved.

In jointly and individually held sessions, we took a look at Jill's early childhood, whence her insecurities, lack of trust, and tendency to retaliate originated. She spoke of betrayal, emotional neglect, living with an alcoholic father, knowing of his repeated affairs, and seeing her mother passively accept the unacceptable.

We spoke of compassion and forgiveness for what had occurred in the past. I explained to Jill that some childhood traumas cannot be forgotten. She began to accept that healing would come slowly as she grew more confident. "I need Jim's tenderness, admiration, and respect," she said. "It makes such a difference."

It turned out that Jim, for all his business acumen and smarts, felt inferior. Even as a young boy he was always comparing himself to his father and brothers, never believing he could measure up. He kept seeing himself in sharp competition with Jill—always coming out on the losing end. He perpetually looked at the downside of their marriage, suffered from "imaginitus," always expecting the worst. For the better part of his life, Jim's cup had inevitably been half-empty rather than half-full. I explained that such negativity and low self-esteem is the breeding ground for a "shadow depression"—a lingering state of pessimism that is disturbing to mood and outlook but is not incapacitating.

More than once I reiterated, "Jim, look at how you negate your worth—as though you are of no value." Gradually he grasped the idea that when he discounted Jill he was projecting his own low self-esteem onto his wife. It was time for Jim to love himself. Time to stop saying, "My wife's smarter than I am." It was time for him to move beyond competition and the coercive tactics that had been so debilitating to the marriage. It was time for Jim to see himself as of equal stature to Jill.

CS: Gains Made

At the beginning of the fifth month, the couple began preparing to reunite. Jill and Jim were apt students, and they reaped the benefits of their CS. The partners made the following impressive changes:

- The couple discovered the importance of being of equal standing rather than resorting to power plays and manipulation.

- Both partners clearly understood their relationship had been undermined by excessive use of alcohol. Not wanting to further malign their relationship, they agreed to drink only in moderation.

- Each spouse was determined to improve communication and willing to confront disagreements in a constructive manner.

Jill said, "We are smart enough to work on conflicts because we recognize the source."

Jim voiced his approval. "That's right. I find it best to deal with one issue at a time and not let it drag on—that doesn't work for us anymore."

The CS gave the couple a combination of the right conditions—structure, guidance, and time—which enabled them to persevere with a sense of safety. They did not have to give up on their marriage. Each had demanded excellence and was rewarded. Being "liked/loved" and having fun had been missing for too many years. Now, compliments flowed and romance was renewed. Sweethearts! I was in awe of their transformation.

Follow-Up

At the close of the couple's six-month separation, I suggested meeting four more times on a monthly basis. "Let us call it follow-up," I said. They consented but never rescheduled.

I had intended to contact this couple so I could write their story to share with you, but then it happened easily on a summer evening five years later when Jill recognized me at a movie theater. She took me to where Jim was sitting. His greeting was expansive. They looked trim and in the best of health. Jill's twinkling eyes locked with Jim's as she spoke. *"We are very happy . . . it is good."*

The resolution of these partners' "stay or go" impasse confirmed my sense of the immense potential of the CS to change the direction of the lives of couples on the cusp. As next we delve into the CS Contract, you'll see how flexible and dynamic this separation method can be.

$\mathcal{N}$egotiating a Controlled Separation Contract

Your Marriage Contract

WHEN COUPLES MARRY, they make contracts and sign certificates that make their unions legal. This is usually the last time the subject of mutual contracting is ever raised. Contracts are recognized in our courts, attorneys love to poke holes in them, and the business world lives by them. But once the marriage contract is signed, spouses generally set the document aside and get busy with the state of being married.

Making Rules

You and your spouse make all sorts of rules about your daily comings and goings in order to function in some orderly manner. You divvy up the chores, and you have "understandings" of who does what and when. You inform one another of where you will be, and most likely you have a rule about phoning if you are going to be late returning.

Some rules are implied—automatically taken for granted. Others are openly discussed. But I would guess few couples ever think to write down their rules. It is thought that such "formality" kills romance.

The Hunger for Structure

Your CS Contract is meant to be a solid instrument that you can rely on as you attempt to make sense of your "stay or go" dilemma. The comprehensive structure of your contract takes into account the everyday practicalities of living apart. Making an investment in this project is the most potent way for couples on the cusp to mobilize their joint energies and save their sanity.

Without structure we are aimless, as if our lives lack purpose and meaning. We grow restless and impatient, then plummet into the boredom trap, the joy of intimacy going out like a light.

Celebrated psychiatrist Eric Berne, M.D., explains in *What Do You Say After You Say Hello?* that we all hunger for structure, for some direction to our lives; otherwise, our time would become more chaotic than we could possibly manage.[1]

The structure of your CS Contract begins with setting time limits. The impact of this important first agreement cannot be underestimated. As the terms are nailed down, there is no guess-work—your separation path leads to resolution of your impasse in the safest way possible.

How to Get Started

Let's say a CS has a certain dash and appeal to you, but you're having difficulty breaking the news to your mate. If you are too afraid to broach the subject but want to get your partner involved, the following example can assist you in speaking candidly and effectively in the least offensive manner. Use a conversational tone and speak with conviction:

Please hear me out. I am very unhappy, and I'd like a temporary separation. I'm not blaming anyone; it's just that I need time to think about where we are going in this marriage. Before I do anything, I'd like to discuss my ideas with you because I don't want to do anything impulsively.

In this way you are sure to get some dialogue going. If your spouse is in shock, you may need to repeat these sentences two or three times. Do so patiently and courteously. This gives you a chance to mention the CS and make reference to the CS Guidelines and CS Contract. Better yet, show your mate this book.

The following list pinpoints what couples on the cusp might initially gain by a productive separation. Use this information to open communication and supplement discussion with your mate.

- A stop to fighting

- A time to cool off

- Ways to determine your next course of action

- A chance to wait and see how your mate responds

- An opportunity to test how you feel about your relationship

- The experience of living alone

- The means to revitalize your marriage

- Preparation for a civil divorce, if you cannot reconcile your differences

Next, write down three reasons why a CS would help you personally or as a couple.

1. _____

2. _____

3. _____

Then write down three reasons why you think a CS would not be appropriate for you personally or as a couple.

1. _____

2. _____

3. _____

As you open constructive communication, you are in a good position to assess your relationship and get involved in the CS process.

No hard decisions need to be made. It is sufficient that you and your partner are being straightforward in addressing the state of your marriage. So meaningful a conversation can be gratifying in itself.

Don't be surprised if either party says, "I know I don't want a divorce, but that's all I do know." For the time being, accept that answer for what it is, and do not press your mate further.

Be assured you are laying the groundwork and planting some potent seeds for further communication. By this joint effort, don't be surprised when you witness an abrupt turnaround in your mate's behavior right then and there.

Whether you and your partner respond in the same vein or differently, your frank discussions clear the air far better than hedging or making vague insinuations. How much better to state where you stand and reduce frustration.

CS: Letting Go

In anticipation of negotiating a CS Contract, it is often difficult to let go of the familiar. Mostly, the known, no matter how unpleasant, feels safer than the unknown simply because it is far more predictable.

Prior to your CS journey, perhaps you, like many partners, remain tentative and skeptical of the CS process. In their own way, my clients usually make an effort to be hopeful:

- "What a relief to know we are finally getting on target."

- "If there's a chance to save our marriage, I'm game."

- "This is a good way to keep us involved and still talking without such a hassle."

- "It's not what I want, but I'll do what I can to cooperate."

- "Can't get any worse . . . I'll give it my best shot."

- "If it ends in divorce, I'll have less guilt and know I did my best."

A Common Purpose

Standing at the precipice of the chasm, you and your spouse join together for a common purpose—to determine the fate of your marriage. As you begin the process of making your CS Contract a productive one, the wheels of decision making are set in motion.

Trust that workable answers can emerge from your chaotic conflict when you negotiate as cooperative teammates. A conscious use of time can produce answers that speak from your heart.

Take Stock of Your Attitude

On the eve of your CS journey, how objective can you be, poised on the brink of your unknown future? Are you dreading the losses or waiting impatiently for the fulfillment of your dreams? Are you down in the dumps because you don't want to separate and your spouse does? Are you enthusiastically energized because you want out, at least temporarily?

For the present, trust may be a commodity in short supply. Yours may be a verbally abusive relationship and you're feeling shaky, not at all confident about how to improve your troubled communication.

Are you concerned as to the extent you can distance yourself from your impasse? Or are you imagining dangling like this forever? If you find you are being unduly negative, be advised such an attitude bodes more harm than good. Keep the faith. Clarity and movement are forthcoming.

The Adversarial Trap

In anticipation of preparing for your CS journey, let's look at the disadvantages of perpetuating an adversarial standoff. In contrast, we'll see the advantages of setting aside ill will for the sake of restabilizing lives gone out of control.

Adversaries are bent on war and strife. For whatever reason, these conflicted spouses often show little or no interest in developing a healthier partnership. One spouse is ignored or seen as the enemy to be overpowered by the other.

Adversaries are competitive scorekeepers. They keep tabs: weighing, measuring, and counting each other's contribution. They compare who does the least or the most, who is better and who is worse, who is guilty and who is innocent. Inasmuch as one party is surely found wanting, the worth of the coupling is likewise found lacking.

As inequities are glaringly exposed, the couple's relationship is vilified, slandered, and condemned; each spouse's dignity is diminished. If the worth of the partnership is negated, the demise of the coupling is perilously close at hand.

As mates permit this kind of tyranny to fester, they must cope with burgeoning antagonism, which breeds its own brand of contempt and suspicion. The pettiness and meanness of it all cripples the heartbeat of the marriage. In due time, adversarial marriages dissolve in an all-consuming rage that makes life hell on Earth for the parties at risk. Such toxicity feeds on itself. When people are sick at heart, having had their fill of duplicity and antagonism, they feel justified to move beyond the point of no return.

The Advantages of Being Advocates

Advocates are of equal stature and worth; they foster the good in one another. Advocates gravitate to the spirit of teamwork. The partners' energies go toward building bridges, mending fences, and strengthening their connection. Advocates are motivated to uphold common decency and welcome an opportunity to treat their spouses with respect, and they appreciate the same in return. They grow exponentially as the integrity of the team and the value of each partner is promoted.

Pepper Schwartz, Ph.D., professor of sociology and author of *Love Between Equals: How Peer Marriage Really Works*, explains:

> Egalitarian couples negotiate directly, fairly, and without abuse. They share conversation, even to the point of equal time, and the respect they have for one another creates a speaking style that overcomes traditional tendencies toward aggressiveness or timidity.[2]

To negotiate fairly is to transfer or assign to one another something that is of equivalent value. Call it *compromise*, wherein each party gives up some demands and makes some concessions.

It takes expansive acts of love, compassion, and courage to achieve couple advocacy and to negotiate fairly. As partners dispense with inequality, neither has a need to misuse his or her power in an effort to dominate and control the other.

The concepts proposed by communication specialist Patricia Evans, author of *The Verbally Abusive Relationship: How to Recognize It and How to Respond*, can be adapted to the "stay or go" dilemma. In the spirit of Evans the following chart compares how the worth of adversaries is diminished and the value of advocates is dignified.[3]

Adversaries	Advocates
Inequality	Equality
Competitors	Teammates
Manipulation	Fair play
Animosity	Good will
Intimidation	Invested intimacy
Negation	Validation

The benevolent qualities of advocacy hold you in good stead as you consider the advantages of a CS.

A Word of Caution

You cannot expect the chronic alcoholic, abuser of illegal substances, or the defiant batterer to abide by the rules of the CS. These people rebel against authority and live by rules not culturally sanctioned, and they won't change until they are ready to face their impairments. These immense societal problems are addressed in Chapter 10.

The Negative Trap

The long-term effects of negativity are crippling to relationships. This is a good time to take stock of your attitude. A jaded, cynical, pessimistic approach can become a setup for failure.

I believe that negativity is contagious. When you breathe another's gloom-and-doom attitude, it reinforces your own woeful thinking. It perpetuates bitterness and sabotages your efforts to have benevolent thoughts about your mate and your relationship.

In essence, your negative thoughts are actually digging you into a rigid position from which no good can come, and you are convinced: "My spouse won't change; I won't change."

As you consider these ideas, be aware that you have choices. You can set in motion negative responses, which reinforce negative actions; or you can initiate positive responses, which reinforce positive actions. Let me use an analogy to explain how this happens.

When you plant a tomato seed, what do you get? A tomato, of course.

When you plant a negative seed, what do you get? A negative reaction.

When you plant a positive seed, you will usually get a positive outcome.

When I spoke with Jill (Chapter 3), she understood what I meant: "For me negativity is a vampire that drains every ounce of my energy, and all I want to do is sleep."

It's not so easy to see how you fall into the negative trap, especially when it has become ingrained. Sometimes we are so blind to what we think, say, and do that we don't realize how our lives are affected by what we habitually reinforce in our heads. It doesn't take much for the seeds of failure to mushroom despite what you thought were your best intentions. When you substitute positive thoughts for negative ones, you are on the path to transforming yourself and your relationship for the better.

As you shift your attitude to one of optimism, it becomes easier for you to persevere, to be more objective, and to allow time to work in your own behalf. Notice the response you get as your partner readjusts to the "new, more confident you." This is how relationships grow.

Get Moving, Get Fit

In preparation for contract negotiations, you and your partner will be more productive if you are feeling fit. Get moving. Stretch your body as well as your brain. If you breathe easier, you can think more effectively.

Get off the couch and dust off your Exercycle, rowing machine, golf clubs, tennis racket, volleyball, swimming togs, jogging shoes, dancing slippers, or hiking boots. Loosen up. This is your golden opportunity to recharge the love spark that's been hidden but not totally lost.

CS: Calm Your Nerves

Before your contract negotiations get rolling, there are lots of healthy ways to calm your nerves. If you are wondering how you'll ever scrape your anxiety off the ceiling, if you are near drowning in remorse and regret, if you feel too frail to pump iron or jog around the block, there are other ways to get your blood moving.

Turn on the shower and hoot and holler! Sing! Shout! Scream to raise the roof! Then cool down under blankets. Quiet yourself. Listen to your heartbeat. Meditate and visualize both you and your mate wrapped in a golden light! You may not be sure where all this is taking you, but know that this is not wasted effort. It pays off sooner than you can imagine.

CS: Stay Focused

A word to the wise: stay focused when you work together on your CS Contract. It is easy to get distracted—your spouse is talking about apples and you want to talk about bananas or automobiles. That will never do. If you mumble, something essential can be misconstrued. Listen carefully and speak clearly.

As you move along, the following eight suggestions can keep you on track:

1. Work on one item at a time. If you tackle two CS Guidelines at once, you are looking for trouble.

2. Take on the easiest Guidelines first. Put on temporary hold the most difficult or highly conflicted issues.

3. Play it safe. Be flexible and change the order of the CS Guidelines to suit your own convenience.

4. Do not expect to change everything at once. If you settle on one significant agreement at a time, congratulate each other.

5. Write down your agreements, making note of the sticky ones.

6. If either partner has doubts about any issue, he or she should say so firmly and directly.

7. As you would avoid the plague, stop analyzing what went wrong with your relationship.

8. Remember, your children's problems can usually be distinguished from your marital squabbles.

Each spouse's willingness to act in good faith gets your contract negotiations off to a sane start.

CS: Managing Your Differences

Conflicted issues have a way of sneaking up when you least expect them. You already know the two of you will not see eye-to-eye on some of your Contract terms. In these cases, each party is likely to feel as if "I am right," because you both have different needs.

If you are fearful that you won't be able to keep your emotions in check during negotiations, the following six recommendations can help reduce friction and implement better understanding.

1. Be aware that yelling or screaming is a form of verbal abuse. If you provoke your spouse with hostile remarks, expect your partner to be as miffed as you are.

2. Speak in a conversational tone, and your negotiations will go more smoothly.

3. Practice speaking to the point without beating around the bush.

4. If you get angry over a difference of opinion, do not walk out of the room in a huff. Instead explain, "I need time to

think about this" or "I'm falling apart and I need to pull myself together."

5. Be courteous even though aspects of your spouse's personality rub you the wrong way. In this way you will be more effective.

6. If your CS flounders on the rocks of resentment, get professional help.

When Conflict Engulfs Your Negotiations

Should your negotiations not go as well as you had hoped, should one partner bully or intimidate the other, should either party feel overpowered, cheated, used, or slighted, then call a time-out. Any time your dialogue gets out of hand and voices escalate, stop your negotiations and set a time to resume them another day. This gives you a chance to take a break and see if you can pinpoint the problem.

What is happening in your negotiations that disturbs you the most?

- Is one party not listening, interrupting, or changing the subject?

- Is your mate so competitive or dominating that you feel oppressed?

- Is your spouse insisting on having the last word?

- Are your feelings ignored as if you don't count?

If your negotiations falter or break down altogether, avoid hazardous confrontations, which are apt to incite further vindictiveness.

When Professional Guidance Is Your Best Option

Keep in mind your CS Contract is a potent instrument for change. The following indicators are reason enough to seek professional guidance and spare you and your family needless grief:

- When neither party can be sufficiently objective

- When one or both partners are defensive beyond reason

- When derisive threats rule the roost

- When both spouses are battling it out to see who wins

- When negotiations are on the verge of collapse

- When one or both parties are persistently argumentative

- When one party is passive, resisting engagement in conflicted issues

- When either party's clout is jeopardized

Consider the emotional safety of professional support, which can empower you to make a sane decision without destroying the good in your relationship.

CS: Therapeutic Safety Net

There is a certain comfort level in knowing you have backup when your contract negotiations are bogged down. A skilled therapist, facilitator, mediator, or coach provides a therapeutic safety net and knows how to get you unstuck, makes certain you don't get mired down in the blame battle, and encourages you to persevere and avoid making hasty decisions. This support can relieve you of considerable strain when you and your partner are most vulnerable. Rather than struggling needlessly, using therapeutic assistance can bring the voice of reason to the bargaining table.

With emotional protection available within the bounds of this safety net, you garner support and get a more enlightened slant on the issues that are impeding your progress. Counseling gives you a chance to explore your most sensitive and troubling differences under the most favorable conditions.

Your safety net provides a sense of security when you feel as if you are falling apart. You are allowed to express your innermost thoughts and feelings, knowing you are receiving impartial guidance. Someone is actually listening to what you have to say and is there to pick up the pieces should your relationship come apart at the seams.

In other words, *a therapeutic safety net serves to reduce anxious moments, not only during contract negotiations, but during those crucial days after your CS Contract is in operation.*

With therapeutic guidance, you might agree to temporarily set aside current unresolvable issues as attention is directed to a review of the more favorable aspects of your relationship. This gives both partners time to quietly ask the following questions and listen carefully to the responses:

- What do I find attractive and pleasing in my partner?

- What are the strengths of our coupling?

- What do we have in common that we enjoy doing together?

- Do we take our foibles so seriously that we can't let down our guards and find room for laughter?

Your bleak situation may be no laughing matter, but with therapeutic backup your conversations may shift to a more affirmative direction. This very effort might turn the tide or at least alter your mood for the better. This vital turnabout can minimize resentment and access a more charitable, compassionate connection with your mate. As your attitude changes to optimism, how much easier it is to partake of the advantages of cooperation and advocacy.

The age-old saying "There is no ill wind that doesn't blow some good" is one of my favorites. In difficult times I refer to this affirmation regularly. You are in a rare, pivotal position to rise to the occasion and complete your Contract. Look upon your CS as a time for personal growth so that you and your mate can achieve a more harmonious understanding. In doing so, you are better prepared to let go of your lingering hurts and anger and move forward.

The Power of Prayer

The possibility of separating without burning your bridges is real. In such tentative and uncertain times, many people turn to prayer for solace and healing. It takes a lot of courage and largesse of spirit to face the reality that we are all just a little lower than the angels.

Prayer works wonders in mysterious ways. I often find courage when I pray for strength to get through a tough emotional ordeal. As couples commence their CS journey, I've noticed that many of them voluntarily return to their church, synagogue, or other place of worship, even after years of absence.

The affirmations found in prayer can be priceless comforts when consolation is needed the most. Many people have wondered why it took such an outlandish crisis to lead them closer to God.

Light at the End of the Tunnel

I always shake hands with my client-couples after they have signed their CS Contract, and they shake hands with each other. This gesture of goodwill speaks from the heart, indicating you are about to carve new pathways with a clearer mind. If you can promise not to toy with each other and to respect the boundaries you have worked so hard to establish, your CS can be an impressive learning experience. As you use your apart time to promote appreciation for your joint efforts, you can sleep better knowing you have done your very best.

Next we meet Samantha (Sam) and Paul, who were determined to hang in for seven sessions to work out the terms of their CS Contract. The finished product was a document both could abide by, with rules that helped save their sanity.

$\mathcal{T}$he CS Contract: Tale of a Tenacious Couple

Sam and Paul: Falling Out of Love

FALLING OUT OF love with your partner and falling in love with someone else is perhaps the most somber reason why partners are compelled to think long and hard about whether to stay or go.

It took three months of therapy before Paul felt comfortable enough to confide in me. Speaking of his affectionate interest in a woman named Carla, he described her as "a friend, maybe more—nothing hot and heavy, not yet. Still not sure about the sex part."

Paul's wife, Samantha (Sam) saw him get moody and depressed; and she phoned me, distraught, when rumor had it some other woman was in the picture. Sam, inundated with shame, was determined to save her timeworn marriage.

Paul, a man of few words, found It unthinkable to provoke Sam's rage and court more trouble—certainly not after 19 years of marriage. He thought it would be safer to remain silent than be accused of deliberately antagonizing his wife. Yet he wanted to explore the single life. Paul was lost in a fog of confusion, with no idea how to handle his dilemma.

Couple Counseling

At our introductory meeting, Sam held the floor and lost no time in demanding to know the score. Did Paul really have a secret sort of understanding with Carla? Guarded, her husband made light of the friendship. "Nothing to it . . . met her skiing a couple of times."

After that Paul was noncommittal, behaving as if there were no crisis to stew about. Sam, however, was taut as a drum and suspicious of his icy silence.

Our next two meetings were uneventful as Sam pressed for answers, to no avail. I repeatedly plied Paul with questions: "What do you want?" His stock answer was, "I don't know." I asked again, "Do you want to work on your marriage?" He repeated, "I don't know." His answer remained the same, even when he was asked about wanting a separation or divorce.

Paul's "I don't know" is a common response for depressed people who feel awkward talking about themselves. In the language of therapy, this is called "resistance." For these "silent sufferers," holding their secrets close to the chest seems a lot better than blurting out some half-formed truth they may later regret.

In the hope of getting to know Paul better, I asked him to make an individual appointment, but he canceled at the last minute, saying he preferred to come with Sam rather than alone.

CS Introduced

Sam was visibly shaken the longer I was unproductive in finding out what Paul really wanted from therapy. By the close of the couple's third session, I knew all three of us were *stuck*, as Paul remained noncommittal.

Stonewalling like this is not a good situation for clinicians. So the timing was right for me to introduce the CS, because from experience I knew that the CS Guidelines were the catalyst that would provoke a response—any kind would do—just to get Paul talking. It worked. I got plenty of reaction.

At first Sam was incensed. "I don't see why we need to separate like this. Is this really necessary?" She was totally unprepared for what looked like a drastic measure. But Paul took only a little prodding from me and mumbled, "OK, I guess that's what we have to do." His ready consent was indicative of his privately held doubts about the future of his marriage. Sam bit her lip, hung her head in disapproval, and reluctantly complied. Surely, she could never have anticipated this turn of events.

The Fading Embers

Sam and Paul were a decent, family-minded, hardworking couple who had invested the better part of their energies in their son, Andrew, and daughter, Candy. Both parents were of a like mind, determined to set aside funds for their college-bound teenagers. The children gave meaning and purpose to their lives.

With blinders on their eyes, both spouses had compromised their relationship, had looked the other way when disturbing differences arose. As a result, the couple had grown resentful and indifferent to one another's needs for intimacy. Any outward display of closeness had become a distant memory. Communication had ground to a standstill as neither party dared to test their long-entrenched relationship. Confrontation was much too risky.

Internationally acclaimed marriage and family therapists Augustus Y. Napier and Carl A. Whitaker in *The Family Crucible* eloquently attest to the disquietude that takes over when partners sense something is amiss in the marriage:

> [The couple's] misgivings first take the form of a vague sense of being crowded and constricted by the marriage. Maintaining an intense dependency takes a great deal of work. Since neither can risk rejection, both individuals decide they must suppress many of the feelings that threaten to displease the other. Compromising

their own needs in order to please each other is easy enough for a while, but after several years marriage begins to feel like an enormous set of demands within which they both have a sense of being small and insignificant. The set of demands in which they feel *engulfed* is really a two-sided dependency, but in their minds the jailer is Marriage.[1]

It was evident that any thought of abandoning their union was not to be taken lightly by either Sam or Paul.

Sam's Story

Sam was a feisty woman of 44 who had been a child of three divorces. The feeling of abandonment was as familiar to her as were the men who frequented her mother's doorstep. An assortment of surrogate "Daddies" had come and gone, with never a word of explanation from Mother. Sam felt cheated by not having had a dependable father and shortchanged by a hypercritical mother who continually pushed her aside.

Sam had learned to fend for herself. Proud and tough, she called herself the "sacrificial lamb." She had worked to put Paul through graduate school. Now it was her turn to complete a master's program in psychiatric nursing, paid for by her working evenings in a local department store.

Sam's crusty reserve served her well. She was not one to cry, but when she did, she would apologize and start talking fast so her tenderhearted feelings wouldn't hurt so much.

Sam had a confession to make. As she spoke with me, her eyes moistened. "Lee, I've never told a soul, but once . . . a year or so after we married . . . gosh . . . there was this man . . . I fell hard for him. Guess I've pined ever since for what might have been. I was tempted, all right. But I just couldn't do it, though we stayed in touch for quite a while."

Sam, bitten by the temptation to have an affair, had thought better of it. The image of her mother's behavior as an example was a powerful deterrent. Instead, she wore a mantle of indignation that permeated every facet of her life.

Paul's Story

Paul, 48, manager of a small mortgage company, had been a prisoner of marital misery for the last five years. Not only was he morose, but he had an acute problem in accurately expressing his emotions.

Paul was reared in a family entombed in silence. Nobody talked. The family ate dinner and left the table without a word being exchanged. As a child, he hadn't learned how to express himself. He didn't experience the full range of highs and lows but instead stayed in some fuzzy in-between place where he could shut out the hard feelings.

Contract Negotiations Begin

Paul did his best to focus on making separation plans but had little to contribute, whereas Sam had all she could do to rein in her "bitchiness." She couldn't stop dwelling on their preposterous predicament—another woman, after all those years. Could theirs be only a paper marriage? She hated to think so.

As negotiations began, Sam insisted Paul have the first say, so he would know this separation was his idea, not hers. He conceded, "OK—six months it is." Sam thought month to month would do, then changed her mind. "Well, we'll let Paul have his way." She was making an effort to be conciliatory, but her condescending manner of speech barely concealed her opposition. And Paul's lack of emotionality made it difficult for this dispirited couple to summon any enthusiasm for the project ahead.

Despite these obstacles, Paul soon rented a room in a private residence and prepared to move out. In two sessions we had settled on the following four written agreements.

1. **Moving Out.** I agree to a Controlled Separation from my spouse for six months commencing June 15, 1995, and terminating December 15, 1995.

2. **Legal Counsel.** I will see an attorney to obtain information regarding my legal rights in the event of a divorce. During the life of this contract, I will not file for divorce.

3. Living Arrangements. I, Paul, agree to rent a room in a private home. I, Sam, agree to reside in the family residence.

4. Division of Property. I agree to cooperatively divide household goods to ensure maximum comfort in our separate living quarters.

Money Talk

Sam, looking progressively drawn and dumpy, was particularly uptight about money. She worried about how they were going to manage financially and strenuously objected to their separation's costing her the use of Paul's computer. She depended on it for writing school papers, and she wasn't about to jeopardize any part of her education or deprive herself in any way. This bottleneck was settled quickly when Paul said he would temporarily loan Sam his computer.

When I asked the couple to make a budget, they thought it was a good idea and promptly went to work on it. Meanwhile, it was agreed to put the matter of finances on hold until Paul could better estimate his extra living expenses. Later, Paul picked up some weekend work, and with the help of a reasonably tight budget, they figured they could scrape by.

Child Care

Next on our agenda were their children. Sam was in the grip of motherhood, saying outright she was sure Paul would use work as an excuse to see the children less than he already did. He defensively stumbled over his words and promised not to neglect the children. Sam didn't believe him.

She wanted to tell their children, Candy and Andrew, about the separation in private, but Paul asked for a joint meeting. Grudgingly, Sam backed off. We managed to accomplish the following in one session.

Child Arrangements

 a. I agree that the best interests of Candy and Andrew are of
    primary importance.

b. I am in accord that flexible and cooperative arrangements for child supervision are required. I understand requests for special events are to be made 24 hours in advance, if possible. If misunderstandings arise between us that we cannot resolve, I will ask Lee Raffel to address the matter in a joint meeting.

c. I agree to inform Andrew and Candy of our pending separation with my spouse being present.

Slow Going

The air was getting steamier. Tackling each CS Guideline was getting bogged down, partly because Paul would take his sweet time to deliberate before speaking, partly because Sam had her own brand of delay tactics — a rash of complaints, particularly about how Paul wasn't involved with the kids enough and had so little to say to them.

When it came time to discuss their interpersonal relationship, never could I have imagined that it would become so excruciatingly detailed. Sam wanted to spell out every detail. Draining though it was, we hammered out the following set of complex arrangements in one more overtime meeting.

Couple's Interpersonal Relationship

a. Telephone: Paul will phone Sam three times weekly and talk to the children daily. Sam has permission to leave messages at Paul's office or call on his mobile phone if the matter needs prompt response.

b. Entering Home: Paul will call Sam prior to entering the home in Sam's absence.

c. Household Repairs: Paul volunteers to assume responsibility for minor household repairs if feasible.

d. Family Outings: Paul and Sam agree to take children out as a family every other week.

e. Holidays: Fourth of July: Paul will be out of town for a
business convention.

Shifting Focus

We hadn't broached the tender issue of couple dating. Intuitively, I
knew the timing was all wrong. We needed a breather before
attacking the heavy-duty implications of dating one another, much
less dating someone else. I could foresee the prospect of contend-
ing with "that other woman," and I was intentionally postponing
any part of that equation.

Because we were already on a roll, I suggested we shift the
focus and talk about confidentiality (what to say and to whom) at the
next session. No one objected. I was certain we could wrap that one
up quickly, and we did. In only one meeting we easily accomplished
the following:

Confidentiality

(Paul) I agree to tell my parents and three stepsisters that we have
separated and are working with a therapist.

(Sam) I agree to tell my brother and a close friend that we have
separated. I agree to keep the terms of our CS confidential and will
not malign my spouse or encourage others to take sides.

The Day All Hell Broke Loose

Something was brewing with Sam. I could feel it in my bones when
I walked in the room. She was edgy. Paul was his usual impervious
self. Until this meeting, Sam deferred to Paul, but today she would
have none of that. Her face drawn, she cried out, "I'm adamant! I have
my values. I won't have sex with Paul. I'll never take him back if he
has sex with any other woman. It's a moral thing and more . . . there's
AIDS, you know. How can I ever be sure?"

The room seemed to spread apart, giving Sam a mighty strong
platform to have her say. She screeched, "I'm the one who is dedi-
cated to working out this relationship, without dragging other people in. I would never have sex with some other guy while I'm still
married to Paul. My morals are set in concrete!"

With some effort Paul simply stated, "I don't appreciate your suggesting I don't have values and morals." His words hung heavy in the room.

My work was cut out for me. Talk about "couple dating" is supposed to precede conversation about "dating others." This logical progression is specified in the Guidelines for a good reason. The two issues are very different—a matter of first things first. But Sam would have none of that! Her self-righteous indignation was spilling over like a bubbling cauldron as she insisted on finding out if Paul had any intention of having sex with "that other woman" before she would consider thinking about going on a date with her spouse.

In general I see a logical progression to the couple addressing dating each other before discussing dating others. But in Sam's case there was no denying that the two issues were intricately interwoven.

To bring the couple back to the topic would put us in a bind. Sam had ushered forth the specter of AIDS, and I knew there was no way to separate all the serious sexual implications herein. With the agility of a champion wrestler, Sam made one more swipe at Paul, about "that woman," and once again Paul dodged her. After considerable interruptions it was a draw of sorts. Nothing smacked of romance here. The session went overtime again, but somehow we finally arrived at the following terms:

Couple Dating. I agree to meet with my spouse once per week for breakfast, lunch, or dinner to discuss finances, child-care arrangements, household maintenance, and other practical matters that require immediate attention.

Sexual Contact with Spouse. I (Sam and Paul) agree to the following physical contact: holding hands, hugging, and lying in bed with no demand for intercourse. I understand that this is a risky undertaking in the face of possible rejection. I also confirm that, at this time, "I don't know if I want sexual intercourse with my spouse."

The Bottom Line: Dating Others

We were supposed to discuss dating others, but it didn't quite go that way. Sam arrived looking very attractive in a snug-fitting raspberry jumpsuit, with hair freshly styled and makeup carefully applied. The couple had met already once for breakfast, and things had gone so smoothly she gambled on changing the contract by asking for two dates per week. Paul grimaced but acquiesced to avoid a scene.

A week went by, but Paul hadn't lived up to his part of the bargain. Sam was crushed! He avoided her eyes, making it obvious that he didn't want to date his wife. Bluntly I asked, "Paul, do you want to date others?" Curtly he answered, *"I'd like to have the choice."* With that, Sam stormed out of the room, incensed that Paul might favor someone else. Paul and I sat motionless looking at each other— waiting. After a long five minutes, I left the room and found Sam sitting blankly in the office lounge down the hall. She didn't balk as I gently led her back.

Sam wasn't interested in dating others. Her concern centered on the possible negative effects Paul's "other" dating would have on Candy and Andrew. She demanded that if Paul must see Carla, their children would have no contact with his "date." He let her have her say and agreed not to involve the children. It was stated thus in their Contract:

Dating Others

(Sam) I am definitely not interested in dating others.

(Paul) I would like to have the choice to date. I agree not to involve our children in meeting another woman.

Teamwork

I agree not to cross-examine my spouse or deliberately sabotage the contract negotiations by being negative, coercive, or punishing. [Special requests of this nature can be included in your contract to facilitate your separation.]

Therapy

I will attend weekly, bimonthly, or monthly couple therapy sessions as needed for the duration of this contract. Individual therapy sessions will be arranged as needed. Therapy for our children will be arranged if needed.

Wrapping up the Contract

It was time to bring negotiations to a close. I told the couple I would give them a copy of their final contract the following week. I thought long and hard how to put all we had discussed in palatable terms that both parties would find acceptable. I had no choice but to detail the conditions "word for word" as they had been stated in our conferences:

Termination of Contract

I agree not to break terms during the life of the Contract. Exceptions follow: if both parties agree to reconcile, or if Sam or Paul decide to divorce, this information is conveyed when both parties meet with our therapist.

Renegotiation of Contract

I agree this Contract will be reevaluated and renegotiated as needed in collaboration with Lee Raffel. I agree no alterations to this Contract will be made independently, deferring to conjoint negotiation as the method for change.

Sam reviewed the final document and said, "I'm going along with this thing, but you know I never wanted a separation . . . still, I don't want it to be a hateful thing, either."

Paul looked rather grim as he signed his name, but he had nothing more to add. We all shook hands, and I breathed a sigh of relief after seven long, tedious sessions of negotiation.

Paul's Transformation

Once he was separated, Paul reported that he was looking for magic. Not knowing which side of the fence he was on, he found the experience of separation puzzling—a strange mixture of euphoria and guilt. He called it "controlled chaos." I was seeing a vivacious side of Paul not in evidence before. He became introspective, questioning his behavior as he tried to make sense of his ambivalence.

Blushing, he mumbled, "I don't know if I'm ready for this . . . I'm waiting for a bolt out of the blue or something. I'm still so apathetic. People don't just get divorced . . . I'm bothered by that. I told you before. Married people are married forever."

Not wanting to hurt Sam, not wanting to deny his own bewilderment, he added, "I guess I don't know how to verbalize what I feel—that's a weakness of mine."

Paul was ready to permit his vulnerable side fuller expression when he asked, "Is this something I can practice?" Somewhat embarrassed, he left my office with homework: "Practice experiencing each of your feelings, and make a connection as the words apply to your ambivalence about Sam and Carla." The feelings he wrote down were *mad*, *sad*, *glad*, *excited*, and *scared*.

I suggested Paul keep a daily journal and briefly write something about these feeling words that applied to his everyday experiences. He left the session smiling.

Sam's Transformation

Sam took six weeks to salve her wounds, and when I saw her next, she looked stunning, sporting a broad grin. Without rancor she said, "Paul and I have decided to divorce . . . there was no scene but I did ask him about the computer because he knows how much I need it, and he was nice about it and said I could have it. And the good news is that he's figured out how we'll have enough money to see me through graduation."

Enthusiastically she added, "I have such good friends at school. I am happier and feel better than I have for many, many years. I'm still not sure how things are going to work out with the kids, but we'll just have to wait and see."

Sam had come to the realization that her marriage had died years earlier, and it was time for her to look forward to a more gratifying life.

Follow-Up

The couple's divorce was a civil one. Three years later I spoke with both parties. Each had recently remarried. Sam said, "In the long run, our CS really gave me a chance to hold my head up again—to pull my act together—when Paul dished out his insults, I felt like I could explode!"

Paul said, "The thought of a CS really shook me up at first, but it made me see I couldn't hide what I was feeling but not saying. I don't know how I could have dealt with the whole ordeal without the coaching."

Sam said, "I never would have believed a CS could make me face what I had refused to look at for all those awful years. I'm glad it's all in the past. I have found a guy who understands me."

The couple continue to communicate with one another about their children but otherwise have no direct contact. Both parties stated they still differed when it came to their teen-rearing policies, but for the sake of their kids, they talk it out and make compromises. Both parents said Candy and Andrew had made a reasonably good adjustment to their parents' new marital status. And it was evident the youngsters had benefited by their parents' tenacious efforts to keep the lines of communication open.

6

My Marriage Is Making Me Sick

Partners at Risk

SUZANNE, 48, TEETERING on the brink of leaving her marriage, couldn't hold back her tears. "I haven't been able to sleep for weeks . . . not eating much either . . . choke on my food. My doctor never saw me so emaciated. I know I look like hell. I didn't think to tell him about my troubles with Artie. So I walked out with a prescription for a vitamin tonic that's supposed to build me up. But that's not going to take care of lonesome me. . . . Artie's as cold as a frozen cucumber. He never holds me tight anymore . . . don't know how long I can hold out. If we were separated, maybe I could figure things out . . . but I'm not sure of anything right now."

When you feel beleaguered by the "stay or go" riddle, you are at risk of becoming sick in body, mind, and soul. No wonder you question if you are about to fall apart. Like Suzanne, you may go round and round in circles wondering what will come next. The lamentable truth is that the longer you trifle with marital indecision, the more you risk your health, not to mention your peace of mind.

The "stay or go" question has my indecisive clients making comments like these:

"I'm sick and tired of trying to get through to my husband."

"I'll get an ulcer if my wife doesn't shape up."

"I'm aging fast . . . my marriage is a mess. My life is half over and what do I have to show for it?"

"I get chest pains every time we quarrel. She gets so mean . . . always blaming me for everything . . . wonder if it's worth this much struggle."

"He says he's leaving but then nothing happens. I'm a nervous wreck . . . don't know where I stand."

Such candid remarks are not meant to be a pat dismissal of years of togetherness. They speak of broken hearts, anguish, and despair, as if the whole world has turned on its head. As marriages teeter on the brink, spouses fall victim to a host of physical or mental problems.

Emily's Terror

There was a time in Emily's life when she made no connection between her physical symptoms and emotional state. She said, "I never cease to be astonished by my naïveté in never once associating my physical symptoms—feverish, swollen feet and ankles—with being literally scared 'stiff' of my husband."

At 35 she was diagnosed with Buerger's disease, a constriction of circulation so threatening that without immediate medical treatment, gangrene could have set in, necessitating amputation.

The doctor was puzzled because he had never seen this illness in people younger than age 50 and said he had no idea what had caused Emily's illness. She didn't indicate to her physician that she was living in terror of her husband.

Fourteen years later, after she had divorced, another doctor reviewed the medication Emily was still taking. He talked to her at length and asked if she had been under a lot of stress over the years. Emily admitted she had been terrorized by her abusive husband but wasn't afraid now that she was single.

Her doctor suggested she gradually discontinue her drugs, and in less than three months, Emily was delighted to see the circulation in her hands and feet return to normal. It wasn't until then that she made the connection between her physical symptoms and her emotional state.

She said, "Some insight! It's hard to believe extreme fear could affect my extremities like that. Now I can understand the mind-body connection a whole lot better."

Emily is not alone. Commonly, suffering spouses rush to their doctors, not necessarily correlating their marital misery with their vast array of somatic complaints. And they don't necessarily inform their physicians of their marital troubles.

Food for Thought

As a hypnotherapist, I find that many of my clients request stress or weight management. When I learn their case histories, however, I find marital dysfunction to be a more disturbing issue for them, one that speaks to the source of these clients' symptoms.

If people would only tell their doctors and therapists at the outset that along with their physical complaints they are also having marital troubles, the prospects are good that they would be better served by the professional community.

Close, intimate relationships are an enigma for many couples, writes psychologist Frank Fincham, Ph.D., in his article "Relationship Problems: What Works?"

> Some 40% of the problems for which people seek professional help in the USA concern their spouse/marriage, a proportion that is twice the size of any other problem area. And when marriages go wrong, the costs can be high—marital disruptions are associated with just about any physical or mental health problem you care to name.[1]

Commonly, communication problems motivate people to seek help, Fincham explains.

Your Level of Stress

The grandfather of stress research, Hans Selye, author of *The Stress of Life*, makes the connection between our physiological reactions and mental attitudes when we are faced with acute stress. In such circumstances, whether the threat is real or imagined, we instinctively react as if our survival is at stake. This is popularly known as the fight-or-flight response. However, such chronic overreaction is debilitating to our health in the long run.[2] What better description could we have to the mounting distress of marital indecision than "fight or flight"?

I like the way trainer of somatic psychology Jocelyn Olivier explains what happens to our bodies when we are stuck:

> The chemistry of stress produces changes in our feeling and energy states. Initially it produces a surge of impulse and activity, an urge to action. If the road to action is blocked, the restraint can manifest as a binding or armoring of impulse and be experienced as inertia or being stuck, even as depression, anger or resentment.[3]

Husband and wife medical team Redford Williams, M.D., and Virginia Williams, Ph.D., authors of *Anger Kills*, have conducted groundbreaking research that confirms that raging emotions—accelerated hostility, cynicism, and aggression—are like a "slow acting poison," known to stress the immune system. Unremitting anger can lead to life-threatening illnesses, even death.[4]

As we live longer and become more invested in living longer and staying healthy, couples are finding themselves wrestling with the advisability of staying in their disabled relationships without attempting to make some significant changes for the better.

Measuring Your Level of Stress

T. H. Holmes and R. H. Rahe developed a useful method for measuring your level of stress known as the Social Readjustment Rating Scale (SRRS).[5] As shown in Figure 6.1, the death of a spouse is life's greatest stressor—rated at 100 units. Divorce is second, rated at 73; marital separation is third, at 65; marriage is seventh, at 50; and marital reconciliation is ninth, at 45. These numbers confirm what you already suspected: marital upheaval is a major life stressor.

A score of 300 in a given year substantially increases your risk of illness, a score from 150 to 299 decreases that risk by one-third, and a score of 150 or less amounts to a lesser chance of becoming ill.

Figure 6.1. *The Social Readjustment Rating Scale*

Units	Life Event
100	Death of spouse
73	Divorce
65	Marital separation
63	Imprisonment
63	Death of close family member
53	Personal injury or illness
50	Marriage
47	Dismissal from work
45	Marital reconciliation
45	Retirement
44	Change in health of family member
40	Pregnancy
39	Sexual difficulties
39	Gain of new family member
39	Business readjustment
38	Change in financial state
35	Change in number of arguments with spouse
32	Major mortgage
30	Foreclosure of mortgage or loan
29	Change in responsibilities at work
29	Son or daughter leaving home
29	Trouble with in-laws
28	Outstanding personal achievement
26	Spouse begins or stops work
26	Beginning or ending school
25	Change in living conditions
24	Revision of personal habits
23	Trouble with employer
20	Change in work hours or conditions
20	Change in residence
20	Change in schools
19	Change in recreation
19	Change in church activities
18	Change in social activities
17	Minor mortgage or loan
16	Change in sleeping habits
15	Change in number of family reunions
15	Change in eating habits
13	Vacation
12	Christmas
11	Minor violation of the law

As you tally your score of life events, you see whether they add up to mild, moderate, or major stress. Using this yardstick gives you a greater understanding of the effect of your marital relationship on your overall health and well-being.

Factors That Hamper Resolution

As you ponder the "stay or go" question, you are subjected to certain states of mind that will hamper your ability to make a bona fide marital decision. You can gauge your state of anguish and despair by the degree and intensity of these four factors: ambivalence, polarization, stagnation, and immobilization. Until these states of mind are resolved, they wear down your physical and emotional reserves and give you just cause to feel sick.

Ambivalence

Ambivalence has you running in circles. Like a kid, you seesaw between telling yourself "I won't go" and "I will go." You are tormented with inner conflict, with contradictory sensations pounding at your head simultaneously: love and hate, guilt and resentment, trust and suspicion. Your mood goes up and down like a teeter-totter.

Your logical mind tells you to go, but your heart says to stay. You feel one way at night and just the opposite in the morning. You are wishy-washy. You feel split in two, torn apart. Your head spins. You walk a flimsy tightrope, and your equilibrium is disturbed. You don't like being caught off guard. Ambivalence is not your cup of tea.

One of my clients, Roy, 42, twice married, described it like this: "Ambivalence is like being in a fog as thick as pea soup. . . . I'm so unsure of myself." In time you begin to lose confidence in yourself. Ambivalence can drive you crazy.

- You yearn for the good times, "the way things were," and hope those lost days will return, but logic shouts, "Yes, but look at where our relationship is headed now."

- You say to yourself, "I'm damned if I stay and I'm damned if I go," but that's as far as you get.

- You say to your spouse, "I don't understand why you won't try harder," then you give up trying yourself.

- Your spouse accuses you of being a nag, and you want to fight back, but you hold your tongue.

- You cry your eyes out, sure it's all your fault—or all your mate's fault—and stay stuck.

The chronic nature of ambivalence fuels its own fires and becomes the breeding ground for rage, depression, angst, and grief. The ensuing tension triggers acute stress that holds you in its clutches—until you do something about it. Ambivalence and indecision go hand in hand—they precipitate and activate illness.

Polarized Partners

Polarized partners stay stuck while stubbornly defending their antagonistic points of view. When you are competitive with each other, you hold tight to beliefs and opinions that are poles apart.

- "I am positive about my life, but you are negative."

- "I know our relationship is falling apart, but you think everything is OK."

- "I believe we need couple counseling, but you think we can work out our differences with no outside help."

- "I think you are to blame, and you think I'm at fault."

- "I say the affair is over, and you won't let it go."

When either spouse insists, "I am right and you are wrong," both parties are drawn into a conflicted standoff. Polarized positions of this kind can add up to heavy-duty stress, which becomes unmanageable. You get sick just thinking about it.

Stagnant Mates

Stagnation in relationships discourages the growth of the coupling and inhibits the growth of the person. *Sameness*—ritualized activities that repeatedly occur at the same time and place—preserve harmony for some partners but inflict boredom on others. Boredom itself is an illness of no small order as we shall see in the case of Lucy and Jackie in Chapter 14.

Your marital relationship is a living entity that requires consistent weeding and feeding to thrive successfully. When you take one another for granted and do little or nothing to improve your status, or when you try to thwart your mate's personal development, it doesn't bode well for your coupling. All too soon, your coupling is apt to fall into a state of disrepair.

Immobilized Mates

When both you and your mate are too paralyzed to make a move, you have reached the epitome of stuckness. Immobilized mates are generally frustrated and negative about their marital predicament. You prefer to avoid dealing with your dissatisfactions and let your little irritations mushroom in silence. On the heels of impending tragedy, many of my client-couples have said:

> "There's nothing I can do about my marriage."
> "I'd rather not talk to him about it. Why get him all upset?"
> "I'll duck out of facing her any way I can."
> "I'm not sticking my nose in this mess . . . what's to be gained?"
> "It doesn't bother me" [but it does].

You don't make a move for fear of being on the losing end of a decision to stay or go. You hate the thought of fighting over money or battling over the children, in-laws, friends, or the "conflict of the day." You hate to incriminate yourself. Any and all potential losses hold you and your mate at bay.

Sean, 39, was furious with his wife but too immobilized to do much about it other than complain. "I don't know what's happened to Nancy. She's been coming home at 4 A.M. . . . tells me she's out with the girls and acts as if this is OK. Something's not adding up. If I say anything, she insists everything is going great guns or she just changes the subject. Maybe she wants a divorce. . . . I don't know. She won't talk. I'm shaking inside, like my body is poisoned. I can't deal with it."

Deeply ingrained insecurities and fear for the marriage's survival kept Sean and Nancy immobilized. As long as both mates feared facing themselves and disturbing the status quo, they stayed stuck.

It took a year before Nancy worked up the nerve to tell Sean that she had met another man and wanted a divorce.

Relationship Splintering

A host of factors can provoke a marital impasse. Often, overt changes in the personality of one or both partners breed suspicion and foretell of marital unrest.

Figure 6.2 lists many telling signs of relationship splintering. Check off the ones that fit you or your spouse.

Figure 6.2. *Signs of Relationship Splintering*

❏ Physical and verbal abuse

❏ Unprovoked hostility in mate

❏ Feeling you cannot express yourself adequately to your spouse

❏ Frustrated by frequent, useless arguments

❏ Sudden unusual behavior: frequent shifting employment, excessive dieting, unfamiliar friendships, or unusual personality changes

❏ Aloof and withdrawn behavior

❏ Withholding affection and sexual intimacy

❏ Oppositional and controlling behavior

❏ Increased impulsive spending

❏ Boredom, restlessness, and moodiness

❏ Unexplained absences, working unusually long hours

❏ Lying, acting defensive, or being unreliable

❏ Suspicion of infidelity

❏ False accusations

❏ Unexplained euphoria at odds with current marital stalemate

❏ Compulsive blaming and complaining

❏ Lack of compassion and stubbornly uncooperative behavior

❏ Showing little or no interest in sexual intimacy

❏ Breakdown in communication

❏ Unwillingness to cooperate in decision making

These warning signs are indicators of marital distress that tends to accelerate over time if ignored.

Be aware. There is sometimes an inclination to misinterpret or overlook these signals and pretend they aren't as serious as they actually are.

However, before you get into a real panic about the dire state of your relationship, let's take a closer look at how sickness in marriage develops in progressive stages: malaise, obsessing, and chaos.

Malaise

The onset of malaise begins the first time you become aware that something is amiss between you and your mate. At first you pretend your apprehension is without substance, but gradually the feeling takes hold. A certain uneasiness creeps into your sinews that is hard to explain. You want that nameless, gnawing feeling to go away.

You might not want to admit it, but it is not unusual for two common fantasies to begin to disturb you: disposing of your spouse or attaching yourself to another hero or heroine.

Such intrusive thoughts make it increasingly difficult to have any kind of meaningful and loving relationship.

As malaise takes over, your energy is consumed with solidifying or penetrating stony walls of silence. Or you may be impulsively jumping into jungle warfare. These oppressive conditions infringe on your energy. You can't concentrate or face up to your stalemate.

Partners who are in a state of denial manage to hold out by exerting every bit of their energy to avoid the "stay or go" issue. They assume their spouse's discontent will somehow mysteriously vanish; how or when is not the issue. Rather than incite or exploit the marital predicament, they hope that such entrenched loyalty might provide just enough glue to preserve the marriage, be it for better or for worse.

Obsessing

Obsessing is a stage marked by pervasive worry, like a dark cloud that hangs around and won't go away. Your racing thoughts have a way of taking over your life and driving you crazy. You fret. You lose your appetite or eat compulsively. Sleepless nights are all too familiar. Bouts of panic or depression may be unwelcome intrusions at the most unlikely times. By now you are frightened and rush to the doctor, saying, "I'm just not myself. I'm falling apart. I don't know what's come over me."

Your moods are like a roller coaster's ups and downs. You feel helpless to help yourself. If you abuse drugs and alcohol, you complicate your life further. You question whether life is worth living. You might make veiled threats of ending it all.

Obsessing becomes your unspeakable master as you are crowded with unanswerable questions.

"What do I do next?"

"What has come over my mate?"

The harder you try *not* to think about whether you should stay or go, the worse you feel.

Delving into your past, contemplating your status quo, or reckoning with your future is a hardship. The possibility of an ugly divorce stops you in your tracks. With your relationship at a standstill, you grow impatient and feel threatened. The more you overreact to your impasse, the worse your deadlock becomes. Shame is your nemesis.

Chaos

Chaos is exhausting, as if you are "running on empty." You fear your chaotic mess will go on forever. Then panic sets in. Your heart is thumping away, your palms are sweaty, and that dreaded knot has your tummy so upset you just know you are sick.

In your chaotic state, your psyche shuts down and you can't think straight. Your insides either turn to stone or feel as if they are about to burst. You haven't the strength to deal with this bone-crushing tension. You can't even bring yourself to phone a counselor or minister. That will have to wait for another day.

When you are immersed in the full catastrophe of indecision, you have no choice but to admit you are lost. Your relationship drifts. Chaos is a nightmare.

Imaginitus

Any of the above three stages of relationship sickness can be the breeding ground for "imaginitus" to take root. You begin to focus on the worst-case scenario and react as if it were already happening, even when it is not. In this sorry state you go off on all sorts of irrelevant tangents that do further damage to your coupling. You may be suspicious when you have scant cause or be jealous as your unbridled imagination runs rampant. On the heels of imaginitus, some mates impulsively make decisions they soon regret and have just cause to feel sick about that.

Rejector and Rejectee Status and Sickness

Relationship sickness is not often evenly apportioned between partners. One mate might be content and the other remarkably discontent. The turmoil that might send one spouse scrambling for a divorce will be tolerated by the other spouse with a lot less aggravation.

Although I'm not altogether satisfied with the terms *rejector* and *rejectee*, they are a useful way to define the status of each partner. At times both spouses may reject each other simultaneously, or rejection may seesaw from one to the other.

Keeping in mind that nothing is black or white with couples on the cusp, as either spouse can be both rejector and rejectee, I have identified further subdivisions to clarify these positions: "silent rejector," "reluctant rejector," "shocked rejectee," and "rescuer rejectee."

Silent Rejector

You feel justified in not revealing your privately held doubts about staying or going. You don't want a breakup and grieve at the thought of hurting your spouse. Fear of irretrievable losses makes you think twice about speaking up.

Stewart created the very uproar he had hoped to avoid when he told Mindy, "I love you as a friend, not as a wife." It may be hard to believe, but he was able to hide his feelings for over 17 years of marriage. He always hoped he would feel the passion, but it never happened.

Ironically, at first Mindy would not own up to any major relationship difficulties other than that Stewart was a workaholic. Neither did Stewart have a bad word for his wife: "Mindy's been good to me . . . we've never tormented one another."

Stewart's ambivalence finally caught up with him the day he arrived at work too emotionally incapacitated to stay on the job. He told his boss of his precarious marital state and then went home to tell Mindy the truth. She took his admission as the ultimate insult. Mindy cried, "The worst part of it for me is not having had a choice or any input in the matter."

In the aftermath the couple came rushing to my doorstep, both parties in tears. The couple consented to a CS for five weeks and then reunited. Stewart said, "I'm really the marrying kind."

Undoubtedly, there are many reasons why you would rather not show your hand or let your mate know you have one foot out the door. Perhaps you have a "significant other" waiting in the wings. If so, you bide your time, waiting for the right moment to speak up.

As the silent rejector, like Stewart, you may hold out as long as you possibly can because you are afraid to face the fireworks. But retaining your secret is prone to make you even sicker physically or emotionally or both. (The touchy subject of secrets is explored in Chapter 15.)

Reluctant Rejector

You blame yourself, and you are riddled with guilt. All kinds of physical symptoms may intrude and hang on: colitis, migraine headaches, chest pain, back trouble, and other assorted ailments. The stress is wearing you down.

You have every intention of saving your marriage if you can, but it's not entirely up to you. You keep hoping your spouse will do an about-face, but, unfortunately, even counseling has been to no avail.

Although you would prefer to avoid the word *divorce*, you mourn over being forced to consider this option for the sake of your health and safety.

Shocked Rejectee

Your mate tells you he or she wants to leave, and you are in shock because, like Mindy, you had no idea your marriage was in trouble.

When Stewart confessed the bitter truth to his wife, she was incredulous and accused him of being "quite an actor."

Stewart had convincingly showered Mindy with jewels and loving anniversary cards. How could he live a lie all those years? Why the duplicity? she wondered. The reverberations of this shocking news plunged her into a state of depression.

Whether it is the devastating blow of an affair, serious financial losses, or whatever bomb your spouse gracelessly drops in your lap, your equilibrium is shattered.

As the shocked rejectee, you are caught off guard by such drastic news, as if you are the last person to know. If your spouse decides to separate or walks out without warning, you find the betrayal unforgivable. With no ready-made solutions available, for the moment you are overwhelmed beyond words. You can't make sense of your marital tragedy.

Rescuer Rejectee

You are in denial, quick to overlook or reinterpret any overt signs of relationship discord.

As the rescuer rejectee, you see your mission as one of taking care of your partner—the "sick" one. You do your best to ensure that his or her symptoms are treated. Should your mate get strong enough to make the break, you feel cruelly rejected because you had pretended your marriage was on solid ground.

Elusive and Invested Intimacy

At best, intimacy in marriage is difficult to sustain. Both divisiveness and closeness in relationships are normal. Conflict is a necessary part of intimacy, as there is no way to avoid misunderstandings and hurt feelings. But if your marital dissatisfaction is not resolved, your smoldering vexation sets off a chain reaction of overt or covert retaliation, which makes for sickness. And then you wonder why being intimate is so slippery.

Elusive intimacy forces us to face our ultimate aloneness. It creates a sense of loss—alienation and isolation—as if you are at loose ends with yourself and out of touch with your partner. You begin to question your own self-worth. And then you question the worth of your marital relationship.

It is not easy to identify our symptoms of illness as messages meant to alert us to pursue and repair those parts of our lives that feel incomplete and unfulfilled. When these symptoms are misinterpreted and not resolved, the subsequent emotional baggage we carry can be debilitating. It gnaws at our insides. It is toxic to our immune system.

Conversely, *invested intimacy* in marriage is built on the premise of heartfelt care, collaboration, and communication that promotes implicit trust, that enhances rather than diminishes the partners' worth.

Psychotherapist Emily M. Brown, author of *Patterns of Infidelity and Their Treatment*, tells us what brings couples closer:

> True intimacy depends on talking to each other about joys and sorrow, the mundane and the profound, the pain and the pleasures, and likes and dislikes together. It means standing up to each other and confronting differences until they are satisfactorily resolved. . . . Above all, intimacy means being honest with each other, knowing that each other's word is good. Any false words cast doubt about the rest.[6]

As long as the torment of elusive intimacy continues to evoke the "stay or go" question, the lack of closure takes its toll. Until you make a definitive decision, closure, much like the golden pear, stays just out of reach.

Who Decides?

Waiting for an answer to the "stay or go" question is like a two-edged sword. If you are the rejectee, you are beset with waiting for others to decide the fate of your life. As your mate tarries, you suffer the angst of second-guessing. If you are the rejector, you are engulfed in waiting to see if you will be your own prime mover. The longer you linger, the more depression depletes your energies.

In either case, your fluctuating moods leave you feeling out of control.

Sociologist Diane Vaughan, author of *Uncoupling: How Relationships Come Apart*, explains that the rejector who holds the secret is at an advantage in having the power, not only to create a crisis but also to control the marital unfolding.[7] In this way privately held doubts are not revealed until the impetus to separate or divorce outweighs the benefits of remaining together.

Because the signals of discontent may be less than obvious, the rejectee is at a disadvantage in being on the outside looking in. It can be tricky to discern what is going on, particularly if the signs of marital splintering are misconstrued.

As long as the rejectee doesn't want to know and the rejector doesn't say, the couple's status quo is preserved. A threatening situation is avoided, and a difficult choice is averted. In some instances the "stay or go" question is delayed for many years or circumvented indefinitely.

In determining the direction or fate of the decision-making process, if you take the course of least resistance, you can live with things the way they are, as long as you are not at odds with yourself. But once your eyes are opened and you face what can no longer be denied, chances are your seething indignation will cause all kinds of havoc and you could become a prime candidate for all sorts of unwanted marital sicknesses.

Next, we'll investigate the broad spectrum of couple separation.

7

The Anatomy of Marital Separation

Lives on Hold

"WE'LL SEPARATE OVER my dead body."

"I don't want to separate and be responsible for breaking up our marriage."

"I'll file for divorce before I'll separate."

"I've mentioned separation, but my spouse doesn't think I mean it."

"I'm separating. The lawyers can figure out the rest."

Marital separation encompasses a complex assortment of arrangements that frequently change shape like an amoeba. Couples in conflict put their lives on hold because they aren't aware of the vast implications inherent in marital separation.

Eminent psychologist Constance R. Ahrons, Ph.D., in *The Good Divorce: Keeping Your Family Together When Your Marriage Comes Apart*, tells us that partners give their own definitions to separation, reflecting the characteristics, needs, and goals—at the moment—of the parties involved.[1]

Contradiction in Definition

Basically, separations fall on a continuum from cooperative to contentious. My working definition of marital separation is this: Husband and wife live either apart or in the same residence by unilateral or joint agreement or by court decree.

Admittedly, this definition is contradictory. The first picture one gets in speaking of marital separation is of some enraged mate packing a suitcase and checking in at the nearest motel, bunking down at mother's, or sleeping on some friendly rescuer's couch. This is actually a close approximation of what is often known as trial separation (TS).

A TS can also take place right in one's own home, as one disgruntled spouse abandons the marital bed after a grisly fight. The result is a similar kind of physical separation for the same emotional reasons. However, couple separation by my definition is vastly more diverse and intricate than either of these descriptions.

Six Basic Forms of Marital Separation

Let's start with six basic forms of marital separation.

1. Divorce

2. Legal separation

3. Situational separation

4. Long-distance separation

5. Transitional separation

6. Experimental separations (Controlled Separation and trial separation)

None of these forms represents a truly distinct category as far as living arrangements go; each can blend or merge into another form at times. For example, one mate might file for divorce and separate with every intention of following through and then have a change of heart.

1. Divorce

Why is divorce placed first? There are several reasons: first, people misconstrue *separation* as meaning *divorce* because the two terms are sometimes used interchangeably. Second, not all divorces represent a clean relationship break, even though divorce is viewed as the ultimate legal separation. Third, some people assume that separated parties, if not already divorced, are well on the path to formalizing the event. Fourth, there will always be those divorced couples who continue to date each other, reconcile, remarry, and divorce again.

In these cases, "finality" is not final to the extent it provides no guarantee that mates will cease living together. Though rare, some divorced couples sufficiently make up to the point of resuming residence in the same dwelling without ever remarrying. Emotionally, these relationships enter a swampland—divorced but still a twosome.

Katie and Hank: The Lost-Without-You Couple

Katie was worried. On several occasions she had caught her husband "ogling" their two budding teenage daughters in the shower. Our counseling focused on her working up the nerve to confront him. Eventually she spoke up, and I met with Hank briefly.

I could see why his wife was having difficulty in stating her disdain. Hank's rationalizations and excuses were like a sieve; they didn't hold water. He minimized his "errors in judgment," failing to see the full implication of his actions.

A year went by, and Katie was still sorely troubled. She didn't trust Hank's promises to stop spying. More than that, she could not abide the thought of jeopardizing the well-being of her children. Divorce had never been on Katie's agenda, but divorce is what it came to. "I had to do it to ease my conscience," she told me.

Hank moved out, and I thought Katie was beginning to make an acceptable adjustment to this major transition. When three months had passed, she informed me that Hank had been reinstated in the house. I verified that their daughters' privacy was being protected.

"Hank wasn't making his rent on his apartment. Um . . . uh . . . ah . . . we had a long talk, Hank and I, and . . . well . . . anyway, he's back home. We fixed up something for him in the attic . . . it's . . . I guess it's working out so far."

2. Legal Separation

SHE: "Lee, when you talk about us separating, I'm not sure what you mean. Are you suggesting a legal separation or what?"

HE: "I might consider a legal separation if I knew the advantages, because I am not in favor of divorce."

Today, legal separation has become something of an oddity. After a quarter century of increasing acceptance of divorce, there is less need for such an arrangement, but it remains an alternative for people who do not wish to divorce for religious or other reasons.

Prior to 1965 and the divorce explosion, legal separation was the "condoned" method of separation, particularly for Catholics, inasmuch as Catholicism prohibits divorce. When droves of staunch Catholic parishioners began to defy the church edict against divorce, the church was obliged to acknowledge that a legal separation was becoming less acceptable to couples than a divorce.

Legal separation is court ordered and subject to state regulation, which can vary from one state to another. For example, the following five regulations apply in Wisconsin:

1. Both a divorce and a legal separation are court ordered on the grounds that a marriage has been irretrievably broken.

2. The same legal procedures are involved for both a divorce and a legal separation; that is, custody is determined, property is divided, and support payments are court ordered.

3. Divorce means a marriage is legally terminated; spouses may remarry in six months (by law in the state of Wisconsin—the time limit varies by state).

4. A legal separation may be converted to a divorce after a year, allowing the spouses to remarry, if they so choose.

5. Spouses who want to reconcile can have their legal separation revoked at any time.[2]

3. Situational Separation

Two types of situational separation exist—permanent and temporary.

Permanent Situational Separation. In reaction to life's situational twists and turns, there are always a few couples who forge a permanent, nonlegal separation. Of course, people have their reasons for choosing this option. Practically speaking, it may be a matter of money, religion, or children. Psychologically, it may be inertia or an abiding fear of being trapped in a second or third bad marriage. Ann and Luke's situation is a case in point.

Ann and Luke: The Indifferent Couple

Ann sought counseling because she couldn't manage the extenuating circumstances that surrounded the care of her elderly parents. At the time she felt very much alone, in need of support, and took the opportunity to tell me about her relationship with her husband, Luke, from whom she had been separated for 10 years.

There was a time when Ann and Luke, a childless couple, were sweethearts, but his gambling proved a source of immense disappointment to his wife. Luke would tell Ann he loved her, but his behavior told her he loved gambling—the stock market, horses, football games, lotteries, whatever—even more. She constantly worried about money, which Luke won and lost easily.

Though she nagged him to get treatment for his gambling addiction, he refused. This rejection was the last straw. She could never forgive him.

Ann had a long history of chronic illnesses stemming from early childhood. Her frail health was a "good enough" reason to withhold sexual intimacies from her husband. Without either of them discussing it, she knew her husband was displeased with her. And she was quite aware Luke knew how much she resented his risky lifestyle. Each partner's rejection took a lasting toll on their relationship.

After 15 years of marriage, Ann summoned the courage to tell Luke she was moving out. He wasn't as shocked as he feigned to be because Ann had recently received an inheritance. Though not large, if it were wisely invested, the money could modestly sustain her.

The couple never spoke of divorce. It wasn't like them to discuss such issues. But what Luke did understand was that Ann would
be in a financial bind without his health insurance.

She described her relationship with Luke as being "quite indifferent." He would attend family functions maybe once a year, but
they never had anything to say to each other. He had a live-in woman
friend, and she dated the widower next door. Luke was so closemouthed, she didn't know how he felt about their separation.

Ann had no wish to change her marital status. "I'm satisfied
with the way things are. We never could get close. I know one thing
for sure, remarriage is not for me—I don't ever want to get stung
again." I could only surmise that Luke's apparent inertia was just
enough to hold this couple to their permanent separation.

Temporary Situational Separation. Couples routinely experience a number of temporary separations resulting from a variety of
situations. The ordinary demands of work, travel, and illness sometimes make it prudent and necessary for spouses to be away from
home for periods of time. The situations that cause such separation
might be brief, temporary, intermittent, and/or ritualized. Parting
may be benign or conflicted. If marital equilibrium is not seriously
disturbed, such separations generally do not damage the relationship. In a stable marriage, situational separations are accepted, tolerated, endured, or condoned.

Family illness can be a sad, difficult time, requiring some degree
of separation. Or the terms of employment may stipulate extensive
travel or frequent moves from city to city, which can be exceedingly
stressful to the family and require mates to demonstrate their
resilience and resourcefulness. In durable unions, spouses accommodate for these inconveniences.

Mary and Ted: The Durable Couple

Mary's husband has been a traveling salesman for more than 20
years. Ted loves his work, phones his wife and children religiously
every evening, and looks forward to their hugs and kisses when he
returns home every Friday afternoon. Weekends are planned for
the enjoyment of the family. Mary operates a small business from

home and has never been inconvenienced by Ted's absences, except "when the kids are sick."

When the love connection remains constant and partners make the necessary adjustments and accommodations required of situational separations, no harm is done to the marriage. Mary and Ted's ritualized, weekly separation is a good example of a situational separation that is benign—perhaps it even enhances intimacy rather than engenders dissension.

But some situational separations do great harm, resulting in immense unhappiness and misery.

Lily and Guy: The Miserable Couple

Lily and Guy expected their parting to be temporary, but when it turned out otherwise, Lily fretted day and night. She had three young children with no husband around to give her a helping hand. Guy had taken a position with a large company in another state, and Lily assumed the family would be reunited within three months or as soon as Guy found a suitable house.

Guy made occasional visits back home, and twice Lily and the children went to visit their father, who was staying at a motel. But after six months Lily couldn't understand why Guy had failed to find a suitable house. She sensed her husband was pulling away.

It was nine months before the family was reunited. Shortly thereafter Lily heard via the grapevine that Guy was courting another woman. The fallout of this discovery was enough to fracture their relationship, and their marriage terminated in divorce.

4. Long-Distance Separation

The long-distance separation is a first cousin to the situational separation. It may be brief or long-standing. If the separation extends for an indeterminate period of time, or if the duration of separation is so tentative that the parties are uncertain when, where, and how they will reconnect, such absences take an ever-increasing toll on the parties' psyches. Military service or other career choices that permit only brief, intermittent home visits may be quite acceptable to some independent mates, but long-term partings often place more strain on spouses than they can bear.

Tori and Jon: The Faraway Couple

Tori was lonely, but she never complained that her husband was working as a movie producer in Mexico, more than one thousand miles away. She and Jon had agreed it would be best to raise their three children in the Midwestern suburb where Tori had grown up. For the first two years, Jon came home for at least a few days every month. But he never knew when an assignment would prevent him from keeping even that much of a regular schedule.

Gradually, his visits home became fewer and farther apart. Tori broached the subject of the children being raised virtually without a father.

When Jon was in town and could spare an extra hour, we would talk. He was restless, tormented, and torn. Many of his cohorts were divorcing. He was drawn into a crowd of yuppies who were suddenly single. Attracted to the glamour of the single life, he realized he could not keep his marriage vows. He didn't want his wife to know, but secrets have a way of being found out. Despite Tori's serious objections, Jon filed for divorce at the close of the third year of their long-distance separation. His guilt and worry had become all-consuming.

The longer and more often spouses are inaccessible to each other, the more difficult it becomes to sustain the commitment to preserve the union. In the absence of a mate, many spouses lose interest, are unfaithful, or find another lifestyle not in keeping with that of their partner. Jon could not sustain a long-term commitment to his wife because his career and newfound lifestyle came first. Tori told me, "I can never forgive Jon for abandoning us at home. We were so loyal to him."

I have met countless spouses who work separate shifts and who, in time, discover their marriages have become, in effect, long-distance separations. With precious little togetherness time that is not consumed with "have-to chores," couples find that a once-manageable separation arrangement has grown tedious and debilitating to the relationship. Alice and Will maintained a workload that provides a case in point.

Alice and Will: The Swing-Shift Couple

Alice had a dream. She wanted to build a house. Driven, she worked three jobs to make her dream come true. Her husband was smoldering with resentment that his wife was so rarely home, that there was no sex, and that the kids were handed over to sitters.

At the same time, Will worked a swing shift. Always "on call," he could seldom predict his schedule from day to day; at best, he could do so only a week in advance. Neither mate was happy.

Alice finally told me, "I'm awfully depressed. The girls, Will, me—we're all screaming at each other. Everybody's mad about something. I'm so tired, but when it's time to sleep, I can't."

I asked Alice if she thought working three jobs was worth all this family disruption. She said she couldn't give up her dream. It mattered not that she rarely had a moment of intimacy with her husband or any real quality time with her children.

Within six months of finally moving into their dream house, the whole family structure came tumbling down on their heads. Deluged by unexpected expenses, the couple lost the house when Will, discouraged and disgusted, quit his job. Communication broke down. Exhausted, the couple found it easier to throw in the sponge and divorce.

Alice and Will had overextended themselves as far as work, money, and good judgment were concerned, depleting their financial and emotional resources.

5. *Transitional Separation*

The transitional separation officially begins when one or both parties decide to file for divorce. Couples generally find physical separation advisable as they grieve for the demise of their marriage. Others are relieved to be living apart, once they are physically distanced from their long-standing animosities.

Couples in transition endure many critical changes in anticipation of divorce. The stress can take its toll. Breaking up the household, minding children's special needs, and tending to financial and legal matters are necessities one never feels quite prepared to meet.

Although most spouses make a clean break as one party establishes a second residence, other couples stay under one roof until divorce papers are finalized. In these cases the parties make this accommodation for pragmatic reasons—usually for the sake of the children or their budget.

Ungainly though it may be, the mates live more or less comfortably under one roof—in separate bedrooms or maybe not.

Putting their animosities aside, these spouses have the stamina, staying power, and presence to carry off such arrangements.

Bryce and Sherry: The Pragmatic Duo

Bryce and Sherry were a down-to-earth couple who felt financially pinched. Taking a hard look at their combined incomes, they agreed it would be more practical if neither party moved out until their divorce was final. Sherry explained, "We don't want any more debt. This way we can pay off the lawyers." Bryce laughed a little and said, "We can be civil about this predivorce thing. We'll just stay out of each other's hair. Sherry's really not a bad person."

Fred and Martha: Just Being Practical

Fred and Martha had a slightly different slant on being practical. Fred said, "We have no trouble being polite to one another . . . so why rush breaking up the household? We'll have plenty of time when the lawyers have this divorce thing figured out." Martha put it this way: "My job is calling for a lot more traveling than usual. I won't be around much. We've been leading separate lives for years, so we might as well keep one residence."

These couples are mature enough to establish a benign emotional environment. They are not offending one another's sensibilities by living under one roof with an intent to divorce.

Some mates see an "at-home" separation as pure hell. It is as if every move the "enemy" makes is designed to perpetrate an evil torture on the other. So it was for Nellie and Dan.

Nellie and Dan: The Enemy Couple

Dan was the "enemy" when he refused Nellie's plea—"Please go . . . please move out." She had been powerless to stop Dan in his successful mission to convince the court that he should have as much time with their three-year-old son as possible. So Nellie was ordered by the court to have Dan live in their home until they were legally divorced.

Nellie would have gladly hightailed it out, but for the life of her, she never understood the rationale for her being "jailed." She tried in vain to get the court order changed. Terrified of Dan's temper, she made every effort to stay out of his range and shuddered whenever the child was in Dan's care.

Nellie retaliated by not talking to her husband. If Dan needed information from her, it had to be routed through their lawyers. Dan was obligated to live with her silence. She could not and would not reconcile herself to her despicable living situation. Rage seethed from every pore whenever I counseled with her. Such venting of emotion was necessary while she waited out the last 3 months of her 18-month transitional at-home separation.

Whereas some spouses are in enemy camps, others remain friends. Jean and George's transitional separation began with every expectation of divorce, and yet George's indifference and circumstance gradually changed.

Jean and George: The Chicken Soup Couple

George was bored silly with his marriage. He filed for divorce, promptly moved out, and prepared to get on with his life. He had as little to do with his wife as possible. Jean never wanted the divorce. Indeed, she could barely bring herself to discuss her circumstances with her attorney. She felt it was easier to close her eyes and "not get involved in the whole repulsive ordeal."

Jean was my client. She admitted, "I was so dependent on George, he might as well have been a leaning post." Ever since her husband had walked out on her, she wallowed in helplessness. She hoped I could sort out the riddles of her "transitioning" through the legalities and other unwelcome disruptions in her once-tidy existence.

Although I never met George, he might as well have been sitting in my office. From afar, as if by radar, Jean attempted to be in touch with his every move—but she knew so little. What she did know was why he had walked out. He'd told her plainly that their relationship had deadened for lack of stimulation.

For six months Jean had virtually no communication with her husband. Step-by-step, I took her through the divorce process. She met with the family court commissioner and signed the necessary temporary papers. Then she heard nothing more. Impatiently she waited.

During this period, George would stop at the house to pick up and drop off their teenage son and daughter. Conversation between the spouses was limited to a hello and good-bye. A year passed and Jean was still in the dark about their divorce status. It simply was not discussed.

Then one evening as Jean was preparing dinner, George lingered a while, ostensibly to help their son with a science project. Jean awkwardly asked him if he wanted to stay for a bite—she was serving chicken soup. She didn't have to beg George, and so the family ate together for the first time in 12 months. "Was this the right thing to do?" she later asked me. I listened and smiled, saying, "Yes, if that is what you wanted to do."

By this time Jean had a hunch George might have dropped the divorce petition, but she resisted having her attorney verify the fact. Meanwhile she busied herself. She enrolled at a local college, began taking a computer course, joined a women's support group, made new friends with other divorced women, and gradually garnered a newfound sense of freedom and independence.

For the next six months, whenever George came visiting, Jean continued to dish out more and more chicken soup. The couple had been separated for 18 months before they were reconciled. From Jean's reports, George discovered his wife's company to be increasingly more scintillating and stimulating. As for her chicken soup, apparently it was more appetizing than bachelor living could ever be.

6. Experimental Separation

As we've already noted, both the Controlled Separation and the trial separation (TS) are experimental ventures that potentially give couples a chance to explore the dimensions of their relationships and the fates of their marriages.

However, the composition and application of CS and TS differ extensively. Whereas the intent of CS is to reestablish order, the TS is a hit-or-miss experiment that can readily get out of hand, making this an emotionally costly enterprise for you and your loved ones.

Whether you want to stay and your mate wants to go or the other way around, tighten your seat belt, as next we travel the bumpy road of trial separation.

8

The Trouble with Trial Separation

Annette and Jeremy:
"Waiting on You, Honey"

ANNETTE: "Jeremy clams up every time I mention anything about our trial separation. After a year you'd think he'd know what he wanted. Lee, I love him. I just can't bring myself to think of divorce."

JEREMY: "Lee, I don't know what to tell Annette. I admit it was my idea to separate. I thought that moving out would help, but all I've got is more guilt. It's eating me up."

The case of Annette and Jeremy had long been a frustration to me and was one that later induced me to implement a CS. The couple had a particularly stormy 10-year marriage. Both parties had brief, torrid affairs. Both were trying to avoid disrupting their two daughters, ages two and four, any more than necessary. Nor did they want to tangle with their complex financial holdings, which made divorce less than appealing.

Annette said, "Jeremy is so blasé with me—his head is in the clouds or on work—sometimes I wonder if he really loves me." Jeremy said, "I don't know if our marriage will ever amount to anything—I'm not sure what I'm doing about us or me from one day to the next."

Annette was contrite—still hoping somehow to resurrect her failing marriage—and Jeremy was sitting on the fence.

By the time I came into the picture, the couple had opted for a trial separation (TS)—a very loose arrangement that caused Annette much torment. Though I encouraged her to set time limits—four to six months—she was skittish and could never bring herself to make their open-ended separation an issue. Annette hadn't dared confront Jeremy for fear he would misconstrue and think she was forcing him to make a decision to leave her. The thought of pushing her husband to call it quits on their marriage was out of the question. As for their TS, they were in charge of it. I was not.

Worried and Waiting

My only involvement in their TS centered on the children. Annette worried that her girls were being neglected during this emotionally demanding period. She brought them to my office several times, which gave the children some valued extra attention.

Waiting for Jeremy to make up his mind was Annette's nemesis. The frustration was often unbearable. It could be any minute, any hour, any day. She knew her husband hadn't been happy, but she never understood precisely why. Was it with her only or with himself? Or both? He wouldn't say. For Annette the waiting was becoming interminable.

Jeremy was in no rush. He talked to me about his high-powered job, his former girlfriend, and his financial dealings, with no thought of what the separation was doing to his wife and children. The months went by, and the most we could do was sit and wait.

Resolution came in a most convoluted fashion. After 21 months, Jeremy extended an invitation to Annette, "Come back and live with me . . . my new place is big enough for all of us, and the neighborhood has lots of children close to our girls' ages." Annette was exuberant. She managed to sell the family residence in two days. She said, "I was so excited Jeremy wanted me after all!" She hurriedly packed and was soon living with her sweetie and more content than she had been in many long years.

The Climax

Then the shocker! After two weeks together, Jeremy came to breakfast one morning and unceremoniously announced, "It's not working out. I'm filing for divorce. Nothing you can do about it. You and the girls will have to leave—the sooner the better!"

Annette was dumbfounded. No marriage and no house! Brokenhearted, she asked me, "Lee, what could I have done to prevent this catastrophe?" My consolation was meager at best. "Annette, you acted in good faith. Don't blame yourself."

Small wonder I was baffled by my own role in this do-it-yourself experiment. The inefficiency of Annette and Jeremy's drawnout TS was reason enough to feel compelled to find a saner way to resolve lingering doubt.

Trial Separation Defined

From the beginning of time, TS has always been a ready option for relieving the heat of angry passion. Little thought and plenty of hostility are the typical thrusts that get this ungainly venture off the ground.

From my experience, *trial separation* is best defined as an experimental arrangement, planned or unplanned, wherein spouses separate, usually for an undetermined time. The decision to separate can be made unilaterally or mutually, and mates can dwell in separate residences or in the same house.

A "Poor Man's Divorce"

When I was growing up, my mother told me that my paternal grandfather had walked out on the family, leaving my grandmother and her two teenage children to fend for themselves. This formidable crisis came on the heels of another dire misfortune. My father's younger sister, Leah, had recently been stricken with tuberculosis. Once Grandfather came home for a short while, but he soon left again to whereabouts unknown. Thus, my scholarly father was obliged to drop out of school at age 14 to support the household.

At that time such separations were known as a "poor man's divorce." They were not rare. From all accounts my grandfather was never heard from again after that one visit.

The repercussions of this long-ago event cannot be erased. Leah—my namesake—died at age 24, and my grandmother, being as closemouthed as my father, never talked about her children, much less her no-good husband.

The loss of this segment of my family history left me with an indescribable sense of incompletion. I can only imagine the disgraceful humiliation my grandmother endured. With her husband gone, she never knew if her marriage had actually ended or not.

Perhaps because of my personal history, I have been called to make sense of the enigma of marital separation. In any event, certain occurrences from my past seem to have come full circle.

Muddling Through TS Without a Rule Book

Perhaps your marriage is already in trouble, and your TS seems to be compounding your problems. More often than not, TS resembles a "fly by the seat of your pants" operation, like trying to maneuver in the fog without a compass. The experience of such a disorganized venture is frequently an ambiguous one.

- "We're separated but I don't know if it's OK to date or not."

- "When we separated, I thought we were divorcing, but now he wants to make up, and I'm afraid to go back—one more time."

- "We've separated so often I've lost count. But we always kiss and make up because I get so incredibly lonely I can't stand it."

- "I had a real high after we separated, thought I'd finally pulled myself together, but that didn't last long. Nothing gets settled between us—no wonder I'm in the dumps again."

When mates come face-to-face with the ambiguous parameters of their TS, they are obliged to cope with some hefty stumbling blocks that diminish their potential to make wise decisions.

If TS is initiated without a rule book, you have no direction. Your apart time becomes a "by guess and by golly" operation. How are you to know how to relate to one another? When should you phone? What about confidentiality, dating, or sex? And how about the children? If so many details of relating are not spelled out, you soon find that TS is risky business.

In reality most people lack the sophistication—the know-how—to muddle through the complexities of a TS. The intricacies are so pressing that the maturest of mates are often at a loss to make sense of what is happening. When you are struggling with being fed up, hurt, enraged, or betrayed, it is hard to "pull your act together." As doubt keeps you guessing, inevitably any choice feels like a bad choice. Any choice is refuted with your own "Yes, *but*." Your marriage may be shoddy, but divorce feels like being shot.

Trial Separation Is a Test

Did you know that TS is essentially so "normal" an event that more than 60 percent of troubled couples separate at least once, usually many times, in the course of their marriages? It is estimated that in half the separations, the spouse eventually returns home.[1]

Ideally, your TS should serve three purposes: (1) to minimize high levels of marital friction; (2) to test the marital relationship; and (3) to help you decide whether to patch up your relationship and try again or end your marriage. But it doesn't necessarily work out that way. For the most part, spouses view their TS as a temporary emergency exit when it gets too hot in the kitchen or too cold in the bedroom.

One of you might take a do-nothing, wait-and-see attitude or cultivate a stiff upper lip; one of you might get sore knees begging the other to come home. Either of you can get a case of nerves trying to digest the reasons why your marriage turned sour. Both of you can inflict permanent wounds and widen the rift between you by resorting to blame—dumping on either your spouse or yourself. Society seems intent on pointing the finger of blame at the closest target.

By and large, TS is an impulse reaction—a casual way of running away from responsibilities and the trauma at home. The rejected spouse is frequently hurt and confused. The rejector often feels guilty or self-righteous.

The success or failure of TS depends on the "temperature" of your relationship. Is it lukewarm, frigid, or too hot to handle? Are you for or against one another—advocates or adversaries—in this TS venture? Too many couples discover that without some nurturing guidance, a reasonable time frame, and practical rules, TS can become a lesson in futility.

Trial Separation Shenanigans

Unfortunately, the twists and turns of experimenting with separation tend to bring out the worst in people. Living apart apparently gives many parties license to be petty, nasty, or rude. Partners find insidious ways of inflicting all kinds of indignities on one another. In no time TS shenanigans exacerbate couple conflicts, and the parties are out of control. Even the most sensible among us can fall into these dismal TS traps:

- Making harassing phone calls at 2 A.M.

- Forgetting to pick up the kids

- Walking into your spouse's home uninvited

- Being inaccessible at home or at work

- Flaunting a brand-new paramour

- Emptying the savings account

- Disappearing for days without accounting for your whereabouts

Although it may not have been either partner's original intention to be retaliatory or vindictive, "get even" tactics soon force your mate's hand. Should you be feeling incredibly "wronged," you might hightail it to the divorce attorney and thereby plunge prematurely into an ugly divorce, convinced it is the only route left.

A Change of Heart

Countless people have second thoughts about a TS. A mix of acute loneliness, emotional attachment, and doubt tugs at the heartstrings and pulls mates back to the hearth. Eminent psychologist Robert S. Weiss put it this way: "Attachment gives rise to a sense that home is where the other is. It persists even in bad marriages, even when the ultimate result of going home is that things, [the bickering, distancing, the whole thing] start up again."[2]

If your differences are not resolved, if promises "to be better and do better" are just so much hot air, what purpose has your TS served?

Possibly Meg and Hal's TS experience would make an appropriate entry for the *Guinness Book of Records*. Certainly, it is one of the most bizarre scenarios I have ever encountered.

Meg and Hal: The "Back Again" Couple

I met Meg after I had been in practice for a short time. By then she had separated from Hal seven times. Whenever she got "fed up" with Hal's alcohol bingeing, she would take her four children and move in with Mother and Dad. She never left for longer than three or four weeks and would return when she became overcome with guilt.

Meg hated it when Hal blamed her for his drinking, but thought she deserved as much. Insecure, she lived under a cloud of self-doubt and depression. She tried to get active—joined support groups, commiserated with others in similar straits, and attended AlAnon—but none of this did anything for Hal, who wouldn't admit he had a problem.

On the bad days, when Hal threatened divorce, Meg told herself he did not mean it. She was afraid to divorce, not yet convinced she could manage her kids and make it on her own. By the time she quit her therapy, she understood it would take a lot more savvy than just talk to make her life better.

Some five years later, Meg recognized me in the lobby of a hotel where I was presenting a workshop. With a great big grin on her face she spoke of her recent divorce. "I finally did it! Would you believe it took 15 separations? Kids or no kids, it was time . . . I couldn't take his verbal abuse when he was drunk. Guess alcohol will kill him one of these days. But not me! I've got a whole lot more living to do; me and the kids, we're doing OK."

I said, "I'm glad it's working out so well for you." At the time I thought there must be a better way to make a decision.

Five Separation Agendas

If you and your mate are separated, you might be the *rejectee*, the spouse left behind. Or you might be the *rejector*, the one who bolted because you needed to catch your breath and settle down. Or, as the *reluctant rejector*, you tried everything until you ran out of gas and walked away from the wreckage.

You might want your spouse back, or you might no longer give a damn. At this stage you probably know little or nothing of your mate's intentions. Or both of you may be dizzy from the impact of a separation that came too fast and too soon. At this juncture neither you nor your partner has made an irrevocable decision to divorce.

As a rule, partners who experiment with marital separation have five recognizable agendas:

1. Last-ditch effort

2. Waiting on you

3. Interrogator

4. Rudderless

5. Preview

1. Last-Ditch Effort: an openly stated final move to save the marriage.

Judy viewed separation as the last stop before divorce. Fed up with her marriage to Harry, she said, "We used to go bowling, see our friends, and have a good time together. Now all we do is argue, and I'm sick of it. I want to separate to see if there's any good reason to hang in any longer."

2. Waiting on You: a separation in which one partner waits for the other partner "to do something" that will prove the coupling is healthy after all.

Helen's alcoholic husband, Rich, was in treatment off and on. For three years his intermittent bouts of alcoholism made for an extremely unstable existence. Her patience was wearing thin, and it was hard on the children, too. Helen told Rich she wanted to leave, and they agreed to separate for a year. Helen said, "I still love Rich. Lee, I'm determined to wait it out and see if I can ever trust him again." Wisely, Helen understood that unless she could rest assured that Rich was committed to total abstinence, their union would not be worth her while.

3. Interrogator: privately or openly questioning if there is sufficient love between the partners to hang in and make the marriage work.

Greg was infatuated with his secretary and questioned if his love for his wife, Debra, could be rekindled. Greg was devoted to his three daughters, very attached to his home, and hated the thought of being a cad. He viewed separation as a way to put an end to his doubts, but it was 11 years before he worked up the nerve to actually move out.

4. Rudderless: a separation to openly or privately collect one's wits and settle one's nerves.

Sylvia told me she moved out because, "My husband doesn't know what's going on with me and our relationship. Adam's a slave to his job, but more than that, he thinks his paycheck is enough. He's set in his ways and has no interest in showing me those little niceties that make being married worthwhile."

Sylvia's life had flattened out so much she felt "rudderless," unsure of her direction. "With the children going off to college in a few years, it's time for me to figure out what I want, but that's not so easy to do. I'm just drifting right now."

5. Preview: a separation seen as a secret or an open preview to divorce, as if one party has one foot out the door.

Carrie was interested in another man and had a hunch she might even divorce Rob someday. But for the time being, it wasn't in the cards. She had too much standing in her way—two teenagers, not enough money, fears of living alone. She told me, "Separation would give me a chance to set up housekeeping and see if I can make it on my own . . . it's so scary."

Check these five common separation agendas from time to time to identify your own stance. Be aware your ideas about separation might fluctuate over time. Be honest and true to what your heart is telling you.

Euphoria: A Fragile State

For some partners the first blush of physical separation can feel like a godsend. They're glad to be away from the bitter tension that was breaking their backs. If you are euphoric, you think this is how life should be. You want it to last, but it is a fragile state of mind at best.

For a while your mood soars high, and you tell your friends, "No more down in the dumps for me." These are exciting times. You're not sitting around moping; you have great plans for yourself. You join a support group such as Parents Without Partners or Divorced and Separated Catholics. You make new friends, and everyone talks about their awful marriages.

You go back to school in hopes of starting a new career. You meet more separated and divorced people and compare notes to see who has had the most wretched relationship. As you physically and emotionally feel better, you tell your family, "I'm beginning to heal."

Then an unexpected event catapults you back to Earth again. One of the kids has an accident, a close family member is terminally ill, you are fired from your job, or your spouse turns spiritual and has a change of heart.

Be that as it may, by some strange twist of fate, you wake up one morning feeling lonely and unsure of yourself. Your spouse is urging you to come back home. And you find yourself in the quagmire once again. You soon learn how temporary euphoria can be.

Clarise and Ralph: The Whirlwind of Euphoria

Clarise, 57, was ecstatic when her husband, Ralph, 62, grudgingly agreed to move out. She saw her TS as "a flight into health." She said, "At first it was phenomenal—I was removed from that whole anger thing—a jet stream of hostility was stripped away."

Clarise's euphoria, however, was short-lived. After six weeks she found herself stifled by her promise to protect Ralph with "a cover of privacy." On tenterhooks she said, "There's nothing I can say if he doesn't want to tell his business partner or let our friends know. Ralph knows I have a few trusted confidants, but I'm fed up with his charade. We are getting together more often in public, and there's a big circle of friends who don't even know we are living apart. It's so sticky . . . so unfair."

By the time I met the couple, they had been married 31 years; had recently suffered through a four-month, fruitless, in-house separation; and were still stuck, unable to bridge their differences. Nonetheless, Clarise was having faint glimmers of "maybe getting to the bottom of our run-ins and making this a workable marriage." Although her previous therapist had been less than encouraging about reconciliation, she could not give up hope.

When Clarise heard about CS from a former client, she phoned me in hopes of persuading her husband to try it, so they could get their TS moving in a more favorable direction. Ralph agreed to one evaluation session and was immediately hooked by the CS Guidelines. The CS worked well for the couple. The partners set a time limit of three months and made rules about confidentiality that both found acceptable. Dating each other was particularly pleasurable for the couple. As Ralph commented, "I'll be darned. We haven't been alone like this in years." Clarise chipped in, "This is exactly what I've been looking for—a time for the two of us to talk and enjoy being together."

When the couple terminated their CS after three months, they had "reinvented" their partnership—communication and all. Clarise said, "The CS was a blessing. It gave us a chance to take the bull by the horns and straighten ourselves out." Ralph said, "It was a relief to get reacquainted again. I could be private about our CS, and I'm grateful for that."

I had compared some major differences between CS and TS with Clarise and Ralph. The following chart pinpoints why CS is reliable and TS often is not.

Reliability of CS Versus Unreliability of TS

CS	TS
1. Couple- or therapist-guided structured plan	"Fly by the seat of your pants" with no plan
2. Well-defined guidelines	No guidelines
3. Oral or written contract	No contract
4. Predetermined time frame	No time limits
5. Agreement to be advocates	Adversarial posture
6. Open communication	Evasive communication
7. Safety net (no-divorce clause)	No safety net
8. More confident partners	Confused and insecure partners
9. Actively doing your best	Worst fears accelerate
10. Closure with relief	Closure with remorse

This compelling contrast leaves no doubt as to the promising features of CS and the dire prospects of TS, which mostly spell doom from the start.

Now let's shift direction. If the idea of separation grabs you, but you are strenuously opposed to packing your bags and moving out, take a look at the intriguing aspects of an in-house separation—the costs as well as the benefits of this sometimes cumbersome endeavor.

9

In-House Separation: Upstairs/ Downstairs Pals

"WE'RE SEPARATED but still living together . . . not at all sure what's going to happen next."

"I've been sleeping on the couch the last few weeks. Feel so indifferent. Couldn't care less. It's like I'm going through a separation."

"We are doing a Controlled Separation, but my husband isn't moving out. I need him at home."

"We've got this 'down-and-out relationship,' we're sharing the same house, it's convenient, so why get a divorce?"

In-House Separation: A Hidden Agenda

When we think of marital separation, we usually see irate partners splitting—one moving out—and the parties making no bones about their separated state. Each is garnering as much sympathy as he or she can from willing listeners.

Not so with the in-house separation. It is far more ambiguous and far less visible. By and large, the in-house separation is one grand hidden agenda. It is rarely broadcast to the neighbors. Couples often prefer to keep their internal disputes a private matter, seeing no point in airing dirty linen in public.

Rationale for In-House Separation

Many couples are so set against living apart that they continue to live together, miserable though they are, for a number of reasons: convenience, complex economic concerns or less-than-adequate funds, a wish to preserve family status and reputation, and a need to perpetuate existing dependency needs.

Psychologists M. B. Isaacs, B. Montalvo, and D. Abelsohn in *The Difficult Divorce* refer to "spouses [who] become self-made prisoners in the same house, each antagonistic, yet unwilling to be the one who leaves."[1]

Thus, the family stays miserably intact. And it seems to suffice that the children's daily routine is not disrupted and the couple can appear in public as the "all-American happy family."

Andrew M. Greely in *Faithful Attraction: Discovering Intimacy, Love and Fidelity in American Marriage* has some provocative statistics on the predisposition of couples on the cusp to be tempted by separation. Greely writes:

> Thirty-seven percent of married Americans admit that there was a time when they were prepared to leave their spouse or their spouse was prepared to leave them. In 22% of the cases both were prepared to leave each other. Of these, 40% say that divorce is still likely. The other 60% say that divorce is not likely at all.[2]

This would indicate that a significant number of discontented people live in make-do marriages.

Boundaries

If you and your mate are going to separate in-house, you must keep the boundary lines clearly defined. However, boundary issues add a degree of complexity to the in-house separation, especially if certain rooms and property had until the separation been treated as common domain.

In reality, the parameters of the in-house separation can be nebulous and difficult to describe. Logistically, keeping a discreet physical distance from your mate in-house can get knotty. How do you discriminate between what is mine and what is yours—the den, television, computer, dishes, bed—when you usually take these matters for granted?

If you two are the orderly type of couple who like to do things the "right way," and if you both stake out your territories and religiously maintain the parameters you have set, then a separation in-house is clearly understood. But if you insist on bending the rules, your in-house separation can lead to all kinds of misinterpretations as you bump into each other in the most awkward of ways.

A Chancy Undertaking

From what I've witnessed over the years, in-house separations are particularly chancy, especially if conceived in haste without rules or much forethought. As with a TS, this kind of arranged split is all too often a surefire recipe for even more chaos.

In-house separated partners, living in so tentative a state of "controlled warfare," are walking on eggshells, each guardedly looking askance at the other. As communication all but disintegrates, living under one roof can become extremely oppressive. The mates either tough it out or find reason to throw in the sponge and give up altogether.

Much like a TS, I see such arrangements as a "by guess and by golly" setup for couples to do their "on-again, off-again waltz" at high speed.

Although separation experiments of this kind are never wasted, the in-house separation is an iffy venture best entered into by the maturest of couples. And even then, without therapeutic guidance, don't be too surprised if the plan goes haywire.

The Invisible Wall

The origins of the in-house separation can be traced to an invisible wall of emotional and/or sexual distancing that stands between couples in conflict.

The antagonistic partners are separated by vehement opposition, bitter stonewalling, and a river of tears that words cannot express. It takes just one disgruntled party to prove a point by physically separating, sleeping on the couch, moving to a different room, or quartering off a section of the residence and designating areas as "my sacred space," where the other is not welcome.

Bedroom Antics

Let's call distancing maneuvers such as a temporary or permanent abandoning of the bed "bedroom antics." Such antics are quite common marital behavior, viewed by the disgruntled partner as a temporary way to get a grip on the self or to trigger the other to "right the wrongs" and make amends.

Judging from the popularity of bedroom antics, I've often wondered if there is some mysterious edict that sanctions sleeping on the couch after an awful spat. Or perhaps dodging the marital bed is merely a way of saying, "Look here, dearie, don't you realize our marriage is in deep trouble?"

The ambiguous nature of this illusory distancing maneuver suggests that bedroom antics are at times frivolous, not to be taken too seriously, especially if the mates are compatible in other aspects of their relationship. But for many couples this maneuver poses a serious problem.

No matter how long or short a time partners have been married, some spouses are unable to initiate or maintain a viable sexual relationship with their partners, even though they were passionate before tying the knot.

The couples who have considerable difficulty sustaining a consistently spirited sexual connection might limit sexual intercourse to four to six contacts per year. Even partners in their twenties and thirties are known to have sparse and tenuous amorous engagements.

In a 1992 study on why people divorce, authors Lynn Gigy and Joan B. Kelly found that, overall, sexual intimacy problems were a major factor for 64 percent of the women and 65 percent of the men.[3]

Surveys reported by Miriam Arond and Samuel L. Pauker, M.D., in *The First Year of Marriage: What to Expect, What to Accept, and What You Can Change for a Lasting Marriage* are an eye-opener. They found that at least 25 percent of newlyweds were having sexual problems.

> [This is] a remarkably large proportion considering that 85% of those surveyed had engaged in sexual intercourse before marriage—and so, we assumed, had time to evaluate and adjust to each other sexually. Our guess is that the high expectations people cherish about sex—as well as marriage—are partially responsible for this striking statistic.[4]

We might question how and why these parties adopt so contrary an attitude once they are married. As couples cope with the demands of marriage, they are obliged to make adjustments that are often emotionally charged. The partners may have very different expectations of who should initiate sexual encounters, when to expect them, and how a myriad of other conditions will be met or avoided. When one partner's expectations differ or shift, the other mate may not be able to read or interpret the new signals. As a result, some mates become remarkably passive, refusing to address such touchy matters. In turn the couple is faced with the hazards of miscommunication.

As sexual contacts grind down to a minimum, if one spouse makes a fuss about the lack of affection or objects to the other's flawed sexual performance, the relationship is placed in jeopardy. If discontent and misunderstanding continue and neither party makes any significant effort to resolve the sexual rift, in time, bedroom antics tend to shatter or certainly diminish the couple's opportunities for invested intimacy.

Audrey and Gil: What Next?

Audrey and Gil, in their midtwenties, had never consummated their two-year-old marriage. In this extreme case, neither party made affectionate advances toward the other, and neither had a sensible rationale for why this was so. Audrey finally thought it was time to look into the matter. As neither was inclined to bridge their sexual impasse, they eventually agreed it would be better to divorce.

Reactions to Bedroom Antics

The invisible walls that separate divisive couples split the parties into quasi-friendly–quasi-enemy camps—a fleeting, fluid, slippery, evasive state of existence. Intimacy is elusive, as the spouses lack the drive or insight to look into the causes or repercussions of their differences.

In general, mates react to the waning of passion and affection precipitated by bedroom antics in four ways: apathy, retaliation, disdain, and confidence.

Apathy

This partner is virtually untouched when the spouse abandons their bed. With a yawn, the apathetic spouse seems to say, "So what else is new?" apparently beyond the point of caring what the other does or doesn't do.

Retaliation

This mate often retaliates when the bed is empty by looking for other friends or playmates, which tends to increase the marital distancing.

Disdain

This partner sees bedroom antics as a tangible sign of discontent, repeated all too often. He or she will recognize the behavior for what it is: a wake-up call to take a closer look at how the marriage has drifted off course. This mate sees counseling as a sensible recourse.

Confidence

This spouse takes sexual-distancing maneuvers in stride. Maintaining a coolheaded, patient approach, the confident spouse is willing to wait until the other cools down, certain the couple will soon be snuggling again.

Inasmuch as the in-house separation is often poorly conceived, many parties eventually reunite, with little or no grasp on how to resolve the deeper problems—sexual or otherwise—that caused the emotional distancing.

Types of In-House Separations

When troubled couples separate under the same roof, the parties usually take one of two different routes: "disengaged and indifferent" or "disengaged and attached."

Disengaged and Indifferent

Mates who are disengaged and indifferent to each other establish a relatively permanent understanding: "You go your way and I'll go mine." This generally means, "We live under one roof and stay out of each other's hair." Such an arrangement may be openly declared or be an unspoken injunction. In either case, the parties have decided to limp along with a scarcely tolerable marriage.

As a rule, these spouses are not troubled with ambivalence about whether to stay or go. If they ever were, they have long dispensed with that struggle of indecision. In such circumstances, these spouses take their marriage vows seriously to the extent that they intend to live together under one roof until the bitter end.

Having come to that understanding, the couple has no need for a CS because a decision not to divorce has already been made.

Molly and Roger: So What!

In this particular case, I never met Molly. It was Roger who requested hypnotherapy for a phobia—a fear of public speaking—that had been limiting his career advancement. At the close of his final session, Roger told me about his strained marital situation, although he had no wish to do anything about it.

He and Molly had stayed in a 28-year marriage in name only, primarily for financial reasons. He also indicated that he had been strongly influenced by his employer, who frowned on divorce.

Roger said Molly could be charming to her friends but show-ered him with her shrewish disposition. I gather both mates had a knack for spoiling a lot of potentially good times. About 20 years earlier, Molly moved to "her" bedroom because she was so infuri-ated with Roger. On occasion he was allowed to visit when they were on speaking terms, but if her "dander was up," her bedroom was off-limits.

Roger said they had a succession of fruitless forays into indi-vidual and couple counseling and after that, "We just gave up . . . and there's no love lost between us."

From what I gathered, this couple had disengaged and had become remarkably indifferent to one another. Whether it was con-venient or inconvenient for them, apparently they were satisfied to go their separate ways while living under one roof.

Disengaged and Attached

Sexual distancing keeps a number of partners intimately disen-gaged, yet they choose to remain attached because of strong roots in family, church, and neighborhood. One or both spouses in a marriage may have developed interesting cohorts in the community and have actively forged separate identities that are fulfilling in themselves.

The couple's sexual conflicts remain unresolved until one party gets in a huff and is ready to put the relationship to a test. Such was the case with Edna, who had her fill of Albert's bedroom antics.

Edna and Albert: Yes, But!

Edna, 56, a schoolteacher, had such serious misgivings about her marriage that she was contemplating separation. But she was afraid to approach Albert, knowing she would dissolve into tears and botch the confrontation. Edna had a strong hunch Albert would object to her leaving in any case. "He's so stubborn, you know."

How was she to get Albert's attention? I took this as a cue to give the CS a big buildup. Edna hopped on the idea and said, "I'd like nothing better than to shove the Guidelines in Albert's face." But soon she had second thoughts and backed down. "I'm too chicken. I can't work up the nerve to do it."

I had counseled with Albert some years earlier, which made it easier for Edna to drag her husband to her next therapy session without giving the precise reasons why. We talked about the CS, and just as Edna guessed, Albert was adamant: "I'm not moving out of the house, and that's that!"

To Edna's dismay, he refused to even look at the Guidelines or discuss anything pertinent to separation. Frankly, the idea of moving out was not high on Edna's list either, because by this time she had something far better in mind. She promptly announced that she was going to retreat to her "in-home haven," a small back room filled with plump pillows and niceties Edna would carefully fashion to her liking.

Later she said to me, "I can't depend on Albert—certainly not emotionally or sexually—so this is my way of taking care of myself . . . I've got to know I have a place to escape to where I can be alone. Albert says he will respect my need for privacy."

As Edna drew strength from her in-house separation, she no longer felt trapped. Rather than attempt to coerce Albert into accepting the CS option, Edna had made her point by convincing her husband the marriage was going downhill fast.

Her independent action jolted Albert into realizing their relationship had slipped beyond his control. To Edna's delight, he agreed to extensive individual and couple counseling. They addressed Albert's inclination to procrastinate and Edna's tendency to overreact hysterically. As their communication and emotional connection were remedied, the mates understood what it meant to be advocates.

Five years later Edna and Albert renewed their marriage vows on a mountaintop. Edna shared her good tidings. "I still treasure my in-home haven, and now Albert is welcome to my nest."

Two Variations of In-House CS

Two variations, the "mini in-house CS" and the "adapted in-house CS," apply some but not all of the CS Guidelines. These types of separation are not conspicuous, so issues of confidentiality and privacy are usually less of a problem. Little is served by telling relatives and friends; there is no need to rearrange your finances, except to improve management; and neither is there call to change the way parents discipline and spend time with their children.

Mini In-House CS

The mini in-house separation is limited to testing whether sexual intimacy and romance can be revived. Time limits are of the essence, living and sleeping arrangements are clearly specified, and the terms of the spouses' sexual behavior must be found agreeable to both parties. Generally, such a contract might be difficult to establish without therapeutic intervention.

Valerie and David: Who Cares?

Valerie and David agreed to a mini in-house CS because Valerie wasn't at all interested in having sex with her husband and neither was she concerned about how this was affecting her marriage. Although she didn't care about being physically close with her mate, David was fit to be tied. He had felt cheated almost all of their 15 years of marriage, and he made no effort to contain his disgust.

Valerie had been date raped as a teenager and after that trauma wasn't interested in getting close to any man, not even her husband. It galled David that she didn't seem to care one way or another about sex, although otherwise, he acknowledged, she was a very good wife and devoted mother. At the time I was treating the couple, Valerie's lack of affection was not deemed sufficient cause for either partner to consider divorce.

For this reason we applied only the guidelines relating to dating and sexual contact. The couple agreed to date once a week, and David was allowed to hold Valerie's hand and put his arm around her, but nothing more. It was agreed they would sleep in separate bedrooms, and David promised not to push his wife for sexual attentions.

The mini-CS was useful. Once David stopped pleading for more affection, it became evident that Valerie wouldn't budge an inch in allowing David to demonstrate how much he loved her, despite the warmth of his caresses and display of caring.

In time, David went looking elsewhere for companionship, and within a year he filed for divorce. Despite the couple's incompatibilities, they remained on friendly terms for the sake of their four children. Their mini-CS had revealed the intractability of their impasse and laid the groundwork for a good divorce.

Adapted In-House CS

An adapted in-house CS can be effectively handled as long as both parties abide by the established boundary rules. But if the contract agreements are obstructed, as they were in the case of Roz and Scott, it is bedlam.

My good-faith effort in the couple's behalf was complicated by the fact that Scott was hiding his alcohol abuse from his wife and me. As a consequence of the couple's adapted in-house separation, this vital information was ultimately bound to surface.

Roz and Scott: Upstairs/Downstairs Pals

The day Roz found out about Scott's affair she demanded a separation. Scott didn't want to leave and insisted they go for counseling to untangle their web of disenchantment. Roz wanted her husband out of the house and couple therapy as well. This is when I got involved.

The partners worked different shifts, had limited finances, and were strapped with the heavy demands of three children under six. Roz often felt on the ragged edge, relying heavily on Mother for socializing, shopping, phone gossip, and children's visits to Granny.

Scott felt cast aside, as if all that was important was his checkbook. He made no excuses to me about being preoccupied with fantasies of affairs.

Roz told me, "He ogles every skirt that walks by," and this only served to fuel her jealousy and suspicion. She hated the way Scott tried to control her—sexual intercourse being strictly on his terms and not hers. It made her feel so small.

Scott had no wish to move out and came up with an idea: "Couldn't we separate inside the house so I can still be around to help? . . . it would make it easier on Roz."

With that entrée, I proposed an adapted form of the CS Guidelines that would suit this couple's needs. Principally, the couple contracted for time limits of three months. Scott set up temporary residence in the basement, where he put a bed, his clothes, and a computer, with work space for completing some career-related projects.

I questioned how much the partners loved each other and wondered how committed they were to their marriage. I was convinced their CS experiment would produce answers to these questions.

Boundaries Sabotaged

Roz and Scott were amenable to an adapted in-house CS, but it was difficult for them to maintain their agreements, and their venture soon turned into a farce. Their comings and goings took on the complexion of an Abbott and Costello routine, "Who's on First?"

Distractions took on a new dimension that was hard to nail down. When Scott wanted quiet time with his computer downstairs, Roz insisted she "needed" his expertise as chief cook and bottle washer "upstairs." The changing of diapers daily and other "urgent errands" never seemed to end.

But when he was feeling lonely in his dingy dungeon, which was often, Scott would sidle upstairs looking for romance. The couple hadn't anticipated indiscriminate confusion, yet at every turn they persisted in crossing the boundary lines between his quarters and her domain. Inasmuch as both parties were irresponsible, there was no defusing their in-house fiasco.

After nine weeks of living in such a turbulent environment, the couple called a halt to their contract. At Roz's request I continued individual counseling with her for another six weeks.

Follow-Up

I had always felt unfinished with this case, as if something had fallen through the cracks. Six years later I spoke to Roz, and she opened my eyes to a situation I had not been privy to before.

Not only did Scott have girlfriends on the side, but he had cleverly denied his drinking habit. When he binged, he became physically and verbally abusive as well. This was the couple's secret.

Roz explained that after the couple quit their adapted in-house CS, Scott's addiction became intolerable. She gave him an ultimatum: "Leave for three months and get help for your drinking problem or else I'm getting a divorce." Scott complied, but their TS didn't make a difference in their relationship. He went back home for another year, all the while still in denial, still getting abusive when he was drunk.

Roz finally divorced Scott. As she put it, "I thought he would change for me, but he didn't." Roz urged me to let others know about her most important therapeutic lesson: "I thought I could, but you can't change someone. As much as you love, if you have doubts [about the relationship], don't hide from the truth of your situation."

Roz said she is happily remarried and has another child. Scott has also remarried.

My follow-up with Roz substantiates my premise that users and abusers do not make appropriate candidates for a CS. In the very next chapter we find out why.

Part II
Relationship
Transformation

10

*U*sers, Abusers, Losers: Twisted Minds—Twisted Lives

Twisted Minds—Twisted Lives

CHRONIC USERS AND abusers are society's losers. Like children playing a cruel game, they treat their lives and the people around them with disdain. They have nothing but contempt for the damage they perpetrate.

To avoid confusion, the term *user* is synonymous with the *addict*, whether that person is addicted to alcohol, marijuana, cocaine, heroin, or any other legal prescription or illegal drug. It is understood that this person *cannot control his or her use of these substances.*

The term *abuser* is synonymous with *the perpetrator of violence*, sexual and physical. Perpetrators are violence-prone individuals who reverberate to the pulse of their own power to control others. *But it is the perpetrator's life that is out of control.*

A Mockery of Marriage

Both users and abusers make a mockery of marriage, like children playing house, playing with fire, making mischief, throwing caution to the wind. But the harm they do is not make-believe. A river of ruin contaminates families exposed to hard-core usage and violence.

Alcoholism spawns violence as family members are tyrannized physically and sexually with remarkable abandon. The mate is treated as the victim, someone to kick around. This dehumanizing of the spouse and the blatant disrespect for life make the home an alarmingly unsafe habitat.

My Story

I'll never forget my first counseling experience when my marriage therapist told me, "You have a bad marriage!" I nearly fell through the floor. No one had ever said that to me before, and the words left an indelible mark on my psyche. A pacifist at heart, I had worked so hard to fabricate an image of the "perfect marriage" for all the world to see. And now I had to face my inability to maintain my delusion.

Because my parents kept no liquor in our home, the last thing I expected when I married was a life cursed by physical and verbal abuse and alcohol misuse. My awakening began innocently enough after our honeymoon. In a fit of peevish disgust, I slapped my husband hard on the face to show him I was fed up with his "childish" temper tantrums. I thought that was what wives did when they got mad at the men in their lives. I learned about all that from the movies. Bette Davis, Barbara Stanwyck, Carole Lombard, Jean Harlow, and others regularly slapped the guys for emphasis—as if to say, "I'm pissed."

Growing up I thought this was "SOP"—standard operating procedure. Ruefully, my one and only slap unwittingly unleashed a raging torrent of violence that my husband wouldn't contain. After that I stayed scared, as my children and I were violated by his intermittent episodes of abuse, which accelerated when he was under the influence. Intimidated and brainwashed, I cowered in bleak submission to my mate's insidious tyranny. But even then I was convinced I could not be held responsible for his all-consuming rage and lack of remorse for holding his family hostage.

At the time I was too humiliated to speak. For 24 years I stayed silent, our secret shame too disgraceful to own. No one ever knew, although my in-laws suspected as much. Nothing was ever done to stop his reign of terror. The police were never notified; I was afraid my spouse would kill me if I called them. In those days violence in the home was considered "just a family affair." Back then there were no procedures for a formal court-ordered indictment of batterers as there are today.

Use and abuse destroyed our family's self-respect, squelched our creative endeavors, besmirched our dignity, and blackened our lives. Once I met with a minister but never mentioned the violence. I kept myself in denial, had no reliable support system, and felt too insecure to face the big, bad world outside, too immobilized to make a change.

Foolishly, I relied on my husband to change. How grandiose to think he needed the help and not me. I wasn't sick, he was. Little did I understand that my very silence stripped me of my power. But in those days, the thought of having people know of my predicament was stigmatizing beyond endurance. Better not to deal with this blight on my life, better to cry myself to sleep rather than risk indictment from our community.

In the fifties and sixties, who spoke of such secrets? Women silently lost their dignity and self-respect instead. Feeling unworthy and undeserving, I stayed with my husband until I could stay no more.

A Shift in Focus

When I began to work on this book, I had intended to state my premise as *users and abusers make inappropriate CS candidates* and let it go at that. However, the problems of hard-core use and abuse are so abhorrent, so visible and yet so submerged, that the issues surrounding them demand fuller explanation. Countless spouses are desperate to get their mates into treatment. How many unhappily married victims are daily tormented with uncertainty, doubting themselves while wondering if they should simply abandon their marriages and save themselves instead?

Abuse Statistics

It is apparent that excessive alcohol and drug use and physical abuse are related. Recent studies on use and abuse confirm that 36 percent to 52 percent of those who are physically abusive to their spouses also abuse alcohol. Richard N. Mack in *Treating Couples: The Intersystem Model of the Marriage Council of Philadelphia* writes about spouse abuse: "According to the National Institute of Mental Health, physical violence occurs between family members more often than it occurs between any other individuals or in any setting other than wars and riots." Shocking as it may seem, Mack indicates that the U.S. Office on Domestic Violence found that only 1 in 10 cases of spousal abuse is being reported to authorities.[1]

Losers and Abusers: Big-Time Losers

"I'll Attack You Before You Hurt Me!" glitters in gold on the front of the user's and abuser's sweatshirt.

"The Joker Is Me!" blazes in scarlet on the back.

The evidence is clear: chronic users and abusers lose out, relationshipwise. They have the most difficult time cultivating stable marriages. Who can reason with a drunk or an otherwise impaired individual? How can anyone exist in the hazy wastelands of use and expect to bring sanity into his or her life? Alcohol and other drugs loosen inhibitions and tamper with our brain power.

Clinically, I have long understood the reality that violence, incest, and child molestation often go hand in hand with use and abuse. One incites the other, sometimes with little evidence of remorse on the part of the perpetrator.

Victims of use and abuse generally grow up feeling inferior and undeserving. Sometimes they grow up terrified by their parents' drunken brawls and discouraged by their recklessness and irresponsibility. It is easy to identify with parents who have tolerated and condoned the least, rather than the most, life has to offer. To grow up in the shadows of such a life script leaves one prone to perpetuate that dysfunctional lifestyle—either as a victim or as an abuser.

Perpetrators of use and abuse hide behind a mask of tyranny and self-indulged power. As children, they grow up in an environment so deprived of love that as adults they have scant ability to bond or empathize with anyone. Their self-esteem is so discouragingly low, they often place small value on life and limb. They grow up being told they were unwanted and labeled "bad" as children. So the youngsters fulfill the wicked witch's prophecy by acting bad and are referred to as "the black sheep in the family," maligned and misunderstood.

Deprived of adequate parenting, perpetrators believe their worth is manifest only when they can overpower and subdue their spouses or children or other people's children.

Codependency

Users and abusers are a riddle to self and spouse. They hop from one bad relationship to another. They marry, separate, and divorce. They try and fail. They are self-destructive. In marriage the spouses collude to form a toxic symbiosis. Codependency is a "sick" relationship.

Melody Beattie, author of *Codependent No More: How to Stop Controlling Others and Start Caring for Yourself*, explains how codependent spouses relate to one another:

> Codependents are reactionaries. They overreact. They underreact. But rarely do they act. . . . Codependent behaviors or habits are self-destructive . . . [and] can lead us into, or keep us in, destructive relationships that don't work. These behaviors can sabotage relationships that otherwise may have worked. These behaviors can prevent us from finding peace and happiness with the most important person in our lives—ourselves.[2]

Frequently, codependent partners, men and women both, are born of a lineage of users and abusers. The sins of the fathers are repeated from generation to generation. Parents, grandparents, sisters, and brothers all perpetuate florid use and abuse as a lifestyle.

Children who grow up watching a parent be an enabler or a patsy—playing nurse to the "sickie" in return for a roof over one's head—often learn how to be self-destructive in taking care of their own bodies. Frequently they also have no viable models for how to be in healthy relationships.

Then the child grows up, gets married, and takes for granted that is how marriage is supposed to be. Losers propagate more losers.

We see codependents attached at the proverbial hip, living fractured lives. These mates are subjected to layers of destructive manipulation. It is abuse of power to maintain dominance and control. One partner is the controlling sickie or tyrant. The other is the submissive spouse who capitulates and lives as if jailed. All told, it takes the fallout of calculated lies, injurious secrets, flagrant suspicions, and lumbering communication to perpetuate these contaminated relationships. Degraded and deprived of the respect and dignity that should be their due, the mates unfortunately don't know how or when to break the loser cycle.

Losers' Loss: Perpetuating Victim Status

What kind of perverse injustice keeps perpetrator and victim clinging to such "indecent exposure"? Why do people stay in relationships that have so little to offer? Addicts, perpetrators, and their victims consciously and subconsciously collude to perpetuate the myth, "I'm weak, I'm no good. My rotten life with you is all I deserve. I'm terribly lonely and pathetically helpless, so I better never leave you." Essentially, both mates are victims. They lose out and so do their children and society at large.

Partners damaged by their own parents' destructive marriages are prone to repeat the insults they learned growing up. If they had no examples of common decency on which to model, they are obligated to find appropriate role models to make their marriages fruitful.

If one mate has the strength to leave, antagonism will escalate, as more wounding of body and soul occurs.

The experiences of my clients inspired me to formulate profiles of the perpetrator and victim. Ironically, as my work took shape, it became clear that both parties have several fundamental character traits in common.

Perpetrator and Victim Profiles

Perpetrator

Purpose:	Revenge/power
Conscious feeling:	Rage/suspicion
Posture:	Secretive: lie, cheat, steal
Attitude:	Secretive/arrogant
Behavior:	Aggressive and passive/aggressive
Denied feeling:	Pervasive, uneasy depression
The threat:	The world will discover I'm the joker
Belief:	Life is cheap/people are expendable
The hook:	Sweet-talking con artist
The stay:	Brainwashing victim
The rub:	Robbed of dignity
The delusion:	I won't get caught
The collusion:	To perpetuate the loser system

Victim

Purpose:	Rescue/caretaker
Conscious feeling:	Fear/shame/mistrust
Posture:	Secretive/enabler
Attitude:	Insecure/arrogant
Behavior:	Passive and passive/aggressive
Denied feeling:	Pervasive, uneasy depression
The threat:	The world is an unsafe place
Belief:	I'm no good/I'm a failure
The hook:	I can save him/her
The stay:	Tomorrow will be a better day
The rub:	Robbed of dignity
The delusion:	I get what I deserve
The collusion:	To perpetuate the loser system

Why Users and Abusers Sabotage CS

Batterers don't batter because they drink; they drink in order to batter, according to Michael Groetsch, author of *He Promised He'd Stop: Helping Women Find Safe Passage from Abusive Relationships.*[3] On their good days, chronic users and abusers may be intelligent, industrious, and charming companions, but by the very nature of their addiction(s) and inclination to violence, their word is not to be trusted.

These mates can be expected to sabotage a CS because they are irresponsible—neither reliable nor dependable. You can count on them to deny their impairment, attempt to control any negotiations, belittle their spouses, and exhibit an overall disregard for selves and mates. Adversarial behavior of this type spells failure for a good separation.

From my personal experience, users and abusers all too often stubbornly defend their lifestyles as their God-given right. If you are trying to reason with them, forget it. You are only fooling yourself if you presume your partner will comprehend your point of view. *Practically speaking, a CS will not work until the user or perpetrator has been fully rehabilitated and can be trusted to keep his or her word.*

Ginny and Vic: An Ultimatum

Ginny was referred to me by a neurologist. He was her fifth doctor, and I was her last resort. None of the physicians had been able to shed any light on her ailment: she had difficulty walking on her left leg. The neurologist correctly guessed she might be having psychosomatic symptoms.

Ginny limped into my office complaining about Vic. He was drinking too much again. He had spent 28 days in a treatment center the year before and had stayed sober for nine months. Ginny shook her head in dismay. "But then he went on a hunting trip with the boys and that's when he started drinking again . . . Just a few beers . . . Now it's gotten out of hand again . . . I can't believe this is happening to me twice—my first husband was alcoholic." And then she added, "It's like I haven't got a leg to stand on."

I explained to Ginny that our physical symptoms often reflect what the mind is thinking. With this insight firmly entrenched,

Ginny straightened up, having no further need to limp around. She promptly stood up to Vic and confronted him. "It's either me or alcohol—you choose."

Vic, for his part, continued to make excuses, procrastinate, and ignore his wife's ultimatum. Within three months, Ginny filed for divorce.

It takes nothing short of an ultimatum to stop use and abuse and retrieve your lost soul. Ultimatums take on an urgent meaning when you stand up for your basic rights as a human being—to live in the light and maintain your integrity.

> "This is it! Either you get help or I'm leaving."
> "You treat me like dirt. You think I haven't a brain in my head.
>   I'm getting some help so I can get out of here."
> "Your addiction is driving me crazy. I'm not going to let you
>   control me anymore."
> "I woke up this morning and said, 'Enough is enough!' I'll see you
>   in court."
> "Guess I had to hit bottom before I got smart and got help."

Statistics Tell the Real Story

Victims of battering need to be acutely aware of potential danger when they are on the verge of separation or divorce:

- By the most conservative estimates, one million women annually suffer nonlethal domestic abuse.[4]

- One out of every four men will assault his partner in the course of their relationship.[5]

- In 1992, it was reported that 51 percent of victims of intimate violence were attacked by boyfriends or girlfriends, 34 percent were attacked by spouses, and 15 percent were attacked by ex-spouses.[6]

- About 75 percent of calls to law enforcement for intervention for domestic violence occur shortly after the victim leaves the relationship.[7]

- In 1994, among all female victims of murder, 28 percent were slain by husbands or boyfriends. Only 3 percent of the male victims were killed by wives or girlfriends.[8]

The above statistics point out a heightened danger in the event the perpetrator learns of a possible separation or divorce. In many cases the abuser will continue to stalk, harass, and threaten the partner with bodily harm. These behaviors should not be minimized. Victims of battering must be prepared to take action to save life and limb.

Heed the Warning: Create a Safety Plan

Create a safety plan. Contact domestic violence agencies or shelters in your community and request a protection plan and checklist of what you need to know and do if you are in an abusive situation.

Don't be so naive as to consider confronting your physically abusive mate with any news of your leaving. Don't try to reason with this person; you are wasting your energy. You wouldn't try to tackle a raging bull to save your skin.

No one is expected to stay calm when being threatened with physical abuse: "You better shut up . . . just watch what happens if you don't . . . you won't be able to talk for a month!"

Patricia Evans, author of *The Verbally Abusive Relationship*, has somber words of warning for victims of domestic abuse:

> If you are feeling stunned, shocked, or in too much pain to speak,
> if your mate seems to go out of control with anger, if you are feel-
> ing fearful of him, if he has threatened you with any harm, if he has
> hit you, or threatened to hit you or hurt you, you should not be
> dealing with his abusive behavior alone and you must question the
> health of staying around him.[9]

Treatment for the Victim

Get professional guidance, talk to advocates for battered women, and use their shelters to protect yourself and your children.

Fortunately, supportive community services for victims of use and abuse have proliferated in the past two decades: Alcoholics Anonymous (AA), 24-hour crisis lines, legal advocacy, increased police awareness and temporary restraining orders, to name a few. Help is available when life, limb, and sanity are at risk.

Individual therapy teaches victims of abuse to trust their hunches, grit their teeth, and protect themselves and their children by making a decision to be free of an abusive relationship. If your mate refuses to be rehabilitated, restoration of your sanity comes *after* you feel physically safe—and that could be sometime *after* a divorce.

Treatment for Users and Abusers

When I was a clinical novice, I observed that 90 to 95 percent of my clients were users and abusers or had family members who used and abused. As I honed my skills and learned more about the nature of substance abuse and violence, I became increasingly convinced that the primary issue of treatment for users is the need for total abstinence or at least sobriety. For perpetrators of violence, rehabilitation, then marital and family therapy are essential.

First things first. Couple therapy will inevitably fail if addictions and/or violence are ignored and not treated first, before digging into the couple's relationship issues.

With this mission statement firmly entrenched, my own pathway as a clinician was clearly reframed.

Foremost, the user and abuser must admit the following:

- "I am a substance user, and my life is out of control."

- "I am a perpetrator of violence, and my life is out of control."

- "I am ready to stop using. I am ready to stop my acts of violence against family members and be cleansed."

The user and abuser is ready to receive treatment when truly remorseful and fully committed to change. Only then can treatment be effective and help the sick member of the family get back on the road to wellness.

If the user and abuser is in denial, many families arrange an "intervention" to shock the party into getting the help he or she sorely needs. With skilled intervention, the success rate is very good—about 75 percent. This is the best way to ensure your marital relationship's healthy survival.

Substance users and abusers are potential candidates for a CS only after they have been rehabilitated, not before. The following conditions must be met: complete in-patient or day-treatment program for substance abuse, maintain total abstinence, attend Alcoholics Anonymous (AA) or Narcotics Anonymous (NA) meetings, and make a serious commitment to stay in individual or group therapy. In this way the user demonstrates a willingness to be responsible for aberrant behavior.

Making amends is a lifelong task. Many recovering substance users find the camaraderie of AA or NA, which are founded on a 12-step program, a welcome support. This program, initiated by recovering alcoholics, provides a buddy system for maintaining total abstinence. The AA and NA meetings are a congenial place where people of all ages, social strata, and professions come to tell their stories, to receive guidance, and make a lifetime commitment to remain sober and drug-free—one day at a time.

Unfortunately, many mates are divorced long before the loser reckons with the destruction of lives that are left in the wake.

Treatment for Perpetrators

There are many special community programs available for perpetrators of violence, including Batterers Anonymous. Seek them out. Your local mental health association, crisis lines, or telephone directory can be a good place to start.

When I work with batterers, I ask them to make a "No-Violence Contract," meaning they agree to stop all acts of violence against other family members. This contract can work reasonably well if I am also meeting with the other family members.

In conclusion, to the victim of use and abuse I say: Your marriage is starved for lack of trust until your home is safe. Believe your life can be better. You have already reacted; now it is time for action. Tomorrow is mañana. Too many times, tomorrow never comes. You owe it to yourself to look in the mirror and make a decision to be home free today!

11

$\mathcal{B}$roken Hearts, Broken Children: A Call for Compassion

Broken Hearts

WHEN CHILDREN UNAVOIDABLY fall into the abyss of the marital cri-sis, they become vulnerable to the family trauma. At first mention of the word *separation* or *divorce*, youngsters are apt to break into tears. They are terrified of the unknown and don't want to think about a broken home, but they do. They can't imagine something bad happening to the family, but here it is happening to their own mother and father.

What are conflict-driven parents to do when they are standing on the brink of uncertainty about their marriage? What are our chil-dren to do when they cry themselves to sleep at night with worry?

Children at Risk

Given these tenuous circumstances, children are at risk of emotional injury. They feel lost, neglected, abandoned, and alone if they aren't convinced that either parent cares enough to be close at hand to nurture them. They are tormented by fears of being deserted and tortured by having to choose between parental loyalties. They don't want their family to be split apart.

More than anything else, our children need to know they are loved, cared for, and given room to grow on healthy turf. Children suffer when their parents suffer. They breathe their parents' turmoil and anguish, which activates their own. Like sponges, children absorb the seepage of your marital storm.

Your conflicted emotions, painful rancor, and unplanned separation or potentially hurtful divorce all put youngsters at risk. They, too, become entrapped in your web of indecision. You may be able to tune out your misery by escaping in work or play, but your child's unspoken anguish will fester in unseen and untold ways.

Childhood Symptoms of Despair

Fears of a potential family breakup can threaten the physical and emotional health of our youngsters. One 15-year-old girl developed a severe case of hives in reaction to the pressure of her parents' separation and later divorce. Frequent headaches, tummy aches, and colds are common ailments that head the list of physical complaints.

Children at risk are prone to anxious states, nervousness, nightmares, and sleepwalking. A child who is constantly apprehensive about Mother's misery sometimes develops a phobia about going to school and leaving the distraught parent home alone.

Adolescents bearing the brunt of a divisive home environment often mask their depressed state with deviant behavior. A recent study by the Carnegie Council on Adolescent Development found young adults are currently getting far less parental supervision than they did just a few decades ago. Lack of parental attention is thought to be a significant reason why one-third of all adolescents consider suicide and why half of these young people turn to alcohol and drugs. They underachieve, drop out of school, get pregnant, or become juvenile offenders.[1]

Medical epidemiologist Etienne Krug of the U.S. Centers for Disease Control gathered statistics from 1990 to 1995 that point to the high divorce rate as one of the leading causes of childhood suicide. These findings, which were reported in February 1997, substantiate the fact that the United States has the highest suicide rates for children 14 and under—double those of other industrial nations.[2]

The Potential for Child Neglect

As you are preoccupied with the "stay or go" issue, your children's needs frequently fall through the cracks. How can you attend to your youngsters when you are inundated with your personal and spouse-related torment?

Moreover, some children are more sensitive, difficult, and demanding than others and require more attention. Unfortunately, swamped as you are with your own marital troubles, it is hard to concurrently be alert, informed, and proficient in decoding your child's emotional state.

Some parents overlook their children's distress, calling it "just going through a stage," or they minimize the problem, saying it is "just schoolmate squabbles."

Troubled adolescents typically attach themselves like glue to their peers and stay as far removed from the marital strife at home as possible. These not-yet adults frequently feel deprived. They may not be able to express it, but they yearn for the emotional security that only parental discipline, nurturing, and the setting of norms and limits can provide.

Tragically, too many neglected adolescents ruin their lives trying to fill a well of emptiness any way they can. When parents make themselves inaccessible, when they lack the skills, energy, or common sense necessary for good parenting, their progeny, who need parental wisdom the most, suffer the consequences. Left to their own limited resources, these young ones flounder and are lost.

Sad to say, if our young people don't receive some measure of emotional support and treatment for their symptoms during these troubled times, their "woe-begotten baggage" follows them into adulthood.

Childhood Fantasies

Children are smart enough to pick up clues of marital distress without your knowing. Kids often sense the marriage is in trouble before Mommy and Daddy are ready to face up to their own polarized predicament. When perturbed children talk among themselves, they speak of "divorce" in hushed tones. Some youngsters console themselves with thoughts of parental reconciliation while others close their eyes to the unimaginable.

It is natural for youngsters to dream of living in harmony with two loving parents, but when their tranquil hopes are fractured by reality, they tend to resort to one of three disquieting fantasies: (1) they blame themselves, (2) they want to fix the marriage, or (3) they try to avoid family adversity at all costs.

1. Self-Blame: Children frequently assume they are the cause of the marital calamity. When they hear their parents arguing about them, they naturally blame themselves for their parents' marital split. Children see themselves at the center of the family constellation. From that perspective, whatever naughty thing the child did must be why Mother and Dad are in trouble.

This assumption is validated time and again when parents scream at the kids: "You're bad!" "Don't bother me!" "Get lost!" "I never wanted you in the first place!" It is a tough grind for our youngsters to rise above such "don't be/don't exist" messages.

2. Fix the Marriage: Some youngsters fervently wish they could fix their parents' relationship. They imagine ways they might be helpful or show their battling parents how to be loving with one another again. When this fantasy fails, they are devastated. To carry the weight of a parent's trials and tribulations on their small shoulders is too much, and they soon become depressed.

3. Avoid Adversity: Defeated by their frenzied home front, other children "white out" the marital wreckage. They switch gears and fantasize removing themselves from the mayhem. Denial seems to be the simplest way to insulate themselves. Many youngsters

withdraw and refuse to express themselves, holding tight to their misery. Others will fantasize of happier times past and better times to come. In this way the family misfortune doesn't hurt so much.

Fallout of Parental Guilt

Parents often feel incredibly guilty for putting their children in the midst of their marital strife and therefore will placate their young-sters to soothe their own souls. What parents must understand is that in times of marital crisis, children are most in need of loving direction and control by the parent. Erik H. Erikson, a pioneer in the field of psychoanalysis and human development, gives us the basis of child-rearing practice in his book *Childhood and Society*: "Man survives only where traditional child training provides him with a conscience which will guide him without crushing him and which is firm and flexible enough to fit the vicissitudes of his his-torical era."[3]

If kids are sassy and naughty, they expect the boom to be low-ered. But the neglected child learns that naughty behavior begets negative attention, which in the child's eye seems better than none at all.

Our children have a radarlike way of knowing if they are loved and valued by their parents' consistent words and deeds. It bears repeating—consistency is the key to garnering trust and respect. If no such demonstration is forthcoming, our young people are sadly deprived.

The case of Micky and his parents has long disturbed me. In hindsight, I have a hunch that if I had had the CS option to offer the parents, their son would not have become as emotionally ill or felt forced to resort to such desperate measures.

Micky: A Boy with a Solution

Micky, a beautiful 10-year-old child, earnestly wanted to "fix" his parents' broken relationship. He was absolutely convinced he had a good solution for his animosity-driven parents. This smart young-ster told me his bright idea: "I don't know why my parents can't just compromise for a change. They argue and scream past midnight. No way . . . so stupid. How do they think I'm gonna sleep with all that racket? It's every night . . . terrible . . . bothers me . . . It's all I can think about."

Micky's mother knew her son's agitation was worsening. The father, however, was in denial. Counseling the parents was to no avail, and their raging arguments continued. Micky's emotional state deteriorated rapidly, until early one morning the mother found the boy attempting to hang himself.

Micky spent the next three months in a child/adolescent in-patient treatment center. The mother filed for divorce when he was released. She wisely moved her children to a distant state, where they could be close to their loving grandparents and gracious extended family.

CS: Benefits to Parents

In the interest of sheltering children from suffering needlessly, CS partners agree to keep their marital squabbles out of earshot of the kids. With the CS in place, parents can be more alert to how their youngsters are adjusting to the move. Children are less likely to fall through the cracks if their emotional and physical needs are being met.

As you become more involved with your offspring, they take notice. Children know beyond a shadow of a doubt when they are wanted, cherished, and protected. Such a potent investment in the best welfare of your kids benefits everyone in the family constellation, from grandparents on down.

Some cases are more difficult than others, depending on the parents' history of generational dysfunction. Although the CS gives parents a fair start at constraining marital fires, circumstances might preclude the typical "Hollywood happy ending." The case of Tyler makes this point.

CS: Tyler, an Abused Boy

When Tyler, 15, slit his wrists, his distraught mother, Sophie, contacted me. The boy, born out of wedlock, had been physically and verbally abused by Sophie's first two alcoholic husbands. When she married Wilbur, she vowed never to allow her son to suffer abuse at the hand of a stepfather again.

Tyler was essentially the family's emotional barometer. When the adults behaved themselves, his grades improved; but when the parents were at war, Tyler sulked in his room and no one could get a word out of him. Try as he might, he couldn't be indifferent to their nasty brawls. Despite his attachment to his mother, Tyler's respect for his parents diminished considerably, and in time the boy became alarmingly depressed.

The family situation was a time bomb waiting to explode. The situation spun out of control as the full brunt of Sophie's wrath fell on Wilbur after Tyler's attempt at suicide.

Sophie, 35, worked long hours as an assistant manager of a large restaurant. She was the product of a verbally abusive, alcoholic father and a long indentured, subservient mother. Although exceedingly protective of Tyler, Sophie lacked the stamina and know-how to properly guide him.

Wilbur, 44, a former jockey, owned a riding stable. He planned to teach Tyler the business, hoping the two would get closer. But Wilbur had never had children, and the only way he knew to control Tyler was to ram discipline down his throat like a drill sergeant —just as his dad had done to him.

Tyler hated Wilbur, and that put the couple's already smoldering marital conflict at risk of exploding into one big bonfire. Sophie said to me, "I'll never trust Wilbur again—I can't forgive him for hurting Tyler like he has. I've had all I can take. I know Wilbur will hit the roof . . . but I've got to get my own place and get Tyler and me out of there."

Once I alerted the divisive parents to the benefits of cooling off with a CS, they agreed to give it a try. Sophie moved out with her son, and Wilbur did his level best to make amends and cajole his wife into forgiving him, but she would have none of that.

Sophie had no qualms about parting from the house, which she despised from the start. Wilbur couldn't have cared less about the house but mourned losing contact with Tyler. As a result of some counseling with the two, both stepfather and stepson came to a warm understanding. But Sophie was adamant: "I forbid Wilbur to have any contact with Tyler." She rationalized, "After all, we've only lived as a family for less than three years—most of the time it was pretty raunchy . . . and besides, Wilbur is Tyler's third stepfather."

The couple's six-month CS agreement was aborted in less than two months when Wilbur heard via the grapevine that Sophie had begun dating a former boyfriend. There was nothing I could do to save the family's cohesiveness.

Although their marriage ended in divorce, the couple's CS was a limited success in that Sophie and Wilbur negotiated who got which VCR and TV in a way that was fair, sparing themselves additional heartache.

I was glad to see that with the help of some brief therapy, Tyler, now 16, was showing signs of maturation. He took a job as a short-order cook, which he was responsibly handling. As he learned to accept what he could not change, Tyler found he could move beyond a long line of generational dysfunction.

CS: Tina—Pay Attention to Me

Kim, 35, and Colin, 39, were both in second marriages. Tina, seven, was Kim's out-of-wedlock daughter, and the couple had two younger boys of their own. After five years Kim asked for a CS because she couldn't stand Colin's domineering ways. She said, "My husband is so paranoid . . . doesn't want to let me out of his sight . . . always giving me the third degree—where were you, what were you doing? It's gotten so I can't concentrate on my job, and I've got a whole crew I'm responsible for."

Kim knew Colin wasn't particularly interested in Tina's welfare. She also suspected her overcontrolling spouse would try to manipulate the child-care agreements to his advantage by favoring his own two sons with his time, leaving Tina to feel unwanted. And he did.

Heated couple dissension ensued, and to no one's surprise, Colin bowed out of their six-month agreement after 28 days, issuing an ultimatum that he was filing for divorce.

In the wake of the flak between the adults, Tina drew attention to herself by pulling down her panties in front of her schoolmates.

Kim was horrified when Tina's teacher phoned to say the child had brazenly repeated this routine for a week.

Fortunately, Kim had the good judgment to call me immediately. In turn I consulted with both the school counselor, vice principal, Tina's teacher, and then with both mother and child. Within two weeks Tina's exhibitionist behavior had abated.

In a follow-up call 18 months later, Kim enthusiastically spoke about how she had profited from her encounter with a CS, brief though it was. "It made me realize how dumb it would have been for me to tangle with Colin . . . the CS showed me I wouldn't get anywhere. So I held my tongue a lot, and in the end, difficult though it was, I kept my wits about me."

In reference to her daughter's inappropriate behavior, Kim said, "Besides, the CS helped me be doubly careful to pick up on what was going on with Tina and make sure it was taken care of promptly." She added, "You know, difficult as it's been, I'm real proud of how I handled getting through the divorce."

When Telling the Children Is Awkward

Some parents are so ill at ease they find it awkward to face their children and talk about their separation. I've heard many naive parents state, "Why should I say anything to the kids—they wouldn't understand anyway!" It's true that nothing good comes of telling your children the gory details of your marital tempest; however, that does not mean you should keep them in the dark about your pending separation.

Ironically, if you think you are protecting your children—freeing them from unnecessary worry—by not saying anything about your intention to separate or your already separated status, you are in fact only protecting yourself and ducking your responsibilities.

You do your children a grave disservice when they get the impression they don't count because you aren't up-front with them. You might get the very reactions you hoped to avoid—retaliation and rejection.

Be aware: your discerning children talk among themselves and sometimes to their friends. They can easily misconstrue any mention of *separation* as meaning *divorce*. To make certain your youngsters are not unduly suspicious or misinformed, take the time to sit down with them and explain the situation as it is.

CS: A Guilt-Ridden Daddy

On the eve of Marge and Henry's CS, Marge tried not to sound alarmed as she explained to Becky, five, and Annie, seven, that Daddy was moving out. Henry, however, was so crippled with shame he couldn't face his daughters. A few days after he moved out, he told me how disgusted he was with himself for being so incompetent. I told him to bring both girls to meet me.

When Henry arrived with his daughters in tow, I asked him to sit each girl on one knee while I spoke for him. Then I asked Becky and Annie to look at Daddy, not me. This special kind of help I call a "Royal Rescue."

I began, "Becky and Annie, do you know why Daddy brought you here today?"

Each child shyly murmured, "No."

Knowing I had gained their attention, I said, "You already know Mommy and Daddy have just separated. Let me explain a little more. You see, they want to try to work things out, but right now they aren't sure. I see your parents regularly, and I'm trying to help them decide what to do. Now, do you have any questions?" Each one shook her curly head, "No."

Then Henry swept his daughters into his arms and with a big bear hug said, "Annie and Becky, even though I'm not living with you right now, I'm staying close by. I promise to call you every day, and I'll see you as much as I can . . . you are mighty important to me, and I love you so much!"

With that, I could scarcely contain my own tears, and a solemn Henry continued to hold his girls tight. Relief flooded the room.

CS: Guidelines for Telling the Kids

What your children need at the outset is your presence, support, comfort, and caring. If they don't receive this nurturing, they are apt to be bewildered and suspicious when they inadvertently learn the truth or half-truths, as is usually the case.

The following guides for telling your children can spare the whole family undue angst.

1. Discuss your pending separation after you set the time limit and you know which parent will move out.

2. Do your best to arrange for both parents and the children to get together as a family unit to talk about your pending separation. Plan to meet two or three days in advance so the youngsters are not taken by surprise when one parent moves out.

3. Explain that your separation is a *temporary* arrangement. *Emphasize this is not a divorce.* Expect your children of any age to react. Comfort the kids if they cry. Whether or not you cry right along with them, don't apologize; instead explain, "Tears are a normal way for people to express grief."

4. Expect your youngsters to be afraid. The uncertainty of your marital status is bound to be disturbing because they fear for their future. Reassure them that both parents will still take care of them.

5. Encourage your children to ask questions, and expect them to want concrete answers. Do not be vague and say, "Oh, you're too young" or "You don't need to know." This is a put-down.

If you are confused yourself, say so directly. For example, "I'm not sure right now when Dad/Mom is coming home, but I'll let you know as soon as I know what is happening." In this way your young ones feel included rather than brushed aside and treated as nonentities—as if they and their apprehensions are being trivialized.

6. Allow your children adequate time to express their feelings. Make certain your youngsters understand both parents are involved in the decision-making process.

A Call for Compassion

In times of formidable stress, it is imperative that you keep your own body and soul together. With the emotional drain of marital indecision, you may ask, "How much positive energy can I conceivably expend on behalf of my kids, my spouse, and myself when I'm not sure if I'm staying or going?"

There is no way to be sensitive to the subtle nuances of raw conflict in yourself, your spouse, or your children all at once. In the process of making dual living arrangements, some parents will become so absorbed in their children's demands that they neglect themselves.

Fretting over the sorry state of your marriage, you don't feel in good shape. You feel vulnerable and needy. Your children see you teary eyed, and you are torn apart by trying to hide your feelings. When you can't, you feel guilty.

In a bizarre way, though you're in no shape to get yourself unstuck, some of you may be worrying more about your spouse and the kids than yourself.

To have compassion for yourself as a parent and a person is to accept that you will always wish that you didn't have to deal with your marital mess. To be hard on yourself because you can't fix yourself, your spouse, or your children—it's all too big for you— is tough on your morale.

To tell yourself "I shouldn't feel sorry for myself" is to be unsympathetic and will make you feel worse than ever. This is what I tell my dejected clients: "Take a few minutes every day [if needed] to feel sorry for yourself. After all, if you don't, who will?"

To blame yourself for being angry or fearful is a short route to a down-in-the-dumps mood. Tell yourself, "These feelings speak for who I am—my fundamental self. Rather than fight with my emotions, I accept them for what they are and move on."

I believe our attitudes and actions speak for who we are. Rather than diminish your feelings or bemoan your flaws, consider what you do well—what you do right. Then do what you can to change your unskilled behaviors.

Be good to your children and be good to yourself. As you take an interest in improving yourself through healthy living, you will be in better shape to competently take care of your youngsters.

Using Children as Commodities

Haplessly, in all too many cases of separation and divorce, children are used as commodities. The young people's worth is reduced to custody and dollars—who lives the most with whom and for how much money.

I hate to see parents using their children as "political footballs" in a play for power, tossing them back and forth. No wonder youngsters are disturbed. For some parents, the income derived from a custody settlement is of more value than reaching out to the child's heart and soul.

Therapeutic Support

If you find your children unreachable or unmanageable in reaction to your marital upheaval or trial separation (TS), consider the merit of professional help to see you through these taxing times. No point in beating yourself up for not being perfect, for thinking you are incompetent or not good enough because you let your children down.

Consider parenting classes, personal-growth workshops, and family therapy to get a better handle on stabilizing yourself and rearing your children. Reach out to your community resources during these trying times—they can benefit not only you, but your entire family constellation during the decision-making interim.

Gifts of Caring

Marriage and family therapists Craig Everett and Sandra Volgy Everett, authors of *Healthy Divorce: For Parents and Children—an Original, Clinically Proven Program for Working Through the Fourteen Stages of Separation, Divorce, and Remarriage*, point out that children remember the way they were told by their parents of their decision to separate or divorce. If the decision is explained poorly, the consequences can be devastating, as basic trust is destroyed—the trust that is so essential for good parent-child relationships.

In planning for a constructive separation, the Everetts suggest the following seven gifts:

1. Gift of honesty

2. Gift of choice of how to feel and think

3. Gift of patience and time

4. Gift of accurate information

5. Gift of trust

6. Gift of security and continuity

7. Gift of making children your highest priority[4]

Guides to Avoiding More Trouble

No matter what your status, be it planning a CS journey, taking a transitional separation, or still mulling about what comes next, you will spare yourself considerable grief and do your children a great service by heeding the following guides:

- Don't be tempted to "use" your children to gain allies for yourself.

- Don't share with them the gory details of your ambivalence or why you are immobilized.

- Don't malign your mate—no put-downs.

- Do discuss your children's school assignments and their other current concerns.

- Do go to their games and special events.

- Do make dual living arrangements flexible and as reasonable as possible.

- Do tell your children you love them every day and then do lots of hugging and patting of heads and give them the comfort they so desperately require.

By following these guides, you act out of consideration and respect for your youngsters' welfare. Whether your journey includes a CS, family therapy, plain common sense, or a combination of all three, your family can grow closer; and parents and progeny can all thrive in a compassionate environment—a goal worth striving for.

$\mathcal{M}$oney Counts: Different Hats/Different Spats

Money: Power and Emotion

MONEY IS IMBUED with power and emotion. It is a commodity that can facilitate or hinder the decision-making process. Finances—be they enough or not enough—motivate some unhappily marrieds to stay in "make-do" marriages rather than risk the expense and trauma of divorce. Others, in a panic about money, abandon an unstable union only to regret their premature decision.

Money means different things to different people. It can represent a promise of financial security equated with love and approval or a controlling means to further corrupt a faltering relationship.

Money and Survival

At its root, money is equated with our sense of survival. Our physical and emotional security seems to depend on it. When marital separation is in the offing, the first thought that comes to mind is how are you to stay afloat? "How am I going to keep the roof over my head and pay the kids' expenses? Will there be enough to pay the mortgage, charge accounts, and all the other bills?" For those in dire financial straits, there is another worry: "Will I have to go on welfare?" You fret, "Do I have the strength to fight with my spouse over money? Isn't there an easier way? I hate this."

Very few of us can actually divorce ourselves from money issues. Our attitudes are formulated in childhood by the conditions of our birth, our station in life, and how our parents handled money. These early experiences influence whether our attitudes remain the same or change when we marry, separate, or divorce.

Mad Money and Exploitation

The phrase "marital separation" is so emotionally loaded that people are prone to reach for their pocketbooks first and think about everything else second. This is especially true in trial separations (TS). Terrified of losing out financially, many people put thoughts about money even before the welfare of their children. They worry about not having sufficient resources to get through the crisis. The chafing spouse sees money as a valid reason to nail down specific material goods, just in case.

If there is a hint of suspicion or threat of separation, spouses frequently behave as if they are on the road to divorce, even when they are not. Their relationship is further riddled with holes when either or both parties hoard "mad money," secretly empty the checking and savings accounts, or withhold pertinent financial information. All too often, unfortunately, these events take place with little or no communication between the partners. Then one day papers are delivered, and the shocked rejectee wakes up to the reality, "We are divorcing!"

Though hostile mates might prefer to deny the implications of their mad-money frenzy, the intent is plain to see. *Money is the driv-*

ing force that fulfills the prophecy of an ugly breakup long before it might be a confirmed fact!

Couples seriously handicap efforts at constructive relationship repair when they allow the specter of money to drive a wedge between them. In no time the divorce contestants are raging over distribution of the last pot or pan.

Trial Separation and Money

An impasse about money often forces those engaged in a TS to "throw in the sponge" prematurely and fight it out in court.

Adversaries who experiment with TS more often than not find it irresistible to use money as fuel to fire greater mistrust. They lack the vision to see how the torn fabric of their marriage could possibly be mended. Adversaries often fear that money will not be distributed fairly in the event of separation or divorce, a sort of dog-eat-dog philosophy.

Engrossed with getting the most, adversaries are fiercely competitive, centered on "I," with a disdain for "you." Taking a "me first" attitude, adversaries plot and plan how to gain as much financial control as possible. For some this places the major wage earner at a considerable advantage.

Sad to say, when an unstructured separation causes a couple's financial survival to feel threatened, baser emotions are bound to surface. The TS seems to give some mates license to act like barbarians. It is as if the adversary's need and greed create an unhealthy stew dished out with noxious doses of revenge. Such a toxic potion is enough to drive any marital relationship into the ground. Hopes for salvaging the marriage become more remote than ever.

CS: Sane Money Management

Couples invested in a CS, however, are empowered to handle the issue of money with reason and dignity. These partners do not let money destroy the remaining good in their coupling. They aim to minimize hassles over finances; thus, they profit by establishing trust rather than exacerbating suspicion and greed.

There are four significant reasons why CS couples are motivated to handle their finances constructively:

1. Mates can relax about making binding financial arrangements, knowing there is no urgency.

2. With the major fear of being unilaterally served with divorce papers removed, partners wisely see no need to complicate their lives with money matters any more than absolutely necessary.

3. With threats of divorce relegated to the back burner, couples have fewer reasons to provoke one another about money. They realize it is in their best interests to cooperate, rather than corrupt their CS negotiations.

4. If the final destination is divorce, the CS process sets the stage for orderly, cooperative financial discussion.

Different Hats/Different Spats

The following six profiles describe "hats" as the attitudes spouses wear about money. The "spats" refer to stipulations, concessions, demands, and/or threats that couples impose concerning their finances. Couples in accord accommodate, compromise, and pave the way for a sound marriage or do their best to implement a good divorce. Parties who insist on taking control turn petty and demand retribution. Predictably, they are moving toward a permanent split.

By way of correlating the six different hats with their complementary spats, we see the "conjoint consenter," "willing pleaser," "holdout," "two-faced saboteur," "royal avenger," and "desperado." It is important to understand that some partners are advocates when it has to do with their children but adversaries when it has to do with their money. The reverse can also be true. These profiles depict recurring strife, illustrating how people use money to get closure on their "stay or go" impasse. For example, some partners may not want a divorce but will initiate one to ensure that they don't lose out financially.

1. Conjoint Consenter: The Cooperative Ones

For the sake of expediency, conjoint consenters sensibly cooperate as advocates because they are not looking to provoke more trouble than they already have. Although it is important to get what is considered to be a fair distribution of funds, CS partners tend to see the wisdom of being less grabby and greedy, understanding how hard a long-drawn-out "battle for the buck" can be on their children. "Who needs more misery? . . . The load is heavy enough as it is . . . guess we might as well pull together and make this a cooperative separation [divorce] to save our sanity."

Whether it be separation or divorce, when parties show deference for one another in regard to equitable distribution of their monies, they can take pride in acting responsibly.

2. Willing Pleaser: Secret Agenda

"I'll give you anything you ask for, honey, if . . ." The willing pleaser cooperates about money but secretly has an agenda: "I'm banking on winning you back by acting nice and not making a big stink about money." Occasionally this ploy does work.

Another hidden scenario has the willing pleaser cooperating for a very different reason: "Maybe if I act nice about the money, you won't hit the roof when you find out I've got a prospective replacement for you waiting in the wings."

The willing pleaser has good reason to be financially generous. It is a case of "I'll give whatever you ask for because I've got all this guilt I've got to dump."

Don't be surprised if this ploy backfires, and your mate digs deeper into your pockets. In either of the above instances, the willing pleaser usually does not make much of a fuss about finances and, by default, negotiates a divorce in a fair manner. This is especially true if the parties have negotiated a CS or incorporate counseling or mediation as they proceed.

3. Holdout: Stall Tactics

"You can't pressure me into a divorce. I won't budge." The holdout uses money to throw a monkey wrench into the divorce process.

These stall tactics can be a drag, putting TS on hold indefinitely—for five years or more in some cases.

In terms of finalizing a divorce, if the holdout procrastinates and refuses to negotiate with the spouse or cooperate with the attorney, this mate is using his or her clout to strong-arm the other.

In one case the judge was obliged to force the holdout's hand by setting a time limit on delivery of completed financial stipulations. In the long run, it became an 18-month stall. The drain on emotional reserves during the waiting period was so debilitating that my client couldn't sleep, lost weight, and needed medication for a depression she couldn't shake.

4. Two-Faced Saboteur: Throw You a Curve

"If we stay married, I'll be nice about money and a lot more. If you insist on discussing or threatening divorce, I'll be a bear and make your life miserable."

The two-faced saboteur is generous as long as the marriage is secure, but in the face of divorce, he or she abruptly does an uncharacteristic about-face, becomes incensed, and is downright petty when it comes to parting with "my money." The implied message is, "I'll make you pay dearly for divorcing me."

5. Royal Avenger: Greed Is My Master

"I'll make sure you get your comeuppance." Driven by greed, "my money" counts above all else—kids, spouse, family. The royal avenger feels wronged and is determined to right the wrongs by "deservedly punishing" the errant mate. Efforts to "even the score" are nailed down by securing "my material goodies" to the very last teaspoon.

In the course of TS, many mates are extremely agitated about how much they stand to lose financially and materially if it comes to divorce. It takes only a minor misunderstanding before one spouse seizes the initiative and speaks with a lawyer about filing for divorce. In the process of resolving divorce stipulations, the money-hungry royal avenger gets stingier and meaner. Lawyers have a field day with these cases. They can get downright expensive.

6. Desperado: Handicapped to the Max

"Don't bother to call me! I'll see you in court." The desperado gets an unlisted phone number and refuses to discuss money or anything else relevant to separation. Thus handicapped, the desperado forces the issue, and the parties are obliged to talk through their respective attorneys.

Generally, these parties have splitting headaches trying to make any sense whatsoever of where they stand moneywise as their ugly divorce drags on and on.

A Better Way

No matter what the outcome, if you and your spouse lay the groundwork for sensible money management and division of assets, you are wealthier by far than trying to outwit one another down to the last dollar.

13

$\mathcal{S}$exual Excesses: Perverse Pairs

An Overview of Sexual Excesses

AFFAIRS CAN BE the knock-down-drag-out reason for catapulting spouses into an ugly divorce, or they can be a catalytic force for healing scarred relationships, drawing couples into a more intimate, durable marriage.

On your wedding day, how comfortable it is to assume your mutual love will mean loyalty, trust, and fidelity forever. But when the roof comes crashing down on the unfaithful one by the sheer weight of the discovered affair, you have a full-fledged marital catastrophe.

I define *sexual excesses* as any sexual liaison(s) occurring outside of marriage that precipitates a crisis in the marital relationship.

Sexual wanderings—the fling, liaison, affair, rendezvous, sneaking around, one-night stand—usually embody a secret fantasy of making some sexy dream come true. The exuberant lovers' encounter with intimacy would appear to be everything the marriage is not. The tryst tantalizes with its promise of fresh romance and elation a humdrum relationship doesn't supply. In turn, it becomes an effort for the lovers to suffer relentless annoyances on the home front, and then there is double trouble.

Some disenchanted spouses feel powerless to change their sexually or emotionally irresponsive mates, and they will betray their partners for the exhilaration of the first blush of that which is forbidden. Some make a habit of it.

Every case of infidelity has some similarities, but each case is unique. The tale of Faye and Judd speaks to the foibles and drama of the sexual addiction affair.

Faye and Judd: The Perverse Pair

Judd knew that big trouble was brewing when Faye started to cry and wouldn't stop. She cried every day but would not speak. Judd encouraged her to talk but she turned away, silent and unreachable.

It was 10 days before Faye unleashed her secret—one more extramarital affair. Disgusted, Judd cried out, "That's enough now. We need help!"

The couple had much working against them. They were a humorless pair, living from paycheck to paycheck, their nerves frayed. Their social life centered on extended family. Faye had no girlfriends and no hobbies or special interests other than Wednesday night bingo. Judd relieved the daily tedium by "shooting the breeze with the guys at the tavern."

Judd was discouraged. "We've been married nine years now, and it ain't getting any easier . . . hard to stay afloat. Trouble is, I'm not quick on the trigger to do the right thing . . . got no idea what to say when Faye goes on a crying jag. She sulks for days and I get pissed. I go visit my sister and her kid 'cause I gotta get out of there. I get home and first thing Faye jumps down my throat and says I don't care about her."

Judd paused to catch his breath and went on, "I'm no good at this relation stuff. And now with all her chasing around, she's ruining it for us."

The first time I counseled this childless couple, Faye had just miscarried and was told she could never bear children. Acutely depressed, the couple requested I help them work through their grief. It was two years later when Judd contacted me to get their marital relationship straightened out.

Faye's Story

Faye, 34, was a scrawny, mousy woman with stringy blondish hair. She worked as a cleaning lady and took pride in seeing other people's interiors sparkling fresh when she finished her day. But what was it going to take to clean up her own life? And how could she ever hold her head high? Her only thought was that she should separate from Judd; beyond that, everything was a blur.

Faye had been very attached to her father, who was killed in a hunting accident when she was seven. She could never forgive her mother for remarrying two years later. She took an intense dislike to her stepfather, who was brusque and critical of timorous Faye. Her mother was unsupportive. Faye said, "I really had it in for my mother, and I told her so. She never took my side, so who did I have to turn to?"

Faye had a brazen side that cropped up as a teenager. At age 13 her stepfather made several passes at her. In a rage she kicked him in the shins and sought solace in her room. "My ma refused to believe me, and after that I avoided the two of them and holed up in my room. I hated everyone and everything. I cried a lot. When it got real bad, I would sneak out and go looking for guys."

Vulnerable and left to her own devices, Faye became promiscuous within the year. She met Judd on a hayride. They dated a year and married when she was just 17, despite her mother's disapproval.

Faye explained, "Everything was getting to me, and I had to get out of the house. I was awfully young to know much about marriage. I'm still so insecure, scared of my shadow." But she could be brash when it came to latching on to men—single or married. The men she chose were close at hand—a second cousin, a youngish

uncle, and even Judd's brother-in-law. Judd forced Faye to apolo
gize to his sister, but things were never the same. Holidays and
special occasions were uncomfortable for all concerned.

Judd's Story

Judd, 45, worked as a gardener for the park department in the
summer months and took on maintenance jobs in the winter. He
referred to himself as "a farm boy at heart."

A burly man, he would come lumbering into our sessions in his
grubby overalls, ready to pour his heart out about his wandering
wife. He pictured himself as boss, principal wage earner, and pro-
tector of Faye but never saw himself as "the disturbed patient."

Judd's parents were divorced when he was 12. "I took it real
hard. Mama had to go to work 'cause Dad moved away. He was real
slippery, never paid no child support. So Mama sent me and my little sis to live on the farm with the grandparents. We all pitched in.
Nobody had much to say . . . nobody ever said they loved me—or
anything like that."

Judd said he had "sort of forgiven" Faye for her sexual transgressions. Later he admitted to "playing the field" himself shortly
after Faye's first dalliance. He admitted, "I probably was mad at Faye
for cutting out on me like that and wanted to get back at her. But
such goings-on make me queasy—I know it ain't right."

Introducing the CS

By the time I came into the picture, Faye's mother had recently filed
for divorce. The significance of this cannot be underestimated, as
it apparently gave Faye the impetus to view separation as a first step
in facing the decline of her own marriage.

Faye remarked, "I'm depressed, have no appetite, and feel burnt
out from crying about Judd and me. I don't want a divorce, but I
wish I could live on my own . . . only I don't have the nerve to do
it. I can't tell Judd, he wouldn't understand."

I wasn't sure how Faye would respond to my introducing the
CS as a way to undo her stuckness. I half suspected she would have

serious reservations. As it turned out, money was the first major obstacle. She couldn't afford her own place, and she wouldn't move in with her mother. But worst of all, she knew Judd would oppose her moving out.

Her shoulders slumped, dejectedly she said, "It's too much for me to get into a hassle and all that. Judd gets so up in arms and huffy he won't listen. Besides, he's so negative it drives me nuts." Pensively she added, "Guess it's contagious. I hate being so mixed up and not knowing what I'm doing. Then I get negative, too."

Faye, too uptight to mention a CS to Judd, settled down when I suggested we could discuss the CS with Judd, if she were willing.

A week later in my office it happened just as Faye anticipated. In a burst of temper, Judd thundered, "I won't hear of this CS stuff. I'm here to get Faye and us straightened out and not screw up our marriage any more than it already is!"

After that Faye sunk into a disturbingly morbid state, and a frightened Judd grudgingly gave in within two weeks, saying, "I guess a CS looks better than any sloppy sort of separation." In private, Judd expressed his worst fears—a bitter divorce.

CS Contract Negotiations

The couple contracted for a three-month separation. Neither party was interested in talking with an attorney. Both said they would not file for divorce for the duration of their CS.

Faye said, "It gives me some peace of mind."

Judd said, "Glad that worry is out of the way," but he fretted nonetheless.

Faye rushed to get a furnished apartment and in a flurry of activity moved in with three other women she scarcely knew.

The couple contracted to talk by phone three times a week and date on Saturday nights. Faye felt duty bound to keep her promise, but neither one knew how to have a good time. They weren't adept at making small talk, and visiting relatives wasn't a comfortable thought. The couple would go to the tavern for a couple of beers or watch television at Judd's place. Faye was bored and saw her life as dull and going nowhere.

As for sexual contact, Faye hedged, "Oh, Judd can hug me I guess, but I don't want to promise more than that." I didn't push her.

To Judd's dismay, Faye refused to say she wouldn't date other men. He firmly stated he had no interest in seeing other women.

The couple contracted for joint sessions twice a month, and Faye opted for weekly individual therapy. Judd would wait till he couldn't hold out anymore and then call me, wanting an appointment the same day.

CS: The First Month

The first ray of light was quickly extinguished when Faye discovered her new living arrangements were impossible. With little privacy, the television blaring all hours, the telephone usually tied up, and the noise level deafening, Faye thought she would lose her mind. Ten days later she went back to Judd.

But by then she was so down on herself, I suggested she look for a quieter place where she could settle her nerves. A month later Judd was generous enough to help her move into a tiny furnished one-room apartment, a good deed considering their fragile circumstances.

Faye had never lived alone, and she didn't like it. The lonely nights were the worst, and when anguish mounted, she would furtively turn to one or another of her former paramours.

Unaware of this turn of events, Judd was pleading with his wife to "come back and all will be forgiven." More confused than ever, Faye hated herself for being so wishy-washy. Judd was heartbroken when Faye braced herself to remain separated.

Heightened Drama

Faye heard via the grapevine that Judd was threatening suicide and abruptly packed up and went back home. But that move was short-lived, and she returned to her apartment within 10 days.

A few days later, a very distraught Faye told her sister she, too, had thoughts of suicide. When Faye didn't show up for a luncheon appointment with her sister the next day, the police were notified; and 12 anxious hours later, she was found. Faye said she "forgot about the lunch and went shopping instead."

She spent another few days with Judd and left again. Dismally insecure and pitifully dependent, she stayed attached to one man or another. Wretched wherever she lived, she felt an urgency "to settle it between Judd and me once and for all."

CS: Faye's Transformation

In desperation Faye said, "I can't keep hopping from bed to bed like this. Where do I draw the line?" Working on her marriage was not her highest priority, but she saw the CS as a way to achieve two other goals: to halt her sexual addiction and learn to love herself.

Using a modification of the Alcoholics Anonymous (AA) 12-step program, Faye avowed:

- "I admit that I have a sexual addiction, and my life has become unmanageable.

- "I trust a higher power can guide me.

- "I turn my impairment over to my higher power and hold to the vision that I will overcome my sexual addiction and begin to love myself."

To reinforce this program, I asked Faye to practice the following affirmations:

"I am lovable."
"I am valuable."
"I am capable."
"I am worthwhile."
"My life counts."

As Faye rehearsed the words every day, a stunning change came over her. She brightened up and began to understand her underlying motives: "It used to be every conquest was like a jolt of power, but the letdown was so awful, like I was beating myself up. I feel so different—like I can really get rid of a terrible burden."

When the couple's three-month CS Contract came to an end, they did not renegotiate for additional time. Faye told Judd she wanted to continue living apart, and divorce was never mentioned by either spouse.

The couple kept in contact and occasionally would talk by telephone or meet for dinner. I continued to work with Faye individually for another six months, until she terminated therapy. It was yet another year before Faye felt stable and secure enough to ask Judd for a divorce. The couple had no qualms about making it an amicable one.

Follow-Up

Five years later I spoke with Faye. She is happily married to a considerate gentleman with four children. With a lilt in her voice she said, "I always wanted four kids, and now I've got them."

She indicated Judd had remarried, but they had minimal contact. I wasn't successful in contacting him.

I asked Faye how she had benefited from the CS. She replied, "I was so unsure of my marriage. The CS opened my eyes a lot and helped me know I had to get myself straightened out first. I've grown up a lot. I found out I wasn't helping myself by staying with Judd."

Faye concluded our conversation on a joyous note: "I'm glad to say everything in my life has finally come together."

Sexual Excesses and Gender Differences

There is good cause for marital mistrust, judging by current reports that upwards of 70 percent of those married admit to being unfaithful according to Arond and Pauker.[1]

My research indicates relatively few clinical studies are available on marital infidelity. Shirley P. Glass and Thomas L. Wright report approximately 25 percent of couples request marital therapy because of infidelity, and another 30 percent disclose adulterous relationships in the course of treatment.[2] And these numbers don't account for the partners who never seek treatment and never tell.

In years gone by, it was commonly thought that men had affairs more often than women. However, the unleashing of sexual freedoms during the sixties and seventies has given today's women vastly more opportunities for infidelity than ever before.

Annette Lawson, author of *Adultery: An Analysis of Love and Betrayal*, notes that affairs are occurring earlier in marriage than ever before. Women are catching up fast—and even passing up the men. She reports that within the first five years of marriage, approximately two-thirds of the women and nearly one-half of the men have affairs. In contrast, only one-fourth of those married 20 years or longer have affairs.[3]

Glass and Wright found that men can readily separate sex from love, whereas women believe love and sex go together and feel an affair is justified if they have fallen in love.[4]

This difference in perception accounts for why women will more often perceive an affair as justification for divorce, and many men will not see an affair as a substantial enough reason to part ways.

Lies and Deception

It takes a web of lies to sneak around. Infidelity represents a flagrant violation of trust and is bound to incite merciless retribution for most married folk—at least in the United States. In our culture sexual excesses are considered "just cause" for divorce.

Marriage and family therapist John Amodeo, Ph.D., in *Love and Betrayal: Broken Trust in Intimate Relationships*, tells us, "Although we may presume we are successfully concealing an affair, the truth has a way of seeping out in subtle or dramatic ways."[5]

Apparently, the betrayer subconsciously wants to get caught and apprehended. Not so mysteriously, evidence of the affair is exposed—unaccountable extras on the phone bill, unfamiliar ticket stubs, and questionable items on charge accounts. When the unfaithful spouse is nailed, a reign of terror is apt to follow. It is not so unusual for some contrite betrayers to experience a surge of relief when the truth comes out.

According to Constance R. Ahrons, the staunch, faithful mate considers the sneaky lies the worst affront of all—harder to swallow than the actual affair(s).[6]

Types of Affairs and Hidden Agendas

Marriage and family therapist Emily M. Brown calls the affair "a giant wake-up call" indicative of marital troubles that overtly or covertly involve both partners.[7] Drawing on Brown's provocative insights, I've identified five types of affairs—and their hidden messages—that correlate with the "stay or go" enigma.

1. Conflict Avoidance Affairs

"I'll make you notice me, one way or another." The discovered affair forces couples on the cusp to face a crisis they don't know how to handle. As a rule, conflict avoiders are pleasers who assiduously avoid conflict for fear of being rejected. As controversy is ignored, resentments pile up. The adulterer deludes the self into believing "if I don't tell my spouse I am angry and annoyed, the problem doesn't exist."

Conflict avoiders feel justified looking elsewhere when sex with a spouse is waning. When the infidel goes on the prowl, he or she gets into double trouble, trying hard to avoid getting caught.

All hell breaks lose when the conflict avoider's affair(s) comes to light. The very conflicts they have kept under wraps put couples on the cusp in a precarious position. It is not uncommon for the rejected spouse to "call foul play," seek individual or couple therapy, insist on a TS, or threaten or actually file for divorce. The CS is generally a welcome alternative, as further anguish is spared and marriages are often saved.

2. Intimacy Avoidance Affairs

"I'm afraid to get close for fear you'll reject me, so I'll look elsewhere to get my intimacy needs met." Intimacy avoiders feel inadequate and uncomfortable in being emotionally close with their mates. The unfaithful one has insidious ways of upending the coupling, finding the affair more exciting than putting his or her energies into working on marital intimacy. How tantalizing to be accepted with no strings attached!

Intimacy avoiders and their partners can benefit from a CS by confessing to the affair and looking inward to determine if admiration, commitment, and love can be rekindled or if the marriage is ultimately washed up.

3. Sexual Addiction Affairs

"Fill me up; I feel deprived of love and I'm insatiable." The sexual addict is emotionally unfulfilled and thirsting for power. Self-absorbed, he or she often feels no concern about being found out. Deprived of love as children and feeling unwanted, sexual addicts find the sexual act provides a lift, but not for long. Sexual excesses won't fill their empty hearts.

It is not unusual, as in the case of Faye and Judd, for both partners to have similar profiles. As each party is unable to exert an uplifting influence on the other, the parties feel trapped in an uncomfortable codependency.

There is no predicting the fate of the sexual addict's relationship. If sexual indiscretions are condoned, the marriages endure. A case in point is the current interest in infidelity as the affairs of politicians and other public figures come to light. As a rule, the wives turn the other cheek, apparently taking their husbands' unquenchable sexual appetites for granted. It is assumed to be far better "to put up and shut up" rather than bring public disgrace to the entire family.

Conversely, other rejected spouses, tormented by incessant jealousy and suspicion and eager to break the mold, will find sexual excesses reasonable grounds for divorce.

4. Empty-Nest Affairs

"I'm fed up with you, but I'd be miserable without you." The empty nester who "plays around" complains the marital relationship is devoid of sexual warmth and caring. The adulterer leads a life of duplicity. Overnight absences are lamely excused by work demands, overtime, out-of-town meetings, or other lies that appear to suffice. These long-term marriages, 20 years or more, endure despite limited access to open communication and sexual intimacy.

Gladys, age 55 and married for 35 years, told me, "My husband wasn't interested in sex for such a long time that twice I deliberately arranged to have sex with an old family friend. He was tender and made me feel alive—like an attractive woman again. I wish my mate would be that attentive. The dog gets his affection, not me!"

More often than not, the unfaithful empty nesters hold firm to their marriage vows, committed to "make a go of it somehow." Although empty nesters divorce less frequently than shorter-term marrieds, their divorces can be just as abrasive.

The CS is a sound method for helping these couples successfully restructure their marriages or avoid ugly divorces, as the case may be.

5. Out-the-Door Affairs

"I've secretly decided to divorce, but I can't make it out the door without your help." The unremorseful infidel has lost interest in the partner and subversively plots to "get kicked out."

Out-the-door affairs can seldom be kept secret for long, although the liaison can be relatively brief or stretch out for years. When news of his or her "friend" eventually leaks out, the couple have heated arguments over who is "at fault." The third party is looked upon as the villain, and this gets both spouses off the hook. In this way the couple is spared facing up to their joint responsibilities for the demise of the marriage.

Should the out-the-door mate initiate a TS, it is usually with the intention of not returning home. In contrast, conflict avoiders and intimacy avoiders see TS—or, better still, CS—as a true test of the marriage and hope to reconcile.

If the out-the-door spouse remains immobilized, then the rejected mate is left to decide whether to divorce or not. In the case of a split up, the CS reduces the trauma and prepares the parties for a constructive divorce.

Disclosure of Sexual Excesses

A word of caution: do *not* disclose sexual excesses if you suspect violence or destructive divorce litigation. Use discretion and take every precaution to protect your safety! It is essential to use good judgment in such potentially threatening situations.

Furthermore, you are not obliged to expose all sexual indiscretions when the damage done would far outdo the benefits of telling. What good is to be served by talking about affair(s) from the past?

CS: The Gateway to Honesty

The CS provides a forum for honesty whereby covert liaisons can be frankly discussed in a prudent manner. As you negotiate your CS Contract, a heavy dose of frank communication can be refreshing and lighten the load for parties who have had their fill of lies and deceit.

There are cases, however, when vulnerable rejectees find a candid admission of an affair a bitter pill to swallow. More than one grieving mate has said, "I wish I didn't know—somehow it would be easier."

If you are riddled with guilt and remorse, however, then disclosure—under the protection of the CS safety net—provides a sensible way to look at the hidden agendas that have placed your relationship in jeopardy. I know of no other therapeutic model that matches the CS in intent or serves such a lofty purpose. Here is a timely and humane opportunity to bridge your chasm and mend broken hearts.

Therapeutic Intervention

Many rejectees choose individual or couple counseling to cope with the pangs of infidelity. Whether you opt for a CS or not, should it be too taxing to plunge into the devilish area of sexual excesses, then use a skilled facilitator. You wouldn't chance exploring the Amazon jungle without a guide, so consider therapeutic intervention before losing your way in your own treacherous marital jungle.

The Identity Crisis: Discovery-Zone Mates

The Tale of Lucy and Jackie: Mothers Each

EVERYTHING SEEMED TO have fallen into place for Lucy, 42, and Jackie, 37, who were drawn into an affectionate lesbian bonding. Lucy told me, "Meeting up with Jackie was the best thing that ever happened to my daughter and me." Jackie spoke in a similar vein, "I could always rely on Lucy to be my best friend and loyal companion, and our girls get along well, too."

Despite their differing temperaments, Lucy and Jackie had molded a partnership that flourished for 14 years. Jackie was flamboyant and blustery, whereas Lucy was demure and placid.

They had met at a garage sale and discovered they had much in common. Each was at loose ends, each had a young child, and each had almost no social life.

When I came into the picture, Dolly, Jackie's daughter, age 17, was planning to go to a state college; and Lila, age 16, Lucy's daughter, was hoping to follow suit in a year. The first time I met Jackie, her dark hair was askew and her clothes were rumpled, as if she had slept in them. She had called for an appointment because Lucy had walked out on her two days earlier, leaving a scribbled note: "Went to Harriet's. Don't call. Lucy."

With no indication of when Lucy was coming back, Jackie was reeling from the shock. Livid, she let loose with a torrent of grievances: "I'm eating myself up alive. I can't understand what's come over Lucy . . . and now she's left and won't talk to me! Looks like everything we've built together is going right down the drain."

Jackie's Story

Jackie told me, "All I ever wanted was to give Dolly a stable home life. Being with Lucy gave me a chance to rise above a past I've tried hard to forget."

Growing up had been a grim ordeal. A feisty, fiercely determined child, Jackie's temper tantrums could be heard a block away. She called her father, a bullish and overbearing man, "the asshole." She said, "He made it plain he was always right and I was always wrong. I never had any use for the guy."

At 12, she had been abused by an older brother, not once but three times. As her face flushed with rage, I asked her to pause and take a deep breath so she could temper her heated emotions. Her eyes bulged as she said, "So I told my mother about the incest . . . a lot of times. That stupid woman had the audacity to laugh in my face, said I was making it up. To this day she still doesn't believe me. I'll never forgive her."

At 15 Jackie was a virtual hellion, defiant and uncontrollable. That's when she took to making a nasty habit of slitting her wrists. At 16 she spent nine months in a child adolescent inpatient treatment center. When she was released, she lived in foster care.

At 17 Jackie got stone drunk at a party, and when she awoke from her stupor, she knew she had been raped. She finished high school with a swollen belly and made no apology for the fact. The rape was the crowning blow. Jackie came to hate men.

By the time she was 19, she had forsaken her parents and was living in a rooming house, where no one questioned her about her daughter, almost two. She had taken a job at a floral shop and worked long hours, and by some incredible stroke of good fortune, her soon-to-retire employer offered her an opportunity to buy into the business. Jackie almost broke her back working hard but within seven years became the proud owner of a well-established enterprise.

Lucy's Story

Lucy told me, "I had to get away! I was at the point of losing my mind. . . . With Jackie everything's got to be her way—everything by the clock—doing the same stuff all the time. It's hard to say what's going on with me . . . have to find myself somehow. At first, Jackie gave me lots of security. We got along, and I had a chance to give Lila a home and garden."

As a child, Lucy knew tragedy. She was five when her drunken father shot himself. Mother and child went to live with her aunt and a cousin, Harriet. Lucy was content there. She described herself as "the bashful sort . . . used to think I was a burden to Mama . . . Still go around saying 'I'm sorry.' I even apologize to Jackie just to get her off my back."

Lucy liked having no men around. No one bothered her, they ate well, and she got chubby.

After graduating from high school, Lucy married, although her mother didn't approve. She had one daughter, Lila, her pride and joy. Lucy's husband was on the wild side and drank too much on occasion. Tragedy struck again when Lucy's young husband died in a motorcycle accident. Despondent, she and little Lila moved in with Harriet, where she knew she would be safe.

Lucy's Identity Crisis

One day by chance Lucy found herself facing her own mortality as never before. A coworker at the hospital where Lucy was a nurse's aide had been stricken with ovarian cancer, and another staff member's husband had dropped dead of a heart attack.

On the heels of this news, Lucy tried to fight off a scalding indictment of her own life. She scolded herself for working so long at the hospital and never becoming a registered nurse. In the next breath she chided herself for being lazy and not getting out socially. The new crew at work was learning line dancing and taking country-and-western dance lessons. She envied them.

Lucy took another hard look at herself, and her self-esteem sank a few more notches. She could see that she let Jackie boss her around just like her husband used to do.

In a flash, Lucy knew she had taken a detour into the waste-lands of stagnation. On the heels of this alarming insight, she realized, "I'm bored silly. The same routine, dinner at 6:30, same Friday night fish fry at the same joint, same vacation, always whatever Jackie wants."

And then came the awful punch line: "I don't want to grow old living like this."

Lucy was ripe for change. But with each new activity she tried—meeting her cohorts after work and taking dance classes—Jackie became moodier and more impertinent, which irritated Lucy all the more.

Rather than respect their individual differences, the couple had tried to blend their personalities into one—and the enterprise split apart on an impossible premise.

Lucy Leaves First, Explains Later

Lucy had been forced to come to grips with the fact that she had never been able to stand up to Jackie. She had furtively plotted a way to separate. She had thought, "Why not just leave and figure out the rest later?" She had known she could always stay with her cousin, Harriet, for a while. She hadn't been sure if or how this would ever happen, but she had nursed her secret, too unsure of herself to breathe a word of her plans to Jackie.

Jackie's Perspective

Jackie hadn't been able to keep up with Lucy's changes, they were happening so fast. "She's so different. From one minute to the next, it's something new. First she whacked off all her ringlets. Then she goes crazy on this health kick. Next she leaves the dining room table loaded with nursing school catalogs . . . not that I'm opposed to her being an R.N. Next she goes dancing with this bunch until all hours of the night. So much for our Friday night fish fry!"

The wall between the couple had grown several notches higher when Lucy stopped acting like Jackie's friend and then refused to talk about what was going on with her. Misunderstanding between the two women had created a hardship.

Sameness: A Static Relationship

When a couple's relationship falls into a comfortable kind of complacency, as Lucy and Jackie's had, it can feel much like an old shoe that wears well. Lucy and Jackie, however, had tried to merge their differences into a seamless partnership, which left no room for personal growth. Their enterprise was built on such a rigid structure, it was just a matter of time before their relationship split at the seams.

Some couples stay in static relationships for a lifetime. The parties may grumble and complain at times, but breaking out of old established roles—divorcing, for example—is simply not done.

For Lucy, *sameness* had meant loyalty and reliability, two essential staples, but one day it was no longer enough. She felt as if something were missing in her life. Lucy said, "Jackie is dragging me down. Sure, I know she's on her feet all day, and she's got her customers to contend with, but she's gotten so stuffy lately. She comes home, collapses on the couch, smokes her cigarettes, and sips her brandy when I'm ready to get out and kick up my heels."

When a couple's relationship sinks into a static state of sameness and repetitive, ritualized partnering, lack of creative input tends to discourage growth.

Introduction of CS

For two weeks the weather had been stormy, matching Jackie's frenzied mood. She had hoped Lucy would be the first to phone, but when the waiting became interminable, Jackie called me for an emergency appointment.

With Lucy stubbornly digging in her heels, I knew it would take some doing to bring the two together. I saw my introduction of the CS as crucial to getting both women actively involved in Lucy's separation. Jackie was cautious but soon saw the merit of possibly opening the lines of communication. It wasn't easy for her to swallow her pride, but she phoned Lucy, told her she was in counseling, talked about planting a garden, and hinted about the CS. Jackie said just enough to pique Lucy's curiosity, and within a few days the two women were sitting in my office.

CS: First Meeting

Although the shifts in the couple's relationship had started out innocently enough, it took Lucy's separation to lay bare the serious cracks in their once-compatible partnership.

Lucy was standoffish and not particularly responsive. Jackie was put off. The two women were visibly nervous and guarded, wanting me to take the lead. Jackie made it clear she wanted Lucy to come back home, "if she wouldn't act so weird." Lucy said she resented Jackie calling her "weird" and grabbed her purse as if she were ready to leave.

Explaining the details of the CS was not enough for Lucy. I needed to restate that the break between the couple was serious. I emphasized that this separation was a wise choice. With that Lucy backed down and was ready to be reasonable.

By the close of their first meeting, Jackie and Lucy had agreed to a three-month CS. Lucy said, "What happens after that . . . well, I'll just have to see how I feel." Jackie would have liked more of a commitment, but that was all the energy Lucy could summon for the moment.

The CS in Process

It was agreed Lucy would garden twice a week; the women would talk by phone once a week. They would meet with me in another week to talk about the dating aspect of CS.

I suggested individual counseling for both women. There was no quarrel with these arrangements. Both parties knew they could call me for additional sessions, if need be. When we met again, the partners agreed to meet for one dinner date on Sundays, but these arrangements got off to a slow start. Initially, Lucy held back and had little to say. Jackie was stiff and ill at ease. A turnabout in their relationship came in progressive stages.

Lucy's Questions

"What has happened to me that I've changed so much so fast? It's like I'm two people. It's like I'm barely surviving and dying to live." Lucy asked the question time and again.

I explained her split self was a normal phenomenon—an identity crisis. Lucy began to grasp what I meant. "No wonder I got so alarmed and overwhelmed, rushing around wanting to do all the things I had let slip by. So many choices—sometimes I don't know what I want to do first." With a half smile she said, "I'm like a kid at the circus. I want it all and right now!"

Lucy began to see the importance of her being optimistic about her new experiences. I explained it would be best to take her time to prioritize and decide what in her life she wanted to keep and what she could leave behind.

Brightening a bit, Lucy said, "I see what you mean. It's good the CS can do that for me." Then she giggled. "I guess I'm just a late-blooming baby boomer."

As Lucy grasped that her identity search would enable her to make sense of and find new meaning in her life, she could relax and let down her guard. By the close of summer, at harvest time, she could decide if she needed and wanted to be connected to Jackie in a committed, stable relationship.

CS: Discovery-Zone Mates

As Lucy was taking more of an interest in her personal growth, Jackie in turn was discovering more about her partner and herself. When Lucy questioned what the couple's relationship meant to her, Jackie was obliged to look at herself and decide how much she was willing to change to keep pace with her partner. Jackie repeatedly said she wanted Lucy back if she would be nice again, but Lucy hesitated—

not at all sure of herself. She stated it this way, "The problem is, Jackie just wants her way all the time and that gets to me."

The two women had a lot to learn from each other. Our joint sessions gave them an opportunity to practice communicating directly. Coping with conflict wasn't easy for Lucy: "I'd rather run till my legs drop than get into it [argue] with Jackie." In turn Jackie said, "I'm starting to see how I get sort of bossy."

Back and forth they talked and tried to listen without interrupting as they struggled with their conflicted issues. But at this stage of their growth, they were more absorbed with self and what "I want" and thinking less about what "we want." A large part of the couple's transformation hinged on each partner's developing a more empathic ear.

The Dimension of Dating

Dating presented a hardship for both women. Lucy complained to me that Jackie would try to coerce her into coming home, and, not knowing what to say, Lucy would break into tears.

Jackie complained, "I know I get heavy-handed and I'm sorry, but what are we supposed to do on a Sunday afternoon? You know we used to go to flea markets and antique stores and that sort of thing, but I'm afraid to say anything anymore."

I interceded, "Are you afraid Lucy will reject you?" With that Jackie's eyes misted as she contritely admitted, "I am such a mess. I don't know how to handle myself—it's awful."

I suggested that Jackie express herself to Lucy just as she had to me at our next joint session. It worked. As the women began to look forward to "rummaging around" at their favorite haunts, their Sunday dates began to take on a more pleasing dimension.

The Search for Self

If your coupling is already in jeopardy, nothing can rock the status quo quite like the onset of an identity crisis. To be swept into the vortex of self-examination is to travel uncharted territory. The intriguing convolutions of an identity search all but defy explanation. Like inhaling the mists of a foggy future, the experience becomes too cloudy to comprehend.

You encounter wistful dreams, and you're intrigued with spirited visions of events yet to come. My clients are inclined to refer to their experience as "a weird feeling that's hard to explain."

Midlife Crisis: A Developmental Stage

Never underestimate, however, the potential of a midlife identity crisis to take its toll on a partnership. The impact of this fateful event varies from couple to couple, depending upon the strength of their foundations. Experts in the field of human development view the identity search as a natural occurrence, a stage in our midlife cycle that produces a catalytic force for change.

Psychologist Edward P. Monte, Ph.D., gives us a dramatic sketch of this personal discovery in his article, "The Relationship Life-Cycle":

> It is a stage of self-examination, upheaval, major life transitions, crisis, reorganization and increased tension on most fronts. It is perhaps the most perilous stage for any relationship in that so many fundamental issues are at question at one time with so few answers immediately available.[1]

The Split Self in Midlife

Your midlife inquiry may parallel that of a rebellious teenager as you struggle to be your "own person." At once you are beset with questions: Who am I? What do I want? Where am I going? You have a compelling urge to be different, to feel competent, to be important and of value in the scheme of things. You feel split apart, consumed with an urge to put aside the old in favor of the new.

Compulsion to Separate in Midlife

You have a compulsion to pull away, to separate from your mate, but you can't put your finger on it. You feel dissatisfied. You question the worth of staying married. You measure your own worth against the worth of your partner. You look at your life through a different set of lenses and see it as flawed. You get depressed. You see your mate's shortcomings, and you are angry. Your coupling makes a mockery of all you have or have not accomplished. You live with regrets.

If your partner is the one with the midlife crisis, you wait and cautiously walk a tightrope. You ask, "What's going on with you?" If the answers don't make sense (because people generally don't have the words to express the experience), you are left with a gaping hole in your relationship.

If you are the party who is inundated with thoughts of separation, you may feel unprepared, at a loss where to turn, afraid to take action. In this case you live with a disturbing sense of being incomplete, and your life feels like a contradiction.

Two Opposing Forces

The desire to separate in midlife ushers forth a conflicted interplay of two controversial life forces: a push for independence at the expense of togetherness and a pull for dependence at the expense of individuation.

Togetherness refers to what is most familiar in the relationship. *Individuation* refers to breaking free and growing beyond currently acceptable relationship boundaries. This push-pull places a heavy demand on relationships and commonly precipitates a crisis that appears to come out of nowhere.

If couples are ever going to save their unions, the parties must first wrestle with an immense assortment of differing perceptions and possibilities that weave a web of complexities that touch the very core of their being.

To maintain the relationship, each party must sort out his or her priorities. A shift in attitude, from negative to positive, helps establish a viable connection. If no attempt is made to change and improve the relationship, then couples are prone to give up—seeing the old ways as expendable.

Composite Forces of a Midlife Crisis

The compulsion to separate may be so deeply entrenched in the psyche of one partner that it can throw the whole relationship out of kilter. Extrapolating from Monte's work on the midlife crisis,[2] I see nine major life forces, which operate sequentially, alternately, or simultaneously:

1. The compulsion to self-examine is a developmental process born in the genes.

2. The search for self in midlife gives rise to the same dynamics as an identity crisis in adolescence.

3. Stable couple relationships can generally withstand the onslaught of ambiguity and stress embedded in this growth process.

4. Partners who are at cross-purposes bear the full brunt of a major relationship upheaval, as if the couple's rule book has been dumped on the garbage heap.

5. The "searcher" experiences a sudden dramatic change in demeanor, attitude, feelings, and personal goals but has difficulty explaining what is happening.

6. The other partner is caught off guard, finding these drastic changes too formidable to tolerate for long.

7. The "searcher" also is caught off guard, rent by leanings to separate from the partnership. Alternately trusting and doubting these inner longings, the "searcher" is torn by indecision.

8. Intuitively, the "searcher" knows the couple's intimate relationship needs a major overhaul, but intense emotional conflicts thwart quick resolution.

9. The CS helps partners bridge their differences, openly communicate on an equal footing, reforge their identities, and amicably resolve their impasse.

The Rest of Lucy and Jackie's Story

When Jackie said she wanted Lucy back home if she would be nice again, Lucy was noncommittal. I realized their formerly close bond had yet to be restored. At this juncture I had an idea that might heighten both parties' affinity for one another.

Although Jackie and Lucy knew something of one another's early family life, I thought it might bring them closer if the two women knew more of the grisly details that had been told to me. It was reasonable to expect that if the partners spoke of their feelings, they might be able to generate more empathy and compassion for one another.

Storytelling

Lucy was the first to tell her tale of woe. A week later Jackie worked up the nerve to share her sordid story. Each woman took a full session to relay bits and pieces of history they would just as soon have shelved. Their recitations were interspersed with lots of questions and requests for more specifics.

In the telling and listening, both women got a new slant on the meaning of their relationship. Both were starting to savor their differing temperaments and appreciate their similar philosophical standards and values.

At the close of their storytelling Lucy said, "It's good to open up like this. It helps me to piece together the changes I've made over the years. I'm glad we had a chance to talk like this."

Jackie said, "This was a hell of a lot of work, but it's worth it when you think of all the territory we've covered. I want to keep talking like this. I'm hoping we can become better friends."

The Value of Sharing Stories

The experience of sharing stories can be an invigorating one. If two lonely people are at odds with one another, it is a safe way to develop a keener understanding and appreciation of the worth of the other. Storytelling opens us to the infinite possibilities of connectedness. It is a beneficent way to transform relationships.

CS: Termination of CS Contract

At the close of six months, the CS contract was terminated and Lucy was ready to chance moving back. By this time the couple had tempered their rift and were of a mind to compromise.

Jackie said, "I guess I can kick up my heels and go line dancing once in a while." And Lucy replied, "And I guess we can still have our Friday night fish fry—I've got to say I've really missed it."

The couple's CS was an indispensable vehicle, providing a safety net as each partner took the time needed to uncover lost parts of herself. Here we see the challenge of invested intimacy met anew.

Follow-Up

Two years later I spoke with both women by phone. Jackie said, "We're getting along a whole lot better. At least Lucy isn't scared to tell me what's bothering her." Then she shared another insight, "It has taken me a while to figure it out, but I used to think because Lucy and I were like soul mates, it wasn't right if we didn't think the same way about everything. I know better now."

Lucy was in nursing school and working part-time. Their daughters were having their share of boyfriend problems, but otherwise she had no complaints. About the benefits of CS, she had only praise. Elated she said, "I never realized how much I gave my power away. Without the CS I'm afraid our relationship would have been done for . . . but now I feel empowered, and Jackie and I can talk plain to each other. That feels right. I like the new me so much better."

$\mathcal{T}$he Well-Kept Secret: Partners in the Dark

Secrets and Skeletons

EVERYBODY KEEPS SECRETS and every family has skeletons in the closet. We hide the good and not so good from our partners. It isn't possible to make commentary on all the comings and goings of everyday living. We forget, don't remember, or attach little importance to some events and grave import to others. Discriminating between which of life's experiences are meant for sharing and which are best kept private is a measure of wisdom and maturity that can take a lifetime to learn.

Secrets come in many shapes and sizes—from inconsequential white lies to hidden agendas of momentous consequence. Secrets are not easily categorized, especially as they relate to one's "stay or go" impasse. There are family secrets, marital secrets, personal secrets, and sacred secrets, with considerable blending of all four.

Secrets and the "Stay or Go" Question

Partners who feel the pressure of the "stay or go" question can be made dizzy by the hidden agendas they keep from each other. Why bother to talk about your twinges of doubt? Your spine shivers at the thought of suggesting you should separate. What good is it to stir up more bad feelings? How much easier to say nothing and put your guilt on the shelf for another day.

The Tale of Ruth and Ed: Partners in the Dark

Ed was frantic. His wife was depressed and unapproachable, he was worried about his boisterous four-year-old twin boys, his marriage was out of his control, and he was disappointed in me.

Ed bellowed into the phone, "What are you doing with my wife? It's been almost two months and she's going off the deep end. It's not a good situation. . . . I don't think she's doing the children any good. You know, I hardly have much of a marriage left. I don't understand what's taking so long."

Gently trying to soothe Ed, I asked him to be patient and give us a little more time. What I didn't tell him was that this was a difficult case, and Ruth had virtually nothing to say to me.

In the Beginning

I can still hear Ed's raspy voice the first time we spoke by phone: "I'm calling about my wife, Ruth. Something's the matter here. She's not herself . . . not acting right. I don't know what to do with her. She won't stop crying. She's mad all the time, and she won't talk . . . won't tell me anything. I don't know what's wrong, but I'll tell you one thing—she's getting impossible to live with! Now, when can my wife come and see you? What's your first opening?"

At the time, I had told Ed it would be more efficient if he would come with her. He promptly snapped back, "She's the one with the problem, not me!" Then I pressed him to keep the appointment whether his wife came or not. "Ed, your input is important," I said. We set a date for our first meeting.

Ruth's Story

Ruth, 28, kept that first appointment with Ed. When we met she appeared preoccupied and sad. Her lusterless eyes and swollen face implied she had been crying. She wore no cosmetics, and her auburn hair was pulled tight to the back of her head. Ruth stared at me, then turned away as if to say, "Keep your distance, lady. . . . I'm tough; don't mess with me!" Getting her to talk about herself was an ordeal. It was 10 weeks before I gathered the following information.

Ruth hated her day job but said she couldn't quit. After her schedule changed from second to first shift, her life felt out of kilter. Wistfully, she said, "I miss the night shift . . . the girls. . . . You see, we used to go out after work . . . a couple of beers, you know, relax."

The raunchy talk with her pals was a hoot, and Ruth later told Ed the best jokes.

Working the day shift was an ordeal because she was forced to rely on her mother to stay with the twins. This was a bitter affront because Ruth didn't like the woman but couldn't afford to pay anyone else.

Ed was taking two night-school classes and had less time to help out with the children and chores. The kids were making Ruth a nervous wreck. Resentfully, she said, "I'm working for my paycheck . . . and that's all I can say!"

I asked her if she had told Ed how she felt, and she answered, "He knows," and insisted we drop the matter. Taking a different tack, I asked Ruth about her father. She was brief. "I never saw him much. He was gone most of the time. When I was a kid, he worked three jobs and that's all there is to it."

Ed's Story

Ed, 34, was a reliable family man with an officious air about him. He took considerable pride in being the father of two boys. A machinist by trade, he always had more house projects and side jobs to do than he could possibly handle.

How could he manage such a hefty load with his wife falling apart? Good reason to be in a panic. Ruth had been the light of Ed's life, a willing helpmate and friend since high school days. He couldn't fathom why the once-charming girl he married eight years earlier had grown so despondent. It was inconceivable that her lovely face should be shrouded in gloom. He, too, was in the dark.

Slow Going

I had verified that Ruth wasn't suicidal, nor was she interested in antidepressant medication. "That stuff makes me feel like a zombie," she had said, and the matter was dropped. Remote and barely audible, she was evidently leery of therapy. It would take time to gain her trust.

My usual greetings didn't seem to get through to her:

"How are you doing, Ruth?"

"Not good."

"What's bothering you, Ruth?"

"Don't know."

"How can I help you, Ruth?"

"I don't think you can."

"You're being negative, Ruth."

"Yeah."

"Is there anything on your mind you would like to share with me?"

"Not really."

"Well, what do you want, Ruth?"

"I don't know."

Around and around we went with this circular, go-nowhere probing. It was not to my liking. I was frustrated.

Ruth's lack of investment in therapy concerned me. Our relationship was tenuous at best. I could only wait it out. I figured she must be coming to me for a reason—I just hadn't been made privy to it yet. Sometimes I tried to entertain her with chitchat about TV or the news of the day. Then back to the same dreary questions.

Guarded, Ruth had descended into her depths, and I felt like an intruder invading her space.

Maureen Murdock in *The Heroine's Journey* offers us keen insights into the feminine experience of depression:

> To the outside world a woman who has begun her descent is preoc-
> cupied, sad, and inaccessible. Her tears often have no name but are

ever-present, whether she cries or not. She cannot be comforted,
she feels abandoned. . . . She enters a period of voluntary isolation,
seen by her family and friends as a loss of her senses.[1]

Ruth could not explain her "voluntary isolation" and "inaccessibility," and neither could I. She hated to complain and considered her tears unacceptable, an awkward betrayal of self. To break through her reserve, I said, "Ruth, I know our sessions are difficult, and I understand you don't want to be here. It takes a lot of strength and courage for you to be sitting here with me." A limp nod of assent was all I could squeeze out of her.

Something wasn't adding up. I questioned if the recent shifts in Ruth's work schedule and child-care arrangements were reasons enough to cause her to spiral into so deep a funk. I, too, was in the dark.

Spurred on by Ed's pressing call, I pushed Ruth to speak. Three weeks later she hesitantly said, "I hate this. . . . But it's getting so bad I can't stand to be around Ed . . . can't look at him . . . don't want any more sex. I don't know any more. . . ." I listened without comment. Then she added, "He's not around much . . . guess he's not interested in us . . . hasn't got much time for me and the kids anymore." Here was a woman feeling abandoned and unspeakably sorry for herself.

With that I launched into a bolder approach. "Look, Ruth, let's be honest; do you want a divorce from Ed?"

After a lengthy pause, she continued, "I've thought about it."

Checking further, I asked, "Do you know what you want?"

Obliquely, she answered, "Not really."

I ventured, "I think you and Ed could benefit from some couple counseling . . ." but she cut me short.

"No, I can't do that, not now."

As if called from some hidden aspect of her private world, Ruth tentatively began, "Maybe . . . I'm not sure . . . Well, you see, I've been thinking about separating . . . Not sure what's come over me . . . Not myself these days."

There was no stopping the flow of events: Ed was on my back to get his wife well and fast, and Ruth was toying with separation. Their marital relationship was being put to the test, one way or

another. I had in mind to get Ed more involved in the most straightforward way I knew how.

The CS Introduced

At my next meeting with Ruth, I spoke about the merits of the CS.
"A CS is time limited. It doesn't go on indefinitely. It is a team project . . . very upbeat. The pressure would be off you, and we can
make sure the twins are taken care of, so you won't have to worry
on that score."

Blankly, Ruth sat listening. No questions. No feedback. Nothing. She wasn't making it easy. I waited. At last she muttered under
her breath, "Ed's not going to like this!"

She walked out of my office with the CS Guidelines in hand. I
planted a seed: "You know, Ruth, I've seen the CS work in bizarre
and mysterious ways."

CS: The Strategy Works

Three days later Ruth phoned to say Ed would come to her next
session. I wondered, would he consent to a CS? If so, I felt sure we
could turn their impasse around.

Ed was glowering when he strode into my office with Ruth trail-
ing behind. He barked, "Lee, what the hell are you telling Ruth? To
bring up separation at a time like this . . . she's in no shape to move
out, and the kids need her. . . . We aren't that rich. This would be
a real hardship. You aren't talking about divorce, are you?"

Whatever Ruth had said about the CS had plainly disturbed Ed.
Obviously, Ruth had not accurately informed him of what the CS
could do for their relationship. He rested his case, saying, "Lee,
this is not for us. I'm a married man and I mean to stay that way!"

"Ed, we're not talking divorce here," I explained. "As you
already know, Ruth is terribly distraught. She's talked about marital separation and that's all. I don't know what she's told you, but I
want you to understand that the Controlled Separation is a sensible
plan. It could help her decide what she really wants."

Later I learned Ruth had flung the CS Guidelines at Ed without
a word of preliminary explanation. He had been less annoyed with

me than stunned by the whole concept of marital separation, surely the last thing on his mind. He was convinced they were one step away from the lawyers.

The more we talked, the more Ed got involved, until he talked himself into accepting a CS. Magnanimously he said, "If this is the way it's got to be, I'll move and find myself a place."

The CS Journey Begins

The ease with which the couple slid into their CS was nothing short of astonishing. Having settled on a six-month separation, they took charge of making the necessary arrangements, scarcely needing me. Ed planned to shared an apartment with a fellow worker. He was concerned about their tight finances. Looking directly at Ruth he said, "We'll have to hold down our expenses." She replied, "I guess I won't be going to the craft fair this Christmas."

Schedules and responsibilities for child care were spelled out. Almost daily Ed squeezed in an hour with the twins at dinnertime before dashing off to school. He took them out on Saturdays, which gave Ruth a free day. As a rule, every other Sunday was family day. The couple found it necessary to speak on the telephone daily to make all these arrangements.

The mates dated weekly, usually on Friday nights. Neither partner had any inclination to date others.

The CS in Process

Our monthly meetings were going well. Ed was situated in his apartment with no complaints. The week after he left, Ruth had commented, "At night the house is so quiet when the kids go to sleep and I don't hear Ed rumbling around. It's kind of a lonesome feeling." But she never mentioned the matter again.

We often spoke of the difficulties of child rearing, and Ruth mentioned that she appreciated the extra effort Ed was making on behalf of their boys. Ed said, "Yeah, we've all got to pull together here. I gotta do this to help out because Ruth's in such a bad way."

If she could have prevented it, Ruth would not have told her mother about the CS. She explained, "My ma is so nosy, she likes to butt in. So, Lee, I did what you said and told her we're seeing a therapist and the rest is between Ed and me." And then in a huff she added, "Frankly, it's none of her business!"

Ed was straightforward with his parents and two brothers, informing them of the CS without going into details. The family was aghast, as they had no inkling of marital problems. Ed said, "When I told them we're getting professional help, they seemed satisfied; and the subject was dropped. Anyway, it wouldn't be like my family to give me the third degree."

The partners made light of their dating, as it was going so well. They liked having a regular schedule so that sitter arrangements could be made well in advance. Ruth commented, "This dating sure is different. You know, what with raising twins and working like we do, I bet we didn't go to a movie more than twice last year. And we never went out to eat all by ourselves—only with the kids."

Ed broke in, "Yeah, this is a nice change for us." Apparently the dating time was strengthening the couple's bond. Overall, both partners were so efficient in managing the terms of their CS Contract, they thought monthly counseling would suffice.

Ruth in a Holding Pattern

Although they had successfully integrated living apart, Ruth couldn't seem to shake her depression. A heavy inertia settled over her as she continued to brood—about what, I didn't know. She had asked for a separation, but something was drastically missing.

Ruth was in a holding pattern. When I pushed her to talk to me, she volunteered that her mother was cold and her teen years were rough, and then she clammed up again.

By this time I was sure she was sheltering a hidden agenda. I could only wait it out. I was confident Ruth would open up, given enough time. Secrets aren't uncovered just by chance or accident; I believe our truth wants to be found out.

Ruth's Secret

Ruth and Ed had been separated almost four months before she trusted me with her secret. She fidgeted in her chair. "Lee, I don't know if I should tell it." Then she stopped. I let her struggle with "it" and was silent. Sullenly, she whispered, "I shouldn't have said anything," and rose to leave. Gently, I suggested she sit down and take a deep breath, reminding her, "You are safe here. We'll talk more about 'it' another time."

A week later Ruth's very presence conveyed a sense of urgency. A pathetic "hello" signaled her discomfort. Her voice quivering, her words barely audible, she said, "Nobody knows." From the depths, her secret was ready to come to light:

"One day when I was nine, I was playing with this friend in the basement. I stayed downstairs after she went home. A little while later, I heard footsteps on the stairs, but I didn't pay much attention . . . I was working on a puzzle . . ."

Ruth stopped speaking and put her hand on her chest, her breathing labored. I moved my chair closer and touched her arm, telling her to breathe deeply. "I know this is hard on you. Take your time. I can wait." All but choking on every syllable, Ruth went on.

"It . . . was . . . my Uncle Amos, Momma's . . . younger brother." She spoke haltingly. "He looked at me kind of funny. Then he did it."

She could not go on. I waited again. "Did what, Ruth?" Shrouded in shame, she gasped, "He . . . he . . . he . . . exposed himself! He came right up to me. I almost peed in my pants. I couldn't look . . . Then, right to my face, he made me promise not to tell. He said bad things would happen to me if I did. He said he'd call me a liar."

Ruth was emotionally spent and ready to call it a day. I asked what happened after that. Weakly, she said, "Uncle Amos lived with us that summer. He used to follow me around a lot and tried to pin me to the floor once. I screamed, and he slapped my face. I still get a weird feeling around him . . . It's awful!" She turned away to hide her face.

Then more questions: "Ruth, did you ever tell your mother?"

Limply, "No, I didn't dare."

"What about Ed? Does he know?"

With a tad more energy, she said, "Yeah, he knows something happened."

"Does he know who?"

Ruth spoke firmly: "No."

This questioning was not easy. "Will you tell your mother?"

Somewhat exasperated by now, she snapped back, "You know I can't rock the boat . . . I need her to sit with the twins."

"And will you tell Ed who it was?"

By this time Ruth raised her voice, "No. I can't say any more to Ed either."

Once she had told me her burdensome secret, Ruth's depression faded fast. To my astonishment her recovery was akin to a spontaneous remission. Having trusted me to be both impartial and caring, Ruth experienced a catharsis—a miraculous cleansing—that touched her very soul. Needing no further therapy to integrate her confession, she was eager to put the whole oppressive matter aside and focus on mending her marriage.

The Fallout of Secrets

Some secrets patently inflict emotional reactions too painful to endure. Unspoken or pushed aside, the secret is never told to the family, or the victim speaks out long after the fact of incest, rape, or physical or mental abuse. When you eventually learn in your teens you were adopted, or are told by virtual strangers the identity of your real father, such a revelation can inflict enough harm to send you reeling for a lifetime.

Personal secrets can include other tormenting matters that seriously affect your coupling: bisexuality or homosexuality, addiction to alcohol or other drugs, life-threatening illness, excessive gambling losses, bad financial investments, infidelity, and any other matter that holds you at bay. Dread of discovery, shame, and recrimination stand in the way of honesty.

You are kidding yourself if you believe you can keep your hidden agendas secret with no cost to your marriage. Inevitably, there is a hefty price to pay for deliberately or inadvertently withholding emotionally loaded truths. The longer you let your secret fester, the more distance you put between yourself and your mate. The longer you stay mute, the more you become disempowered and ineffective.

To perpetuate a lie is to depreciate your self-worth. Many years ago I would cover up other people's tracks at my own expense, diminishing my own value in the process. If we lie to ourselves to protect others, we discount our importance and do great harm to our own integrity. In turn, we deprive our spouse and children of our gifts of honesty and insight. How unfortunate that some people go to their graves never aware of the source of their immense loss.

Telling Your Secret

Secrets are best shared with a confidant you can trust. Drawing on the work of authors Terry Hunt, Ed.D., Karen Paine-Gernee, and Larry Rothstein, *Secrets to Tell, Secrets to Keep*, I have compiled eight guidelines for sharing your secrets:[2]

1. Choose a therapist, minister, or friend who treats you with the utmost respect, someone who cares about you.

2. Obtain a promise that your secret will be kept confidential and indicate who else may or may not be told.

3. Select a confidant who is nonjudgmental and empathic.

4. Be aware of your purpose in telling, and know what you want. Is it support, advice, or just listening? Let the party know beforehand.

5. Be sensitive to the effect your secret will have on your listener. Are you heaping on your confidant more responsibility than that person can handle?

6. Be aware of timing. Pick a time and place where you have privacy to comfortably share your story without hiding your emotions.

7. When you spill the beans, be aware that being overly dramatic can alarm your listener.

8. Reassure your confidant you have lived through the worst of your bad experience, if that is the case.

Sacred Space and Sacred Secrets

We all are entitled to the privilege of privacy, to keep certain life experiences personal. Painful as it was, Ruth was satisfied to have shared the details of her secret with me. Afterward, the past could be tucked away in her sacred space, a place that is hallowed and safe. This gave her much peace of mind.

We all have dearly held thoughts, ideas, and life experiences that are stored in our sacred space. I call these our sacred secrets. They pay homage to our birthright—they give us a spiritual uplift.

My own private life is a treasure-house of sacred secrets, some so precious I'm convinced in the telling something magical would be lost. To witness a sunrise or see a falling star is a special high or thrill of pleasure. But how do we describe the experience? Some events remain in our sacred space, from which we continue to draw strength, courage, and inspiration.

The Rest of Ruth and Ed's Story

The couple never failed to show up for their monthly meetings with me. At the beginning of the fifth month of separation, the partners spoke of reuniting, but first there was more work to do. Both mates knew they needed help in managing their boys.

Ruth and Ed held opposing views on child rearing, and their squabbles would rise to an irritating crescendo. Ruth said, "We argue a lot about discipline . . . you know how children will bicker, hit, and all that stuff."

Ed had a different perspective. "Ruth's too easy; she lets them scream and run around . . . mealtime is a disaster." Ruth countered, "Yeah, well, you just scare the kids half to death . . . your voice is like a boom box. Do you have to yell at them so much? How is that going to help?"

I suggested family therapy, an ideal format for resolving parent-child management conflicts. The twins joined the couple in counseling on two occasions. A lot changed.

Transformation Becomes a Reality

Both partners were eager to learn how to discipline their boys firmly and consistently. Ruth became less of a pushover, and Ed took pride in developing better rapport with his sons. Not only was he becoming a more involved father, but Ed was listening more attentively to his wife. The couple's dating time had allowed him to exhibit his mellow side.

As Ed began to moderate his sometimes bombastic nature, he became more empathetic and pleasant. In turn, Ruth was less annoyed with Ed's brassy side and was more approachable and congenial. Transformation was becoming an everyday reality as the partners grew more comfortable with one another.

Termination of CS

In the beginning of the sixth month of their separation, Ruth asked, "Would it be all right if Ed comes home two weeks early? You see, his roommate is moving out." I answered, "Yes, of course. I'm very proud of all you have accomplished."

The family was having more fun being together, as Ruth was getting the emotional support from Ed that meant so much to her. Indeed, their CS had helped stabilize their marriage, and so much more.

Follow-Up

Two years later I almost collided with Ruth at the grocery store. The whole family was there. I scarcely recognized her as she looked so attractive and confident. She smiled. "It's going so well. The twins are still a handful sometimes, but Ed's a big help."

In answer to how the CS was an assist, Ruth replied, "The CS got us going in a direction that I couldn't have believed was possible. You know how bad off I was. And now all of us are so much better off for having been separated." Ed came down another aisle, and right there the partners joined in and gave me a big hug.

Crippled by Rage and Remorse: Scarred Spouses

Patty and Doug: Scarred Spouses

PATTY: "Why am I always wrong? You never take me seriously. What's the matter with you! Can't you ever do anything right? Where are your brains, anyhow?"

DOUG: "I don't know what I do that's so wrong. I'm sick and tired of it all."

PATTY: "So leave. I'll help you pack your bags."

DOUG: "If that's what you want, I have a place in mind where I can go!"

Doug, 40, contacted me because he was unhappy with himself and miserable in his second marriage. At his initial appointment he said, "I'm ready to turn over a new leaf and start all over again."

Doug had a multitude of problems. He was a recovering alcohol and drug user, he had switched jobs frequently because of personality conflicts, he wasn't getting enough sleep, he had difficulty concentrating, he had hefty past-due child support payments from his first marriage, and other debts were hanging over his head.

"What should I do?" he asked. "Patty and I can't get along, and I don't like it. Should I leave?" I told Doug I wanted to meet his wife.

The partners were uptight when we first met, having tried marital therapy twice before without getting anywhere.

Each party had been married and divorced. Each had dated or lived with others off and on for 12 years before remarrying. Early childhood experiences had scarred each of them for life. Doug was a skilled factory worker, and Patty worked in the shipping department of a large firm. Both had dropped out of high school and had thought of getting their GEDs but feared they would fail and so never tried.

Nitpicking for Flaws

Patty and Doug had a love/hate relationship. Though they professed to care about each other, after three years of marriage the bloom of love was fading fast. It was their antagonism—verbal attack and defend—that ruled the roost. The partners were like two spitfires itching for a fight. Neither liked the adversarial relationship, and the verbal gyrations grated on their nerves. But neither made any effort to stop the ballistic outbursts. Both mates had such short fuses that they clearly felt out of control.

What made matters worse was that each pulled the other down in assuming the position "I am right and you are wrong," as if verbal attack was far better than "taking it on the chin." It was only after I got to know these tightly defended mates better that on separate occasions they willingly admitted, "I'm my own worst enemy."

When we first met, Patty was making noises about separating— innuendos under her breath. She was fed up with Doug "being in my face with his sordid obscenities." Doug hated the way "she makes me feel so rotten." Both had such nasty ways of needling and egging one another on that one night in a huff of disgust Doug walked out.

Frustrated, Patty didn't object. Both knew that they couldn't live under the same roof. Not this way.

Doug's Story

Doug held himself in contempt. He had been designated the "black sheep" of the family by his parents, who couldn't control him. He quit school after the ninth grade and went to work in a foundry and could never rise above this status. His earlier years kept reminding him of a cesspool of iniquities that laid him low. His parents divorced when he was nine, and his four siblings were sent to different foster homes. Doug had a foster father who put welts on his back and a mother who was hospitalized for bipolar disorder.

He had a series of vile relationships with women and overall was crippled with remorse over the evil he believed he perpetrated.

Doug had a string of confessions to unload before he could even consider building an honorable marriage and a relationship built on decency, dignity, and self-respect.

To the good, he spoke of his spiritual connection. "I have this relationship with God . . . not a really good one, but I talk to him every once in a while." Then he said, "I know I'm messed up." I answered, "Doug, you're not incorrigible." His face brightened up as he replied, "Oh, you mean I'm fixable?"

Patty's Story

Patty, 38, had a history of depression and was on and off antidepressant medications. She had no patience with Doug and sometimes regretted she had ever married him.

Reared in an alcoholic and verbally abusive home, she saw her parents raging at each other and learned to match their verbal agility. "As a kid, I became plenty mouthy myself. . . . They didn't know what to do with me." Her father died of cancer when she was 12. After that her mother hung on to her for support and continues to do so. This was a constant drain on Patty's energies. She said, "As much as I love my mother, she's become a mean, nasty old woman. . . . Guess I've become bitter, just like her."

Patty's young-adult years were stormy. She made two suicide attempts after she discovered a boyfriend and later a fiancé were cheating on her. In her words, she was married "too young" to an alcoholic, physically abusive young man. After they were divorced, she rarely dated but had one loveless relationship and got pregnant with Sonny.

Introducing CS: Spouses Regain Control

Patty and Doug had no idea where their sudden trial separation (TS) was going. Both mates were ambivalent and would rather not have separated, but Patty had had her fill of Doug's vulgarities and was relieved to see him go. Not so for five-year-old Sonny, who cried incessantly for his stepfather, asking when Doug was coming home. Patty thought she would lose her mind. What was she supposed to tell the child?

At the close of our second meeting, I spent five minutes outlining the CS. It took 120 seconds for the desperate couple to agree to a six-month contract. Doug added, "It's gonna take 10 years to get me fixed up!" Three weeks later the CS was adjusted to three months because neither partner could visualize being apart six months.

CS: The First Test

Shortly after Doug moved out, in desperation Patty spoke to me in private: "This really gets to me because I don't drink. Here's the problem. You know Doug was in treatment for alcohol a few years before we got married. Well, he mostly stays dry, but with this separation and all, he's been real upset. I know him, and when he gets this way, he goes out and buys booze, and he knows he shouldn't. But what can I say? I can't stop him!"

When I saw Doug alone a few days later, I was determined to find a way to confront him. He had just restated his goal: "I told you at the start I'm ready to turn over a new leaf, but with this move and all the turmoil, it's real hard being separated and not seeing Sonny and all that."

This gave me a suitable lead-in. "Doug, are you drinking now?" He averted my eyes and hedged a little, "Well, yes, only twice I bought a bottle. This separation has been rough, and I thought it would help me sleep."

That admission was all I needed to lay out my rules. In the firmest voice I could muster, I said, "Doug, you are to totally abstain from using one drop of alcohol or any other drugs as long as we are working together on your CS; otherwise, I can't be involved. The CS won't work for you unless you are stone sober!"

I never had to say another word. Doug took me literally, making this an essential step in demonstrating his firm commitment to the CS.

CS: Doug's Living Arrangements

After living with his sister's family for a month, Doug couldn't stand it one more minute. He said, "It's disgusting—these people are all worse off than we are—too much beer, the kids running wild, it's really bad."

Doug was looking at a room for rent across the street from a tavern and asked me what I thought. I turned the question back to him, and sheepishly he said, "Not so good, huh?" "That's right. I'm sure you can find a better location," I answered.

Within two days Doug settled into a furnished room in a private home where he had cooking privileges. He paid rent by the week the people were good to him, and the place was only two blocks from the family home.

Revision of CS to Meet Sonny's Needs

Sonny was belligerent and disruptive in kindergarten, and Patty was vitally concerned. She told his teacher there were problems at home and mentioned the couple's separation. For this reason alone, Patty wanted Doug to spend weekends at home to be with the boy.

In this case the couple stretched their interpretation of CS to mean they would live separately four nights a week and together for three. I conceded this plan was the best the couple could do on behalf of all concerned.

On Sunday mornings Doug took Sonny fishing, to compensate for his absences. And he phoned regularly just before the child's bedtime. Patty felt it was the least Doug could do.

CS: Dating

Dating had been introduced the first month but was cast aside partly because of Doug's hefty work schedule but mostly because Patty was rejecting her husband's affectionate advances.

At Doug's request the issue of dating resurfaced the second month. Patty was adamant: too busy with her sister, mother, job, homemaking chores. Her string of excuses angered Doug, and to her face he complained, "The trouble with you is you don't know how to enjoy yourself!"

A month later Doug arranged a picnic with another couple. When Patty refused to go, he said he would go without her. She changed her mind at the last minute and they all had a wonderful time. Doug dragged Patty out a few more times, and she agreed the change of pace was good. Thereafter, the couple enjoyed dating bimonthly, sometimes with congenial friends.

PMS: A Bummer!

Patty suffered from premenstrual syndrome (PMS). This was the worst time of the month for the couple. Patty said, "When I get so bitchy, I keep telling him to ignore me, but he doesn't." And Doug retorted, "Sure, but how do I do that?"

At the same session he confronted her, "Look, I'm not your garbage pail . . . besides, no matter what I do, it's never right!"

I could see Patty was miffed, so I commented, "At one time or another, partners know very well how to push one another's buttons." The mates began to see how they insidiously irritated one another's souls.

CS: Focus on Crippled Communication

Although I had cautioned Patty and Doug, "Don't discuss your relationship outside this office," as I feared, my words fell on deaf ears. Neither party could keep their mouths shut long enough to give the rule a chance to work. They were sassy, rude, and defensive. The first snide interaction—it mattered not who started it or why—instigated retaliation.

I asked the couple to observe how they got themselves entrapped in the same old attack-attack, attack-avoidance, avoidance-avoidance games. I pointed out how they cunningly antagonized each other.

Patty began to see how she nitpicked for flaws in her most inelegant way and then Doug would take offense and storm out of the room in a huff—sometimes out the door. He asked, "So how do we stop driving each other crazy?"

"Crazymaking" and the "Stay or Go" Dilemma

The "stay or go" dilemma comes devilishly close to being a "crazymaking" experience for many mates, just as it was for Patty and Doug. In *Stop! You're Driving Me Crazy*, psychotherapist George R. Bach and coauthor Ronald M. Deutsch insightfully describe the firm hold crazymaking has on parties in crippled marriages: "Crazymaking becomes a clearly dominating characteristic of most marriages as they approach divorce. And when the hope of covering up and smoothing over is almost gone—so that the old powerful fear of separating is nearly over—there are violent explosions."[1]

When the crazymaking experience sweeps parties like Patty and Doug into adversarial relationships, rational thinking all but disappears. The parties can't think straight; they are in no mind to be reasonable and in no mood to acknowledge their spouse's point of view.

Modes of Crippled Communication

Communication at best is an inaccurate art. We are always communicating whether we realize it or not. Our body language, posture, voice tone, and inflection convey our underlying messages. Two groundbreaking leaders in the field of marriage and couple communication, William J. Lederer and Don D. Jackson, M.D., provocatively explain in *The Mirages of Marriage*:

> Scientists have estimated that fifty to a hundred bits of information are exchanged each second between individuals communicating

actively. Everything which a person does in relation to another is some kind of message. There is no NOT communicating. Even silence is communication.[2]

Let's look at three modes of crippled communication that predictably get couples like Patty and Doug in trouble: "passive," "passive/aggressive," and "aggressive." If you are already irritated with your mate, any of these three modes will incite even more fear and anger. In too many cases, crippled communication will provoke acts of violence.

Passive Communication: "Don't Bother Me" Mates

Passive communication takes the form of indirect avoidance of conflict. Some people are so terrified of their own angry impulses that they won't deal with conversations that evoke their ire. With the first hint of friction, they are so ill at ease they become tongue-tied—as if their brains have shut down. Any kind of verbal barrage is more than their temperament can handle.

The worst of passive communication is the icy silent treatment; it makes your blood curdle. In our moments of togetherness, intimacy is blocked when we avert knowing glances, don't listen, interrupt, talk *at* each other, circumvent, misconstrue, reinterpret, and demean one another in untold ways.

Avoiding the war is *not* preserving the peace. Raw silence can also suggest peevish exasperation, an indirect form of communication that chills the bones. Refusing to speak can so enrage your spouse that the inclination to violence is felt even when not acted on.

All too frequently silence is interpreted as a put-down, especially when one party is demanding to be heard. We get angry and feel diminished when ignored. A wall of seeming indifference hurts and is likely to backfire sooner or later. When people don't express themselves openly or say what they mean, passive communication of this ilk spares neither spouse in the long run.

Passive/Aggressive Communication: Gotcha!

Passive/aggressive communication has a two-sided thrust that can take you by surprise. Your spouse is "passive" when he or she refuses to speak up when he or she is disturbed by something you have said or done. Instead, your mate gets "aggressive" and counterattacks by trying to get you mad about something else. This is a particularly sneaky way of throwing you off balance. Sometimes it takes a while to catch on, but your partner's smoldering resentment is convincingly conveyed by such caustic passive/aggressive behavior.

The name of the game is "Gotcha!" Mocking scorn, snide remarks, taunting smiles, sadistic humor, heaps of ridicule, and other such malicious onslaughts are part of the repertoire.

Passive/aggressive behavior is circuitous:

- You ask your husband to get your suit cleaned because you have an important meeting. Then he makes all kinds of excuses why he forgot.

- Your partner says she loves you but doesn't come home on time or call.

- You have sex with your spouse and then he jumps out of bed, leaving you unsatisfied.

- You agree to her entertainment plans; later, she faults you because she had a rotten time.

The list goes on and on. "Gotcha!" is a dirty game wherein parties know exactly how to get a reaction where it hurts the most. Pouting, insulting, and goading are other modes of passive/aggressive behavior.

Aggressive Communication: I'm the Boss Here!

Aggressive communication is a power play. Patty and Doug took turns being the "boss" or "tyrant," the partner who is at war with the "shrew," the hysterical one. Their crude remarks poked at one another's vulnerabilities, and their escalations got downright nasty. They didn't need me to tell them such fierce antagonism brings out the worst in already unhappy mates.

Though aggressive communication is not as visible as the bruises of physical and sexual battering, the battering of the psyche is thought to be the most insidious—as evidenced by two modes of aggressive communication I call brainwashing and double-duty anger.

Brainwashing No More

Brainwashing is the most diabolical kind of aggressive communication. You cannot be brainwashed unless you permit it. Victims of brainwashing are naive. They believe the trash their spouses lay on them—despicable put-downs that heap cruelty on top of cruelty. They assume the underdog position, as if they are beholden to the top dog. When you are verbally devalued, overpowered, and beaten down, you actually start to behave as if you are less than deserving of the best.

Victims of brainwashing are at war with themselves. You cannot be made to believe you are "less than" your mate unless you already believe it. You cannot be made to feel you deserve less of life's blessings unless you are convinced your life shouldn't be too good.

First, you must believe in your own worth. You are part of the human race. You are a good person. You are lovable. It is time to make a change. You can do it!

Double-Duty Anger

For years I have been intrigued with a misconstrued type of hostile communication I refer to as "double-duty anger" because it so aptly explains two layers of rage occurring simultaneously. I talked to Patty and Doug using the following illustrations.

Scenario 1. The first party, Patty, is angry with Doug because he's too loud and rough with Sonny. The second party, Doug, gives Patty a dirty look. Then he starts to defend himself, but when Patty interrupts, Doug refuses to talk. He freezes, sulks, and walks out of the room. Sometimes he even leaves the house.

With that, Patty freaks out with uncontrolled anger, unable to summon a response from her mate. This sequence constitutes compounded rage, or double-duty anger.

Scenario 2. The first party, Doug, is fit to be tied and dumps long-pent-up resentment on Patty. The second party, Patty, is insulted by having to listen to the viciousness in her mate's voice, and she reacts with a counterattack. Then the first party, Doug, angrily blurts out, "I don't get it. I try to speak for myself and you go nuts." With that, double-duty anger escalates at a feverish rate.

What Purpose Crippled Communication?

Patty and Doug found out soon enough that any of the above modes of crippled communication incite treacherous retaliation, as the ill-fated parties are provoked to "stick it to him/her." Rancid needling and cynical discounting blemish and devalue the worth of another human being. Revenge of this ilk is not so sweet. For what purpose but to court an evil that tugs at your gut? How can you feel good about yourself when your rage magnifies many times over?

Assertive Communication

Assertive communication is straightforward, honest talk, which is not necessarily the way we were taught as children. It is the best way to rise above petty bickering, sniveling, and sniping, and it is a dynamic way to start feeling good about yourself.

Unfortunately, our parents often gave us overt messages that thwarted our communication, such as "Don't rock the boat," "Don't be angry," "Don't make a fuss," "Don't complain," or "Don't cry." Such messages taught us to hide our true feelings and to get along with others despite how we felt. Assertive communication takes practice until you are satisfied you are saying exactly what you mean, expressing yourself effectively and gaining self-confidence in the process.

Constructively Stop Crazymaking

To maintain relationship equilibrium, keep in mind a little criticism is a good thing and a whole lot is overdose. Remember, it is the degree of nagging, the frequent retreating, and the repetitive put-downs that diminish the value of your partnership—often destroying relationships.

Anger can be constructively expressed so that it is neither abusive nor crazymaking. I'd like to share a personal little trick. When Mark and I get into silly bickering, it takes about 60 seconds of potentially damaging communication before one of us will say, "Stop!" We have great respect for this word. It's like coming to a screeching halt at a big red traffic light. For us, "Stop!" means our argument is getting out of hand. It means "take a break." This way neither party feels like a loser. "Stop!" works well for us.

Patty and Doug were in the habit of shouting, "You *always* forget . . ." and the other would counter, "You *never* remember . . ." I suggested they apply a shorthand version when this happens and patently say, "Always and Never!" The couple laughed, relieved to have found a better way to halt their verbal brawls.

Recipe for Assertive Confrontation

Do not underestimate the worth of assertive confrontation. A firm yet blunt expression of your frustrations and resentments has the potential to immunize you and your mate against your relationship going stale or deteriorating altogether.

Patty and Doug had a habit of speaking for one another, by saying "you" rather than "I." Then each party would react with double-duty anger.

The following six guides are a step-by-step recipe for effective confrontation:

1. Begin all statements with "I," not "You." In this way you take responsibility for yourself and dispense with the implication of blame.

2. State honestly what you want to achieve.

3. Acknowledge how you feel about your differences.

4. Verify your partner heard you accurately and ask for feedback.

5. Propose at least two solutions—or more, if possible.

6. Pat yourself on the back for making direct contact without getting distracted.

Confrontation takes practice. You must be satisfied that you are saying exactly what you mean.

The experience of engaging in direct confrontation without being intimidated is an achievement that has its own built-in rewards. Doug said, "It gives me more self-confidence."

Patty and Doug Practice
Behavior Rehearsal

Behavior rehearsal—role play—serves two major purposes: to discern the finer nuances of empathy and to sharpen your communication skills in a fun way.

Role play works like this: both parties pretend to take their partner's antagonistic or polarized position. You continue to reverse roles back and forth until you get a feel for a contrary point of view.

Patty and Doug giggled as I asked them to sit facing each other and maintain eye contact. Soon they had a more accurate sense of what their partner was trying to convey. Patty said, "Do I really sound like that?"

Behavior rehearsal can help people of all ages achieve compassion and thereby enhance their relationships.

CS: Light at the End of the Tunnel

The day Patty came in saying "Doug is the least of my troubles," I knew their marriage was on the upswing. Still feeling unsteady, the couple renegotiated their contract for an additional month. As Doug said, "We don't want to goof it up again."

Ongoing Transformation

After the couple were reunited, they focused their attention on Sonny, who was being a tyrant at home and at school. Family therapy helped Doug get more involved in disciplining the child, and Sonny's behavior improved remarkably at home and school.

Patty got a new slant on her negativity. She relayed, "I hadn't realized how negative I can get. My mother's awfully contrary, too. You know, I've always been afraid if I'm real positive, people will think I'm cocky . . . but I try not to think like that anymore."

Then Patty told Doug to remind her if she was being negative. I thought, "Here is an aspect of teamwork worthy of applause."

Doug changed jobs and for the first time in his life found employers who appreciated his work—a boost to his ego. Having settled into a manageable 50-hour workweek, he was primed for career advancement. No longer defeated, his life took on purpose and meaning, measures that had been sorely lacking.

Transformation was a two-step-forward, one-step-backward journey. Patty said, "It's real hard not to be nitpicking for flaws—it's such a nasty habit, like I gotta put a clothespin on my mouth. . . . It's easier when I don't have PMS."

Doug responded, "Yeah, I'm mellowing out, watching my words. . . . I don't spout off so fast when she's in one of her lousy moods."

Patty had a secret. She said, "I'm under terrible stress at work. I hear all the backbiting, and I never say anything. Then I come home and take it out on Doug."

In amazement, I asked her if Doug knew this. Looking at him she explained, "Nope, never said anything to him—just kept it all to myself." When I suggested she be honest with Doug and tell him when she has a rotten day at work, he exclaimed, "Sure. I'd rather hear Patty say that than take it out on me!"

This case was destined to take longer than most. Three months after the couple reunited I asked them to assess their CS experience.

Patty said, "We couldn't live together . . . we had to separate to cool down. The CS helped us do that without our losing it altogether. Doug and I are standing firm on disciplining Sonny. As for me, I've learned not to be so nitpicky, and I'm trying to overlook the little annoying things that don't matter anyway."

Then she added, "It used to drive me nuts when Doug got up in the middle of the night and raided the refrigerator. Well, not anymore. I get up and we both eat together!"

Doug said, "You know I never wanted a divorce. I don't know how much longer I could have held out. It was the CS that saved us and our sanity, too. The good thing I found out is I can be myself and Patty can be herself, and we can still say, 'I love you.'"

As I have watched Patty and Doug's partnership strengthen, it makes me a believer in miracles as never before.

17

From Blame to Forgiving: How Do I Know I Love Thee?

The Tale of Ellen and Bob: A Not-So-Perfect Marriage

The infamous day Bob told Ellen about his five-month affair with his secretary, Louise, the couple's family life was turned upside down. Ellen went berserk. This was not the same Bob she had married. How dare he betray her and flaunt this Louise woman in her face? How dare Bob, in his unassuming way, say he felt no passion for his wife! On top of the affair, an admission of this magnitude came like a lightening bolt on a bright, sunny day. How was she to stay afloat in such shark-infested waters if Bob didn't love her?

Bob's Conflict Avoidance Affair (see Chapter 13) had the couple wallowing in blame and entrapped in guilt, humiliation, and consummate hopelessness. Ellen stormed into her family physician's office cursing the infidel. Her doctor referred her to me.

When I first met Ellen, her eyes were swollen and red. "I've been crying for three weeks . . . can't stop. It's hard to believe. Bob and I were high school sweethearts . . . I thought he was my best friend . . . I can't understand what's come over him . . . How am I supposed to be with him? How can I show my face in church? I'm sick about it . . . it's too hard on me. What am I to do?"

Ellen's Story

Ellen, 28, formerly snug within the borders of her charming country home, had liked to pretend she had the perfect marriage. She was a good mother, rearing three healthy daughters, ages four, seven, and nine, with the help of a good husband and father. She praised the Lord and considered herself blessed until Bob's infidelity laid bare the flaws in their relationship.

Ellen had been reared in a stable Catholic household, where no one ever divorced. At 19 she became pregnant, quit college, and married Bob. She worked three evenings a week as a seamstress at a bridal shop. She hoped someday to get a college degree.

She admitted to a few "marital ups and downs" but preferred to focus on the positives, of which there were many. The partners had worked hard, saved their money, and shared similar values, and both were invested in their children's welfare. Family outings—boating with the kids in the summer and skiing in the winter—had given her warm, cozy feelings. She and Bob cooperated, and most importantly for Ellen, they didn't argue.

She said, "Bob is quiet and reserved. I'm the talkative one." The couple found it easier to cast their irksome resentments aside rather than face up to their problems.

After the children were born, Ellen lost interest in sexual intimacy with her husband. She said, "When it comes to sex, I can take or leave it—never had a strong drive. By the time I get the kids tucked in, I'm hardly in the mood."

As a teenager, Ellen encountered some scary things. She said, "Not exactly rape—but they turned me off. Hate to say it, but sometimes I just fake an orgasm. I could never tell this to Bob; I wouldn't want to hurt his feelings."

And therein was a critical flaw in the couple's marriage. Groping to make sense of her collapsed world, Ellen frantically prayed for the strength to get through her ordeal, hoped the children wouldn't be unduly damaged, and, God willing, prayed the marriage was salvageable.

Bob's Story

Bob, 29, was a tormented, lost soul. He felt hopelessly forsaken by his God and questioned the worth of his once-steadfast faith. Tortured by merciless guilt, he was torn apart and driven by desire to be with his paramour; yet the thought of separation, much less divorce, was inconceivable.

Bob's identity was built on his career as a human relations director for a large sales organization. He found the company's infighting so disturbing, however, he was trying to locate a better position.

Bob spoke highly of his wife, who had been the only woman he ever dated. Like Ellen, he entertained the notion of a perfect union and aimed to keep it a low-profile, low-stress, low-conflict endeavor. And then he went and loused it up! His life wasn't adding up somehow.

Bob took his be perfect premise to heart, but the contradictions he faced were taking a toll. He had seethed in conflict since childhood. Reared in a cold, barren environment by "perfectionist" parents who never openly expressed their love, the pressure to measure up to his parents' standards was too much for him. At 16 Bob nearly ran headlong into catastrophe when he tried to take his life by overdosing on his mother's medication. Fortunately, he was saved by a neighbor, but this near-fatal experience had traumatized him.

Much to Bob's chagrin, the terrifying thoughts of suicide had resurfaced as a consequence of his unfinished affair. Although he had promised Ellen he would not see Louise anymore, adultery or no adultery, he was driven to see Louise one more time. All else was a blur.

Wallowing in remorse, Bob felt like a spiritual outcast. "I don't know what God is anymore . . . I don't even know why I had the affair . . . I'm not sure what's going on with me."

A Knotty Bind

Sustaining a polite facade was all but impossible. Ellen wished she could run away from the crisis—a typical reaction when people feel defeated. Bob wished he could get rid of his wife, and he hated himself for thinking such evil thoughts. This is a common fantasy when distraught spouses feel emotionally abandoned.

The serpent had reared its ugly head and cast the mates out of their quasi Garden of Eden. The serpent was 'betrayal'; the master was 'blame'. Bob bore the Cross of Guilt. He had betrayed himself and considered himself condemned to suffer. Overwrought, he didn't trust his precarious state of mind. He questioned if he was even capable of loving anyone. "Suicide," he caustically remarked, "looks like an easy way out."

A not altogether righteous Ellen saw her fiery indignation turn to bleak uncertainty. As the betrayed wife, she felt emotionally split apart, helplessly standing by, praying her hapless husband wouldn't do himself bodily harm. And all the while, Ellen questioned how she could ever trust Bob again.

A world-traveled leader in healing and transformation, Jean Houston tells us, in *The Search for the Beloved: Journeys in Sacred Psychology*, that

> trust always contains the seeds of its own betrayal. . . . Betrayals mark the expulsion from our Eden of complete trust into the empirical but evolutionary world of consciousness, growth, autonomy, and responsibility. . . . With consciousness you can transgress, transcend, deceive, evoke, evade, create, enter, and exit—in other words, you can get somewhere.[1]

The couple's situation was further complicated when Ellen surprised herself by enjoying a sexual encounter with her husband. All "a-tizzy" the next morning, her fleeting exhilaration was immediately dashed when Bob pleaded he "had to" see his Louise one last time.

A knotty bind. What was Ellen to say to that? She backed off, fearful Bob would harm himself. Nor was she in the mood to be blamed for what might be construed as her lack of pity. So she acquiesced, and Bob went to meet his lover one more time!

In the Name of Blame

The "perfect marriage" had backfired. Looking at the dying embers of their partnership, both spouses were in the untenable position of not knowing whom to blame for what. Ellen rued the day she had found out about Louise, and Bob was barely coping with his inner demons—his depression would last for months on end.

Introduction of CS

The couple was at the brink. How were they to bridge their marital impasse and save their souls? Ellen's limits were being put to the test. Living under the shadow of infidelity had become a nightmare. To make a statement, she pushed Bob out of their bedroom. "I've hardened," she said. "I've got so much anger I can't get rid of it."

Then, in a fit of temper, Ellen told Bob to "get out if that's what you want!" The couple were on the verge of a TS but neither party could speak of divorce. They remained immobilized as Bob wallowed in a sea of perplexity and Ellen continued to waver.

It was evident the time was ripe for me to introduce the CS Guidelines. Encouraged, Ellen said, "This plan looks promising. I'll let Bob know about it and we'll see." The three of us met a few days later, and the mates declared their marriage had hit rock bottom. They had no better choice but to go for a CS.

CS: Bob Moves Out

The forlorn mates agreed to a four-month CS Contract. Bob said he would move out, and within two weeks he was resettled in a one-bedroom apartment nearby. Neither party wanted to talk with a lawyer. Telling their children about the CS was their primary concern.

The parents got together with their girls and called their CS an "emergency measure." Ellen said that the separation was temporary, and Bob assuaged his youngsters' fears, reassuring them that he would put them to bed on the evenings Mom was working. He promised to phone or see them daily.

The children were taken aback at first, but when Ellen said they could still go skiing as a family and have other outings as well, their little faces lit up. Bob kept his promises to his girls, and they fared well.

CS: Couple Cooperation

Ellen had said yes to the CS, yet she had many reservations. She worried about shoveling snow in the winter and yard work in the summer. Bob quietly said he'd take care of these things, and she relaxed a bit.

Finances didn't need much adjusting, although the couple agreed there wouldn't be anything left for saving.

As for confidentiality, Ellen was close with her parents and drew support from them, particularly from her mother. Bob, however, was distant with his parents and took a month before advising them of his CS. He said, "I know they won't understand."

By and large, it was evident the mates' cooperative spirit was helping make their separation a more tolerable experience.

CS: Dating Each Other

As for dating, Ellen couldn't bring herself to even think of dating Bob until the Louise affair was resolved. Bob didn't protest. Overall, the couple's cooperative spirit helped make their separation tolerable.

CS: The Tempest of Dating Others

Throughout their contract negotiations, both Ellen and Bob stayed composed, but all that fell apart when we discussed dating others. When Ellen raised the specter of their Catholicism, it precipitated an uproar. Bob said that his religion didn't matter to him as he was determined to meet with Louise again and again, if necessary. "I've got to know where I stand."

With that, Ellen gave full vent to her fury. "What about our faith, our religious teachings? Isn't that what we've always stood for?" Her vehement protests did no good. Without saying so, I had a hunch the CS would serve to make or break Bob's open affair one way or another.

It was the lonely nights that Ellen hated. She briefly toyed with the notion of dating an old family friend who was recently divorced and met him for lunch one day. She said, "I was tempted, but honestly, Lee, I don't have the energy. With the children and all, it's just not for me."

Bob's Despair

Whereas Ellen was recovering her equilibrium, Bob continued to have unrelenting thoughts of suicide. In our individual sessions, I repeatedly urged him to get a psychiatric evaluation and consider medication, but he refused. Instead, we made a "No-Suicide Contract," which eased my mind; but it apparently did little for Bob, who sank deeper into despair. Ellen hoped he could find a better job. Perhaps that would cheer him up.

To his dismay, Bob was making no headway with Louise. Although she said she was leaving her husband "any day now," he waited a month, six weeks, two months, until it became evident she was just stringing him along. In disgust he finally broke off the affair but didn't tell Ellen because he was too unsettled to know what to do next.

Living in the Shadows

In the face of infidelity, how do we stop blaming ourselves and start to forgive? Bob was living in the shadows—somewhere between heaven and hell—wrenched by circumstances often beyond his comprehension—rent by frenzied emotions precipitated by adultery and Louise's subsequent rejection.

I urged Bob to forgive himself and told him, "We are flawed, and our lives are flawed. Being a little lower than the angels, we stumble, we see the error of our ways, or the error of our mate's ways, we pick ourselves up and dust ourselves off and keep going. We use our resources, we forgive, and we try to make tomorrow a better day."

Bob wasn't ready to forgive himself.

CS: Ellen's Confrontation

At the close of the third month of their CS, Ellen was fast losing patience. Still unaware that Bob's affair had hit the rocks, she gave

Bob an urgent ultimatum: "Stop seeing Louise or we divorce!" With that confrontation staring him in the face, he broke their CS Contract and moved back home a month earlier than expected.

Ellen was iffy about their reconciliation. When we met a few days later, she was attempting to reconcile herself to forgiving Bob. She said, "It isn't easy . . . I'm asking the Lord to show me how."

The couple elected to terminate their sessions with me, but Ellen and I talked by phone occasionally. She knew the road ahead would be a rocky one—even with Louise out of the picture. The partners still had hefty lessons to learn. Primarily, they were to discover that the healing power of forgiving is possible, but it can't be done in a day.

From Blame to Forgiving

In the final analysis, whether in or out of marriage, we are responsible for our transgressions. Whether we blame ourselves, our spouses, and/or the world, the sins of our past are indelibly etched in our psyches to teach us lessons. No matter the indignity, be it infidelity, betrayal, abandonment, or abuse, we can forgive our mate, but we can never forget the injury and injustice of it all.

Some people erroneously think they can forgive and forget, as if the sorry mess can be whited out—obliterated from our brain. But that is a fallacy. We humans don't operate that way.

Pseudoforgiving

The following statements imply forgiving, but the premise is a pseudoforgiving—a shallow kind of self-deception. Note the contradictions herein:

> "I guess he didn't mean what he did. I try to be charitable and forgive him. But I can't accept what he has done to me."
> "I forgave her a long time ago, but her betrayal eats at me now and then."
> "Said I'd go to my grave before I forgave her, yet I can't leave her. Strange."
> "I thought I was done with the past—forgive and forget. But it all comes back to haunt me. I don't understand why."

Forgiving and Beyond

Love is the force behind forgiving. It empowers us to risk making a commitment. Love gets us into a crisis, and love empowers us to get out of it. Lewis B. Smedes, author of *Forgive and Forget: Healing the Hurts We Don't Deserve*, gives us messages of hope and potent answers for achieving peace of mind.

> Love does not let you blame yourself falsely for long. . . . The same self-respecting love that gets you into the *crisis of forgiving* has the power to move you into the *place of self-healing*. . . . Love will not let you lock yourself in the prison cell of your bitter memories. It will not permit you the demeaning misery of wallowing in yester-day's pain.[2]

Smedes compassionately speaks of those who hurt us:

> [They] are not just lumps of degenerate corruption: they are com-plex people with more to them than meanness and craziness. They have the potential to become better people, truer people, than they were when they stung you. Respect for them will help you to see the *person* behind the rat. And this respect can stimulate you to move in the direction of forgiveness.[3]

To forgive your partner for his or her indiscretions is a gift of grace and love. Yet it frequently takes a spiritual awakening and a lot of self-reckoning to reach a state of forgiveness. Although the hurts are long remembered, forgiving means we blame no more. And the pain doesn't smart as much as it once did.

Follow-Up: A Gradual Transformation

In the face of so momentous a decision as whether to stay or go, the tale of Ellen and Bob speaks to their gradual transformation in the face of love and betrayal, blame and forgiving, and the realization that we are all ultimately accountable to ourselves and our Maker.

Nine Months

When I phoned, Ellen was about ready to pack up her three kids and leave for good, perhaps spurred on by the news Bob's sister was divorcing. She said, "Bob's so into himself . . . so mixed up, still trying to figure out what God means to him. There's no way we can get close."

Two Years

Ellen was trying to be cheerful. "I'm taking it a day at a time. He's good with the kids, but there's a lot I try to ignore. I wonder if I'll ever be able to trust Bob again . . . You know we work well together, we're friends, but truthfully, it's a loveless marriage."

Four Years

Ellen sounded iffy: "The children are doing fine, the marriage is OK but not super . . . I just wish we were closer. Bob's got another job, and we're hoping that will be an improvement. We'll have to wait and see."

Six Years

I ran into Ellen at a local coffee shop. Over a cup of tea, I couldn't miss her bright-eyed enthusiasm about her new managerial position and Bob's satisfaction with the direction of his career. She spoke of the benefits of CS. "I don't know where we would be right now if it weren't for the CS. Actually, living apart got us thinking about how we wanted our marriage to be." Insightfully, Ellen observed, "I had expected Bob to do the work of changing, and all the while I kept holding a grudge about his affair. We've both grown up a lot. Now it is easier for me to see that forgiveness is really a two-way street."

"And how are the two of you doing?" I bluntly asked. Ellen broke into the cutest grin as she proudly said, "Oh Lee, it couldn't be better . . . Bob has finally come to love himself, and we are better lovers than we've ever been."

18

$\mathcal{A}$ctive Waiting: Hurry-Up and Slow-Down Partners

The Tale of Nora and Todd: "What Will My Future Be?"

"There's such a big gulf between us. I want Nora to come back . . . not out of guilt, but because she genuinely loves me."

"It's a rotten shame. Here we are practically newlyweds, and we haven't had sex more than a dozen times. I've got to get myself well again . . . But I'm afraid Todd's going to explode when I tell him I want to separate."

"What will my future be?" went round and round in Todd's head, hounding him with several murky hypotheses. "If we don't deal with the sex part, how can we make this marriage work? Will I lose out a second time? Will I ever stop feeling like a failure? Will I get through this and still be OK?"

Resentment Escalates

Nora, 31, was the frustrated "hurry-up" partner who couldn't get Todd interested in sexual counseling. They were a childless couple, married 18 months, when Nora phoned me in desperation. Worn down by four months of pleading, she said, "I've got one foot out the door . . . the spark is fading fast!"

Nora had colitis, which she attributed to marital distress. Her patience running thin, she had made her first therapy appointment as much to heal herself as to save her marriage.

Nora had other complaints: miffed with Todd's seeming indifference, she explained, "It doesn't seem to matter how I feel . . . it's like I'm not there. He plops on the couch and watches TV, goes in the den and throws darts, and then he takes fishing trips with his buddies. How can he ignore me like that?"

Todd's Version

Todd, 33, thought his first year of marriage went reasonably well until Nora took a job that demanded 60 to 70 hours per week. He blamed his wife for causing a major crack in their coupling. All spring and summer he had an absentee wife, as Nora often worked late into the night. He had condoned her being gone on weekends, but then the partners had precious little time together.

When Todd expressed his disapproval, Nora criticized him for trying to thwart her career ambitions. And with that he refrained from saying any more.

The Couple in a Bind

The couple were in a bind because they had no means to bridge their differing perceptions of their standoff. The longer Todd was diffident—keeping his mouth shut yet seething with resentment—the more Nora could sense he was taking less interest in her. In turn, she felt she had no choice but to retaliate by pulling away sexually.

And so began finger-pointing, occasional irksome accusations, and a debilitating power struggle that took its toll. Although the partners feared failure, neither would stand up and be counted as "causing the crisis." With their relationship polarized, their marriage had come to an impasse.

Nora's Story

Nora married Todd on the rebound, having broken off wedding plans with her former fiancé at the last minute. Tall, handsome Todd looked like a good catch. He was a well-established dentist with his feet on the ground—or so she thought.

Nora knew neglect even as a child. Her younger brother, born retarded, needed far more of Mother's attention than little Nora, who was always a dependable, independent youngster.

She spoke of her dad, so absorbed in holding the family together financially that he never got close or seemed to care what she was feeling or thinking. Nora was left to fend for herself.

Although she made excuses for her parents' mistakes, it was evident Nora expected Todd to somehow make up for those lost years of nurturing.

Nora is typical of women who do not bond well with their fathers in childhood and are shunted aside by their mothers. Her dating years were traumatic: a date rape, a cocaine-addicted boyfriend, another who slapped her around, and others for whom she made extensive sacrifices.

An attractive, intelligent, dynamic woman, Nora always had a man nearby she could turn to. Much to her chagrin, however, each lover became another disappointment. Overall, she terminated no fewer than seven intimate relationships before meeting Todd.

CS Introduced

A month after I met Nora, she flatly said, "I can't stand it anymore. Todd refuses to get help . . . and I'm constantly thinking about separating." She saw TS as a last resort.

Her decision gave me an opening to speak of the essence of CS. Practical-minded Nora was impressed with the commonsense approach of the CS Guidelines. She needed no further persuasion. But she expected the CS was not going to be an easy sell.

"I just know Todd's going to give me a real hard time about a separation now that we've gone through the work and expense of buying and decorating our dream home."

Nora took the Guidelines home but couldn't bring herself to show them to Todd. It was three weeks before she dared let him in on the CS. She knew he would object; after all, if she moved out now, it would be like a slap in the face.

Todd's Story

Todd was the "slow-down" mate who had closed his eyes and tried to delay facing what Nora saw as impending disaster. As Nora had predicted, he hit the roof when he saw the CS Guidelines and made an appointment to see me immediately—alone. Alarmed and stunned by the thought of a repugnant separation, he couldn't believe his marriage had sunk so low as to require such drastic measures.

Todd had an idyllic childhood: good parents, good grades, a star at basketball, prom king. No major obstacles. As a kid he didn't know any divorced families. He assumed all divorced people had some sort of character defect—as if they were hapless, bad folk.

Four years earlier Todd had been shaken up by a humiliating divorce. "This time it could be a whole lot worse. I'm looking at being a two-time loser, and that's bad. I love Nora but she just doesn't get it!" At the time, Todd didn't "get it," either.

CS: Nora Rejects Couple Counseling

Todd was agitated the day he and Nora came to talk about a potential separation. Immediately, he suggested couple counseling as an alternative, but it was too late. Nora wouldn't budge once she had been primed for a CS. Todd felt trapped. Forced to back off, he reluctantly agreed to a three-month separation.

Privately, Todd expressed his concern. "Getting through these next months is going to be rough. I realize the sex part is our biggest hurdle, and I don't know if we can ever bridge that one. Nora's real grouchy these days. Every time I try to hug or kiss her, she pushes me away . . . wish I knew what I'm doing that's so wrong!"

CS: Contract Negotiations

On the eve of the couple's CS journey, Todd felt whipped, his confidence and pride at an all-time low. Nora already had an apartment in mind and moved out within ten days.

Finances weren't an issue for the couple because both spouses earned good incomes. The couple had keys to one another's abodes but agreed they would be used only in an emergency. Otherwise, they agreed to respect one another's privacy.

Nora said she would rather forgo any touching but agreed to hold Todd's hand. They settled for that and said they would date once a week. The couple talked about going to church together, but that never materialized.

Todd said he wasn't interested in dating anyone else, but when Nora said she wanted the option to date others, her husband's look of horror spoke louder than words. He made a weak effort to protest and then, true to form, backed down and let the matter drop without creating a scene. The subject never came up again.

Todd came for weekly therapy, and the couple settled on joint sessions with me twice a month. I saw Nora individually as needed.

CS: Mother-in-Law Troubles

Nora told her parents about the CS and found her mother to be a comfort. Nora said, "My mom is really there for me and so are my friends at work. I've got a good support system going." Nora's socializing with comrades after working hours had taken the place of her establishing a closer bond with Todd.

Conversely, after Todd told his parents about the CS, his mother promptly phoned Nora and laid a guilt trip on her. "Would you believe my mother-in-law tried to make it out that it was all my fault. And when I told Todd about it, he did nothing to stand up for me. No wonder we are in such a mess!"

I listened as Nora poured her heart out. She said, "You know, I used to have a good relationship with my mother-in-law, but now I have nothing to say to the woman."

CS: Rough Going

Although Nora expected to feel better after she moved out, she felt worse, as her physical and emotional state did not improve. She couldn't stop crying. Later I was to understand she was grieving not just for her current marital disaster, but for a lifetime of unsatisfactory relationships with men.

Todd was moody and having trouble concentrating on his work. Ashamed to tell his closest friends of his separation, he shortchanged himself—at least temporarily—because this was the time when he needed his peers' support the most.

CS: Todd's Search for Insight

Todd was taking his CS seriously enough to be brutally honest with himself. For the first time in his life, he was drawn to introspection. Todd had always thought of himself as competent, and now he started to question his capacity to relate to his wife.

Conflict and confrontation were Todd's nemeses. Emphatically he explained, "I've always been a noncombative kid—I detest conflict." He had spent a lifetime vigilantly protecting himself with two coats of armor rather than reveal a side of himself he preferred to keep hidden. The time had come to bare his soul.

Todd's ill-fated first marriage had resurfaced to taunt him, and it compounded the misery of his present marital debacle and unwelcome separation. He couldn't stop reviewing his past. He said, "I deliberately blacked out my divorce. My ex and I had such different personalities, we never should have married."

It seems Todd had been blasé when his earlier union fell apart, accepting it as happening for the best. But this time he agonized as he watched his loving bond with Nora collapse.

His self-examination continued: "You know, after my divorce, for seven years I built a shell around myself to keep from feeling. But I can't pretend anymore . . . This time I'm exhausted and depressed!"

By living alone, Todd was getting in touch with his vulnerabilities. It took his marital tragedy for him to see how he had often placated Nora by saying, "Yes, dear," when he really meant, "No, dear." He was dumbfounded when he thought about how often he had swept his dissatisfactions and resentments under the rug. Our individual conversations gave him an opportunity to speak his mind, grow emotionally, gain insight, and restore his self-confidence.

CS: Todd Contemplates His Future

Todd suspected Nora was separating to spare herself, but not to save the marriage. He feared she wouldn't try very hard, and he matched her lack of effort in kind.

He was sorely impatient, and the nagging phrase "What will my future be?" haunted his reverie, for good reason.

"Maybe I would be better off single," Todd mused, always with the CS outcome in mind. Repulsed by that thought, he added, "I hate the thought of dating again . . . a real rat race!"

Next he pondered if he should or would remarry, and he frequently mentioned being a family man. I gathered this was Todd's lifelong dream. With considerable gravity, he wondered, "Will I ever have kids?"

Our private conversations were a means of laying his worst fears on the table. They also were a way of lifting his spirits. With a half-smile Todd added, "I guess you could say our relationship is still limping along on life support. It hasn't died . . . not yet."

CS: The Curse of Impatience

Couples on the cusp are predictably short on patience, intolerant of each other, and irritable with themselves. Unsettled mates can get incredibly edgy as they impatiently face an uncertain outcome. At least one and maybe both of them want answers right now!

Hurry-up partners like Nora want action fast, having waited long enough for something to happen. Slow-down mates like Todd will either procrastinate or be satisfied with the status quo.

After the partners had separated, they reversed roles. Nora was in no rush to obtain resolution, not wanting to believe she had anything to do with the marital crisis. Todd was in a hurry to get an answer, as the strain of waiting was wearing him down. He wished his marriage was salvageable; but if not, he didn't want to sit around for long to find out.

CS: The Pressure to Wait

In our push-button culture, waiting is hard to do. To wait a day seems like forever. The pressure to wait it out, particularly a TS and in some cases a CS, combined with the wish to divine the future, can be an unnerving experience.

Impatience can't simply be wished away. Who can remain so cool and savvy when a rush of adrenaline sets off anticipatory anxiety mixed with hope and despair? I've seen both rejectors and rejectees be subject to a bizarre blend of ominous foreboding and eager antic- ipation. What will it be: an interminable separation, a revitalized marriage, a so-so relationship, an ugly divorce, or an amicable one? The answer is merely vague conjecture until closure is attained.

Meeting the Challenge of Impatience

To meet the challenge of impatience, I developed the dual concepts of "passive waiting" and "active waiting" to show impetuous couples how to patiently navigate their CS. Be aware that your apart time is not an uninvolved endeavor, but a spirited, enterprising process. In response to the uncertainties of living apart, you cultivate your re- sourcefulness and strengths. When you are energetically involved in a meaningful venture, you recognize that deliberation and deci- sion making take time.[1]

Passive Waiting

"Passive waiting" is a destructive process that leaves couples feeling helpless. It is tantamount to doing nothing but fretting in the face of an uncertain "stay or go" outcome. As we have already seen, taking this tack can lead to immobilization—a debilitating nightmare.

For lack of encouragement and motivation, passive waiting is the precursor of futility and despair, enough to undermine your pathways and the fate of your life. To be uninvolved in your mari- tal turbulence is to deny that you might lose out in the long run.

Passive Waiting Guides

The 12 tenets of passive waiting explain how this happens:

1. Believe nothing in your life will change for the better.

2. Remain negative; expect the worst.

3. Be afraid of the pain of rejection.

4. Lie to yourself—deny or minimize your traumas.

5. Doubt yourself—say, "I don't know what I want."

6. Blame yourself, others, or the fates for your predicament.

7. Believe you are inadequate and helpless to help yourself.

8. Get a multitude of opinions—stay confused.

9. Do not trust your hunches; devalue your own judgment.

10. See yourself and your life as not important.

11. Be bitter, but don't ask for support or help.

12. Stay "spiritually bankrupt."

Active Waiting

"Active waiting," in contrast, is a constructive process—a conscious use of time—that teaches you how to cultivate the high art of patience as you make a positive investment in your future. While you await your CS outcome, active waiting affords you a rare opportunity to maintain your composure and persevere until you get closure.

When I discussed my guides for active waiting with Todd, he nodded, "You've really got it. That's just what I need right now . . . I've got to get through the CS somehow."

Active Waiting Guides

1. Accept that your life is a work in progress.

2. Admit that you are impatient.

3. Look at waiting as a period of incubation.

4. Understand that incubation is the void where something is percolating.

5. Be aware this void can last weeks, months, even years.

6. Recognize your frustration at being obliged to wait. Mentally shake hands with so urgent a feeling.

7. Then immediately make a quick 180-degree shift and focus on a meaningful goal you would be proud to achieve. Say, "I am resourceful. I am creative. I can persist. I can hang in there."

8. Do not be afraid to feel your suffering when the going gets rough.

9. Know life's experiences are opportunities for new learning.

10. Accept that no experience, good or bad, is ever wasted.

11. Develop your spiritual faith.

When you diligently put active waiting into practice, you are on the path to gaining many new insights and making transformation a living reality.

Active Waiting Benefits

As you put the active waiting guides to work, you benefit in many practical ways. You witness the unfolding of your CS journey with a pragmatic eye. You feel more connected to yourself instead of being so isolated and lost. When you are more comfortable with yourself, you have the advantage of viewing your spouse in a better light. As attacking gives way to talking, as obstinacy bends to cooperation, you might be encouraged to willingly respond in kind.

Active Waiting Generalized

The concept of active waiting is applicable in all areas of our lives, from the mundane to the monumental. I have used the principles myself and found them particularly helpful when several publishers were bidding for this book. My heart was racing so fast, the excitement mixed with impatience were all but unmanageable.

Feeling wired and wrung out at the same time, I thought it best I practice what I preach. In reviewing the active waiting guides, I clued into number eight, "feel your suffering," and immediately a river of tears gushed forth, followed by emotional relief. After my nerves settled down, I had the stamina to wait out the hours. It was astonishing how quickly my whole body responded in a healthier way.

The active waiting concept is useful in many guises to enrich your life. Use the guides as an assist in achieving patience, a goal worth your wait.

The Rest of Nora and Todd's Story

By the time Nora and Todd had been separated 12 weeks, it was evident there was no infusion of positive energy coming from either party. Each time we met jointly, both mates admitted their weekly dates were a bust. Todd said, "We just make trivial talk. Who wants to talk about the weather? That gets to me." Nora agreed. "We have nothing much to say. Todd gives me a glum stare, and I want to leave and go home!" In a sense, both partners had backed away from their union.

Despite individual therapy, neither partner could get past the stage of faulting the other. Both had avoided taking responsibility for their own share in the marital breakdown.

CS: Termination of Contract

The longer Nora refused to bring their separated status to closure, the more Todd was fed up with her dawdling. Because he could see no evidence of change on his wife's part, he came to the conclusion he would be forced to take action.

The following week in my office, Todd curtly confronted Nora. "I'm ready to call it quits. I can't wait any longer." She was taken aback by the force of his decisive approach. Their CS Contract was terminated after 13 weeks, and there was little else Nora could say. Neither did she have the will to make a protest.

In a follow-up session two weeks later, Todd said, "I've been such a wreck. The CS made me face up to the fact my marriage was going downhill, when I didn't want to admit it. And I'm getting to know myself a lot better—that's good. I wish it could have been otherwise, but I'm going to make it somehow."

In a wrap-up session with Nora the same week, she explained, "I was getting so sick I didn't have the energy to leave Todd, although that's what I needed to do. The CS helped me to take the first step and move out. But I never would have had the guts to ask Todd for a divorce. I guess it's the only answer. I'm sure we can work out the divorce settlement without getting in one another's hair."

And then Nora put a not-so-surprising twist to the culmination of their CS. "By the way, I've been in touch with my former fiancé. He's settled down a lot, we've had a few dates, and there's still a real attraction. But first I've got to get myself well again."

Follow-Up

I contacted each party six months later. Nora said, "Our divorce is moving along, but every now and then Todd checks in to see if I've changed my mind. I'm just glad the worst is over, and I've got my health back again."

Todd told me, "I still miss Nora. I'm dating now and then, but it's not the same. Thanks for helping me pull myself together. In hindsight, the CS made me see I had as much to do with the breakup of our marriage as Nora did. I've learned there is no way to avoid conflict. It always seems to catch up with you somehow. I'll be better prepared, if there ever is a next time. And I don't plan on making the same mistakes again."

Part III
Operating
Instructions

19

The Good Divorce

"It's over. I have done my best, we'll be in close contact
    because of the kids, and I wish her well."
"I'm so glad we are divorced and I can still communicate with
    him. For a while there I thought I was losing my smile."
"Our CS showed us how to be dignified and not let our
    divorce get nasty."

The Legacy of Divorce

Divorce is about losses and unfinished business. The crushing pain of
severing a marriage involves transition and change. Divorce is an
uprooting, not merely a dismantling, legal process. It is a time of
resettling, pulling together of loose ends, and emotionally recharging.

Marriage therapist Lois Gold, M.S.W., in *Between Love and
Hate: A Guide to Civilized Divorce* tells us:

> Divorce is a legal event, but for the family it is a gradual process of
> reorganizing and redefining relationships and expectations. Fami-
> lies continue, but divorce changes them.[1]

As we approach the twenty-first century, we are not going to dispense with the divorce phenomenon. It is no longer the shameful state it once was. In most of the industrial world, divorce is seen as a natural consequence of marital incompatibility.

The magnitude of divorce is felt in every corner of our society. The experience itself is the second greatest stressor in a person's life, following the death of a spouse. (Refer to the Social Readjustment Rating Scale in Chapter 6.)

The number of people who have or will face such permanent transitions is overwhelming. In the United States divorce rates had been relatively stable until 1965, when they began to skyrocket. They leveled off in 1985 and have remained essentially the same into the late 1990s.

The latest statistics indicate that half of all marriages terminate in divorce, whereas two-thirds of the couples married five years or less will terminate their coupling. More than half of the divorced population will remarry, and some of these same parties will remarry again and divorce again. Overall, better than 50 percent of first marriages and 60 percent of second marriages fall by the wayside.[2]

Divorce takes the punch out of us. Many people drink too much, smoke too much, and generally neglect themselves during this trying time. To make the best of a bad situation takes the stamina of giants. We are immensely fragile and sorely vulnerable in the face of such an insult to our psyches. Divorce saps our strength and takes its toll.

Audrey Hepburn's biographer, Barry Paris, writes that the actress suffered the pain of two philandering husbands and two divorces. Her touching words reveal her anguish:

> [Divorce is] one of the worst experiences a human being can go through. I tried *desperately* to avoid it. . . . I hung on in both marriages very hard, as long as I could, for the children's sake, and out of respect for marriage. You always hope that if you love somebody enough, everything will be all right—but it isn't always true.[3]

Hepburn's words ring true for anyone who has loved, been betrayed, lost out, or lost parts of oneself in a wretched parting of ways. The finality of divorce leaves an indelible mark on us even in the best of circumstances.

Rationale for Divorce

Bestselling author and marriage and family therapist Michelle Weiner-Davis perceptively states in *Divorce Busting* that "you can't make a person *want* the marriage to work if he or she is determined to get out. . . . You may be doing everything [almost] right and it still doesn't work."[4]

There are eight common reasons for divorce:

1. Chronic abuse—sexual and physical

2. Chronic substance abuse

3. Sexual infidelity

4. Trust betrayed by deception, lies, and emotional and/or sexual abandonment

5. Verbal brainwashing, which impairs self-worth

6. Falling in love with another

7. An intent to remarry

8. Personal safety and protection of children

Still Stuck and Waiting

Let's say you are done with waffling and have made the decision to divorce. You didn't anticipate that the question of who would start the divorce proceedings would keep you stuck a while longer. Who, you ask, is going to initiate your divorce?

Let's look at Amity and Warren, who were in the throes of a transitional separation, anticipating a divorce "someday," but neither party wanted to do the dirty work of filing the papers.

Amity had separated from Warren. She was living with her boyfriend, had begun a new career, and was truly enjoying being free of marital strife. The couple's two children, 8 and 12, were living with each parent on alternate weeks.

Warren, a professional man of considerable reputation, was mortified to be sullied by the prospects of divorce. He said, "I would have lived with Amity forever, no matter how bad it got."

However, Warren unexpectedly found himself in an awkward position. He had met Iris, an attractive divorcée, and thought she was an interesting companion; but that was not reason enough for him to file for divorce. Nonetheless, his new paramour had a more permanent arrangement—marriage—in mind. This put him in a most uncomfortable bind.

Although Warren was sure his relationship with Amity was over, apparently neither party was motivated to initiate the legal process.

Good Reasons Not to Divorce

Divorce can be a welcome reprieve from a bad marriage, but it isn't necessarily a panacea for solving all your problems. An increasing number of couples tell me they want to do everything in their power to strengthen their marital bonds, rather than risk immersion in the heated cauldron of a catastrophic divorce.

Many couples, like Amity and Warren, think long and hard about divorce. It was five years before Warren worked up the nerve to close the door to his marriage. Some parties frequently think about divorce, regularly threaten to call it quits, but never follow through.

The 10 most common reasons why people stay in less-than-satisfactory marriages are

1. Loving one's spouse despite the spouse's serious shortcomings

2. Personal values—a staunch belief in the sanctity of marriage

3. Religious convictions—a vow never to divorce, which you intend to honor

4. Limited financial resources or complex financial entanglements that appear to defy and impede reasonable distribution of funds

5. Worry that additional emotional damage will be inflicted on oneself, children, and/or extended family

6. Fear of being a one-, two-, or three-time divorce loser

7. Inconvenience of dismantling hearth and home

8. Poor health and lack of physical and emotional stamina

9. Fear of living alone. Sustained feelings of insecurity, inadequacy, and dependence on spouse

10. Ashamed of being considered a failure

The Ugly Divorce

The crippling consequences of an ugly divorce are instigated by spite, greed, and revenge. When dirty dealings on the part of one spouse incite the other to retaliate, then the tempest escalates, keeping the family embroiled in controversy that often continues long after the divorce is finalized.

I know of knifings at worst, cynical backbiting at least, when parting is not of one's choosing. Vindictive contests only serve to spell more heartache for the "put-upon" mate and do more harm to children, who breathe the venom of parental hostility.

Unsuspecting spouses who are dumped without warning feel entitled to self-righteous rage. You are devastated—in shock—when a uniformed and armed sheriff's deputy suddenly appears at your doorstep one night to serve divorce papers. The experience of rejection is akin to being tossed naked into January waters. Regrettably, revenge can spawn more trouble than you ever bargained for.

One of my rejected clients, a man in his thirties, reported, "This is an insult. What does she expect—that I'm not going to fight back?"

No one comes out a winner in adversarial divorces. Everyone involved falls into the failure trap—feeling like a loser.

Constance R. Ahrons, author of *The Good Divorce: Keeping Your Family Together When Your Marriage Comes Apart*, shares the hauntingly difficult experience of her divorce, replete with the following ugly trappings: "there were private detectives, a kidnapping, several lawyers, and two years of legal fees that took me 10 years to pay off. That painful time was almost 30 years ago, and even today it is hard to write about."[5]

Predictors of an Ugly Divorce

The 10 most common behaviors that incite retaliation and precipitate an ugly divorce follow:

1. Stay suspicious of your mate and expect the worst possible outcome—and you are likely to get it.

2. Blame your spouse—your mortal enemy—but not yourself.

3. Accept no responsibility for the demise of your marriage.

4. Remain defensive, inflexible, and controlling.

5. Insist on winning every argument at all costs.

6. Be unwilling to cooperate with your soon-to-be ex.

7. Refuse to communicate with your spouse.

8. Talk only through your lawyer and remain inaccessible.

9. Seek to punish and get revenge.

10. Get embroiled in a custody battle.

When couples operate within the margins of heated antagonism, how can there be any hope for a good divorce?

The Legal Trap

Unfortunately, the divorce process all too often brings out the worst in human nature. Adversarial partners who say "I'm gonna stick it to him/her" choose the most painful path of all—revenge. There is no denying that divorce hurts. Wounds go deep. As you look at others who have divorced before you, you see people who struggle a lifetime to work their way out of the wilds of bitterness.

The longer you are vindictive and relentlessly bent on getting even, the more you invite upheaval and incur increasing legal expenses. If you take the position that you'll get your just rewards in court, you may be asking for more trouble than it is really worth.

But partners who say "We are divorcing, and we want to stay on good terms" increase the likelihood of making divorce a legal breeze.

Our Adversarial Legal System

Despite no-fault divorce, the adversarial posture of our legal system has played havoc with too many couples, sometimes beyond comprehension. I wish it were otherwise, but for all our smarts, the courts have not been able to avoid, reconcile, or resolve the irreparable damage that adversarial posturing ensures. Neither have our states found a way to make our legal system user-friendly.

When society and the law have an implied expectation that divorcing couples will undoubtedly and unavoidably be contentious, it follows that attorneys will "use" this model to pursue an adversarial premise and swell the couple's breach.

No wonder the attempts of many couples at mediation so often fall short. *How can our family court system be fair or even adequate when it has not been indoctrinated with a premise that fosters couple advocacy?*

Herein our family courts of law are found wanting, having been instructed to assume so negative a posture. The next step is to admonish and dishonor the hostile divorcing parties rather than celebrate those who have chosen to part amicably. It takes very little to split couples further apart. Without a concerned, well-thought-out proactive program that promotes couple advocacy, the courts have devised a system whereby our children—and all parties involved—frequently suffer the deleterious aftereffects.

To add insult to injury, many embittered couples will find themselves having to dig deeply into their pocketbooks when they find out how outrageously expensive and inconvenient an ugly divorce can be. It takes only two determined attorneys representing two caustic spouses. Just watch the deliberate play of antagonisms that pit one against the other. Haplessly, in these instances some attorneys give lip service to mediation efforts but turn around and sabotage what the couple and mediators have worked so diligently to accomplish.

To be candid, I believe our family court system is sorely outmoded. There is little in the divorce process that is made emotionally palatable. Furthermore, the roadblocks on the way to finalizing a divorce are often a legal nightmare.

Major Legal Obstacles

If you have decided that ending the marriage is the right choice for you, spare yourself and your loved ones unnecessary heartache by selecting your attorney with care. If you discover you don't like the attorney you have, switch to someone with whom you feel more comfortable.

Not all lawyers or judges are disposed to making divorce a cold, cruel experience. Some attorneys are altruistic and willing to listen to your woes and will arrange for joint meetings with your spouse and his or her legal council.

There are seven serious obstacles that divorcing mates may encounter:

1. Divorce settlements languish and expenses mount as the courts are in no rush to render a decision and get the job done.

2. Lack of cooperation between lawyers causes delays.

3. Occasionally, lawyers are disinterested in suggesting mediation even when it would be a godsend.

4. If the lawyer-client relationship is not spelled out, it can lead to misunderstandings and prolonged delays.

5. If communication between spouses is shattered, attorneys who speak for their clients might complicate matters more than necessary.

6. Some attorneys are prone to sabotaging your mediator's recommendations by ignoring them.

7. Marital strife is exacerbated when attorneys goad their clients to squeeze all they can out of the marital pot.

Enhance Attorney-Client Interaction

Realistically, the legal profession cannot be expected to look out for your psychological well-being. Divorce stipulations are hampered by the imbalance of power between the parties. It helps to understand what you must do to avoid turning the divorce experience into a legal battlefield. Take nothing for granted, know what to expect from the legal system, and you will operate more efficiently.

You can enhance attorney-client interaction by using Gold's seven operating instructions.

1. Make sure nothing inflammatory leaves your attorney's office.

2. Be aware of the difficult issues.

3. Anticipate your spouse's reactions.

4. Use legal tactics to bring your mate to the bargaining table.

5. An apology to your spouse goes a long way in removing stumbling blocks and encouraging cooperation.

6. Agree to negotiate—you have everything to gain.

7. Noneconomic benefits are also achieved through negotiation.[6]

Good Divorce: Parting as Friends

The idea of parting as friends is not for every divorcing couple. Some people want to nurse their wounds and keep an ocean of distance between them and their exes.

Parting as friends has been a fairly recent phenomenon in our society. In the midseventies all we ever heard about were the ugly divorces. Before I remarried, more than 20 years ago, no one spoke of a friendly divorce—a few barely civil ones but mostly nasty ones.

My husband, Mark, was a trailblazer, determined to stay friends with his former spouse—and they are still friends. This has made it easier for our daughters—two apiece. With weddings and funerals, we have all strived to be gracious in family matters that call for cordial cooperation. Life is too short for it to be otherwise.

The effort it takes for you and your spouse to be civil surely makes the divorce transition and recovery a merciful one. To be conciliatory is to lay rancor aside and spare your loved ones unnecessary grief.

A good divorce can be yours if you and your soon-to-be ex are inspired to use common sense and treat one another with common decency. What is to be gained by involving families in "taking sides"? How much easier not to become embroiled in a "contest of wills."

Divorce *Pro Se*

Divorce *pro se* is the answer for couples who are amenable to a cooperative split and find their financial picture uncomplicated or extremely limited. Divorce *pro se*, pronounced "pro-say," means "for self" or "in one's own behalf." If you live in a state that has no-fault divorce, you can save lots of money and headaches by this "do-it-yourselves divorce" method, sans attorneys.

You can find divorce *pro se* services listed in your telephone directory. The staff will answer your legal questions, give you the necessary legal forms, and walk you through the process step by step.

Divorce *pro se* is a safe way to avoid the adversarial legal system. Furthermore, it is economical and more efficient than the traditional divorce process. Generally divorce *pro se* services will also provide mediation, if needed.

Divorce Mediation

Trying to achieve fairness can be extremely difficult for those rigid and controlling spouses who are divorcing because they are already at loggerheads. Jay Folberg and Ann Milne, in *Divorce Mediation: Theory and Practice*, state, "The concern for a fair and just result has particular applicability to custody and child-support disputes because children are rarely present or independently represented during mediation."[7]

Mediation is a sensible choice if both parties continue to harangue each other about kids, money, the house, relatives, or anything else that is debatable.

When your divorce stipulations have ground to a halt and you aren't getting the answers you are sure you deserve, consider the fairness of using the skilled objectivity of a divorce mediator. Guarded mates are more likely to listen to reason when they are not under attack. As you gain a better grasp of your spouse's position, compromise comes easier because the voice of reason is offered by an impartial third party. The independent, neutral perspective a mediator brings to your negotiations can make both spouses feel like winners.

Mediation is a wise option if agreement on divorce stipulations is giving you a wretched headache—one you can ill afford.

Divorce Counseling

Couples who opt for divorce counseling have a golden opportunity to diffuse grievances, let go of old toxic baggage, and cut their losses. An exchange of ideas with a professional is a sound way to get vital information and answers to questions that cushion the interminable waiting for the divorce to be finalized. Therapeutic assist during the dark days can lead you along paths of restoration and creative transformation. You help yourself when you accept what you don't have the power to fix or change.

Divorce Guidelines

Once a decision is made to divorce, the following six basic guidelines, adapted from the CS guidelines, can make your transition a saner one:

1. **Moving Out.** Decide which party will move out and when.

2. **Filing for Divorce.** If the decision is made unilaterally, soften the blow by advising your spouse of your intentions before papers are filed.

Caution: this rule does not apply if you are concerned about your safety or that of your children.

3. **Legal Counsel.** It's advisable that you be represented by your own lawyer.

4. **Children: Maintain Sensible Rules.**

- Alert the children two or three days in advance that one parent will make a change in residence. This gives the youngsters sufficient time to react, ask questions, and express their feelings. As you and your spouse express your own feelings of sorrow and regret, the children are spared as much angst as possible under the circumstances.

- Arrange for joint custody or other custodial arrangements that ensure your children are not deprived of reasonable access to either parent.

- Discuss phone arrangements, meeting times, family events, and sharing vacation time and holidays with your children.

5. Finances: Division of Property and Monies. Anticipate your children's educational needs. Update your will, medical insurance, and life insurance policies to include your children and, at some point, to exclude your former spouse, if so desired.

6. Exes' Continuing Relationship. Discuss potential phone arrangements, personal meeting times, and family events that do or do not include your children.

Modify the rules to fit your situation. Be optimistic as you agree to set aside your animosities for the sake of your own health and protection of your family.

Operating Instructions for a Good Divorce

CS parties have had practice in being separated and are most amenable to negotiating a divorce fairly. Divorce need not be a do-or-die process. The following nine standards of excellence serve to benefit all in shaping a good divorce:

1. Be convinced your decision to divorce is not a choice made impulsively.

2. Agree to dignify your divorce and to be civil, courteous, and respectful to each other.

3. Recognize the benefits of being objective, keep your emotions in check, and be reasonable in negotiating your divorce stipulations.

4. Accept responsibility for yourself. Refuse to be dragged into stale conflicts that won't go away. Stay cool and let your adversarial spouse shadowbox alone.

5. Agree to keep your children out of your marital conflicts. Do not use your youngsters as "political footballs" or as "go-betweens."

6. Keep your communication straightforward and honest.

7. Agree to be advocates on a limited basis to assist one another in emergencies.

8. Accept mediation if negotiations break down.

9. Acknowledge that one or both parties may remarry, that the complexities of blended family kinships cannot be avoided, but that interfamily relationships are handled far better as friends than as enemies.

A good divorce is in reach if you are willing to bend, if you acknowledge your part in the breakup, and if you are determined to minimize the drama and maximize the advantages in store as you rebuild your life.

At this juncture, there is an oasis close by for weary travelers to get off the bus, stretch, and compare notes with friends. As our journey draws to a conclusion, our last stop will be the Land of New Beginnings, where you will learn about my unique structure for a good marriage. Let's meet Gail and Neil, who made some fascinating discoveries about love, invested intimacy, and peer relationships.

20

$\mathcal{T}$he Good Marriage

The Tale of Gail and Neil:
The Lost-Somewhere Couple

Gail, 44, separated from Neil after 24 years. In the early years of marriage she had tried to get close to her husband, but he was often unreachable—reserved and preoccupied. In time, Gail stopped trying, and the pair drifted along, disengaged, with little to say to each other.

Now the couple were empty nesters with two married children. Gail had enjoyed motherhood, neither wanting nor needing to work outside the home. Neil, 48, was the high-powered provider, a successful executive married to his career.

After their younger daughter's wedding, Gail saw no point in continuing to live in Costa Rica with her husband. "I just gravitated to separation. I rarely saw Neil. He was traveling so much on business, and we'd grown so distant." He was blasé when she mentioned separation and supported purchasing a condominium in Wisconsin, knowing Gail was itching to get back to her hometown in the United States. Neil wished her well, and Gail was excited about making a fresh start.

After she resettled in Wisconsin, Neil continued to live in Costa Rica. He rarely phoned and she didn't care.

Second Thoughts

With no anticipation of a reconciliation, Gail had been savoring her four-month transitional separation. Then she had a most disturbing conversation with Neil. His innuendos were so vague and hard to interpret, she was caught off balance, not knowing what he meant. Totally bewildered, she phoned me for an appointment to get her own thinking straightened out.

Was Neil trying in an offhanded way to suggest she come home, or was he just shooting the breeze because he was lonely? The suspense was getting to her. She was losing sleep the more Neil continued to phone off and on, making small talk.

Our weekly sessions centered on Gail's dilemma: her newfound independence and Neil's newfound interest in her. Her voice rose with conviction. "I like living alone . . . I separated to start a new life. This is my time to find out about me. I've connected with old friends, and I'm meeting a lot of new people . . . joined some groups . . . it's fun."

Confusion mounted. Gail had intended to divorce her husband—eventually—but she hadn't seen an attorney, whereas Neil made an appointment with a divorce lawyer but threw his wife a curve when he intimated the two should get together soon.

Gail was in an awkward position. Apologetically, she said, "I thought Neil ought to know I've been dating, so I told him. I don't know if he's seeing anyone . . . maybe his secretary. I would never ask and he would never say; that's just how he is . . . closemouthed."

The couple was betwixt and between, with both mates not knowing where they stood with one another. Meanwhile Gail was getting busier. Besides her casual dating, she was taking two classes in interior design and found time to volunteer for a battered women's group. There was no stopping her drive to rebuild her life.

A few weeks later Gail came in looking pale and more fatigued than usual. "Everything between Neil and me is so up in the air. I'm scared to go stick my neck out like this. He wants to see me. I can't see him ever changing. He's always been so remote. I've got a life here, and now I'm expected to deal with this!"

She resented Neil's intrusion. She looked at me blankly, waiting for me to say something and then impatiently asked, "What do you think I should do?"

CS Introduced

Gail was pulled in two directions at once. Did she want to see Neil, and if she did, under what terms or circumstances? Did she want to put her newly found freedom in jeopardy? She couldn't even think about love—that was too far-fetched. She said, "Just thinking about reconciliation is driving me crazy."

What better time to introduce the CS? Under the proscribed conditions of the CS Guidelines, the couple could meet on neutral territory—if Neil was willing to participate. Gail didn't need a hard sell. She phoned her husband the same day, and within a month he arranged to come to the States.

CS: The First Month

I could not have predicted Gail and Neil would make such a dynamic team. In a sudden burst of energy, the couple agreed to stay apart another six months and not consider divorce in order to give their marriage a fair chance.

As for dating others, Gail indicated she wanted to continue to go out with her boyfriends. Quite naturally, looking directly at me and not at his wife, Neil said, "I've had a couple of dates with my secretary recently. She's got her eye out for me . . . wasn't sure if I wanted this to get serious, but with Gail sort of out of the picture . . . well . . ." His dangling sentence said it all.

Gail said nothing more, and it was settled that both mates were free to date others if they pleased.

Neil said he would be able to return for another meeting shortly. With this much settled, the couple's transitional separation shifted to an experimental CS.

School for Marriage

Six weeks later, at our second meeting, Neil and Gail became intensely involved, as if they were attending a school for marriage. We talked about my ideas on the structure of a good marriage, something I had been working on for many years, and I showed them my illustration of teammates.

Gail laughed, "Your drawing looks like a house with a roof—guess that's good in case it rains."

Figure 20.1. The Structure of a Good Marriage

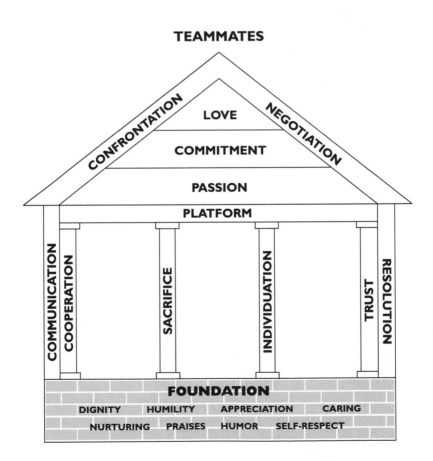

In a more serious vein, Neil said, "I can see you mean teammates can't be 'iffy' about love, commitment, and passion if they expect to build a solid relationship."

Having broken the ice, we talked about a good marriage being a solid and enduring structure—a durable team partnership. "At the apex we see two people coming together as teammates of equal importance. They see themselves as being on the *same team*, working together as advocates. When spouses act as if they are on two *different teams*, they start behaving like adversaries."

I paused for a moment, and Gail said, "I like that you put love, commitment, and passion right at the top. That makes sense to me."

I said, "Yes, this is where the energy and motivation come from. I call this the *platform*. After all, without these ingredients, what do you have in a marriage?"

Neil interjected, "Those four posts or pillars look intriguing. How do you balance them so you get a stable relationship going?"

I explained, "The pillars—cooperation, sacrifice, individuation, and trust—represent the fundamental supports for the platform. In any close relationship these elements are present and in flux. Most importantly, couples are constantly being challenged to put these four pillars to the test.

"It is for this reason that I say *a good relationship thrives on lots of groping, groaning, and growing. It prospers with lots of perspiration and inspiration.* Now let's see what I mean by that by examining more closely each of the pillars.

"*Cooperation* is the comfortable mutuality, the give-and-take between partners that makes living together so inviting and welcomes invested intimacy. You work in concert and you achieve harmony and good will.

"Without cooperation, there is no joy. If your spouse is found wanting and does less than you expect, then whatever you do or give is a chore. And what do you have to show for your efforts? In essence you feel incredibly abandoned—as if he or she is not there for you—and it eats at you. Isolated and lonely, you cry your eyes out.

"*Sacrifice* refers to your special acts of goodness that go beyond the anticipated daily give-and-take. You rise to the occasion and stretch yourself in times of crucial need or crisis, expecting to receive the appreciation you feel is your due. When your spouse recognizes your benevolent efforts with thanks, you are satisfied.

"However, should your altruistic deeds go unappreciated, you are tempted to ask, 'How am I being repaid for my sacrifice?' If no gratitude or reward is forthcoming, then you are immensely disappointed.

"There is a danger in sacrifice, particularly if you overextend yourself on your mate's behalf when it isn't necessarily warranted or requested. When you do not receive the payment you assume is your due, you feel like the angry victim—the nurturing martyr. This is a losing game the nurturing martyr plays for which recompense is in short supply.

"*Individuation* is what each spouse does to enhance his or her personal growth. This could mean your career, schooling, community action, volunteer service, or however you are called to express yourself creatively—the arts, music, dance, or engaging in extracurricular activities with your children.

"If acts of individuation stimulate and enhance your couple interactions, your partnership thrives. If you go so far afield that your drive for individuation is undertaken at the expense of the partnership, your relationship rests on shaky ground."

At this point I reached for Kahlil Gibran's book *The Prophet* and turned to one of my favorite passages on marriage:

> Give your hearts, but not unto each other's keeping.
> For only the hand of Life can contain your hearts.
> And stand together yet not too near together:
> For the pillars of the temple stand apart,
> And the oak tree and the cypress grow not in each other's shadow.[1]

Then I returned to my lecturing:

"*Trust* means partners can count on one another to be responsible, credible, and reliable. You are honest, you mean what you say, and you do what you say. Trust means you own up to your goofs and apologize.

"Game playing, manipulations, lies, and deceit are fodder for mistrust. Any time you have a shred of suspicion about your partner's behavior, or your own behavior is suspect, paranoia takes over and infiltrates your relationship, and there can be no trust.

"With any semblance of betrayal, how can there ever be trust without forgiving your mate's wrongdoings? A grudging sort of acceptance of transgressions won't do either.

"The matter of trust is a tricky one. You can be fooled into trusting when you shouldn't and be suspicious when it is not justified. As you are loyal, give of yourself, and cherish one another; as you are open to learning from each other, you bring to your relationship a good reason to trust."

About Compassion

Gail asked about compassion. "Compassion is a quality that remains obscure if you are lacking in empathy. If you are unwilling to look at your relationship as involving two people, both of whom are imperfect, if you are unwilling to acknowledge your own flaws but focus only on the faults of your mate, then you fritter away the good; and elusive intimacy is the most you can expect."

About Conflict

Directing the couple's attention to my illustration, I explained, "The bricks represent the tough outer mantle of a good marriage. This is the grievous part. To be realistic, you must expect conflict in any close relationship—you can't get away from it. And if you try to ignore your clashes, you compound your troubles.

"This is the bottom line: Without effective *communication, confrontation, negotiation, and resolution*, there's no chance of getting closure on your conflicts." Gail and Neil sent meaningful glances to one another, as if I had touched on a sensitive nerve.

Going back to my illustration, I continued. "We've already talked about the importance of honesty. Now let's get to the foundation of a good marriage. The way I see it, you season your coupling with goodly doses of humility, dignity, self-respect, humor, appreciation, praise, lots of nurturing, and caring. A comfortable mix of these virtues makes for a solid, workable partnership for the rest of your lives."

Invested Intimacy

This second session was becoming an intensive workshop, which lasted over two hours. Neil wanted to hear more about invested intimacy.

"Invested intimacy is like an art form of the soul, starting with how well you love yourself. This sets the tone for all our interpersonal relationships. I like the way philosopher Thomas Moore, in his *Soul Mates: Honoring the Mysteries of Love and Relationship*, tells us that the better you know yourself, the better prepared you are to partake of the provocative richness of being closely connected to someone you love."[2]

Neil broke in, "Invested intimacy looks like a real challenge to me. I think of my parents—especially my father. As a kid I used to think he was lost in outer space. I never remember my parents being close . . . never saw them enjoy being alone together. I think I've been afraid of intimacy for a long time."

I went on, "In truth, we reflect one another's goodness or badness, though we might not be aware of it. We can pull one another down, just as we can lift each other's spirits. This intricate weaving of togetherness is another way of finding out more about ourselves. But if we get so wrapped up in our personal struggles that all we see is the dark side of our marriage, we are unable to envision the possibility of invested intimacy. Instead we are lost in the shadows of our coupling."

Neil had a discerning insight: "You mean if Gail is trying to be nice to me and I'm not responsive or act as if I'm not involved, I'm really pushing her away, and I'm not even knowing I do it."

"Exactly. You've got to be alert to the little nuances of invested intimacy, which sometimes are nothing more than fleeting moments."

With that I grabbed Moore's book, *Soul Mates*, and turned to a page I had marked in preparation for writing this book and read, "Every relationship . . . is an entanglement of souls. The gift in this entanglement is not only intimacy between persons, but also a revelation of soul itself, along with the invitation to enter more deeply into its mysteries."[3]

Setting down the book, I said, "The mystery is that invested intimacy is a balancing act, a give-and-take, ever in flux. Many people are afraid of this challenge because it feels so risky—like you don't want to get burned."

Gail had a thought: "I remember my mother saying you must say please and thank you and show your appreciation when people are good to you. Maybe Neil and I haven't done that. Maybe we don't compliment or try to build one another up. These niceties have been missing. I know how much I like to hear I've done a good job—even if it's just baking a cake."

And Neil added, "Yeah—like I eat her brownies on the run and never say a word."

A Change of Pace

As our school for marriage drew to a close, Gail suddenly looked perturbed. I asked her what was troubling her, and she said, "I'm in no rush to do anything." Though she didn't mention the word *reconciliation*, I knew what she meant. It was clear she needed a lot more reassurance than our conversations would permit.

Neil, sensitive to Gail's reservations, decided on the spot to put their relationship to the test. In his most engaging way, he said, "Gail, what if we took a three-week vacation to the Caribbean and tried out the things we've been talking about today?"

An offer like that Gail could scarcely refuse. Her eyes were moist with tears as she spoke. "We're sure to find out something this way."

The session ended with my saying, "If the two of you ever expect to make it together, you've got to get out of the twilight zone and grab those precious moments when intimacy is awaiting and make your marriage a true partnership."

False Assumptions About Marriage

Categorically, marriage is an institution, an entity unto itself. Although transitions and change come swiftly, it appears that in today's fast-moving world, the pendulum has swung too far.

In my estimation, couples today enter marriage with several false assumptions:

1. "I deserve to have it all and I want it right now." Certainly, young adults today expect to have a lot more material goodies than their parents had at the same early stage in their marriage.

2. Newly marrieds expect the honeymoon to last forever.

3. The notion that marriage is hard work is offensive to a lot of people.

4. Should the conflicted spouses stumble into the lion's den and get their armor and shields dented out of shape, why not get out and find someone else, perhaps again and again? In sociological circles this is called "serial monogamy."

I believe the disruptive consequences of marital breakups will go unabated as long as couples have no comprehension of or instruction on how to resolve their differences.

Many couples will continue to be lost well into the twenty-first century if they haven't grasped the concept of team partnership—two mates working in tandem to raise the flag and staunchly preserve the state of the marital union. When no firm commitment to this premise is forthcoming and with no particular interest in personal and interpersonal growth and transformation, what other option is there but to cry and run away?

The Traditional Marriage

In the "traditional" marriage, loyalty is revered above friendship and sweeping the conflicts under the rug is more crucial than investing in the kind of intimacy that would draw the couple into a more endearing friendship.

When I was growing up the traditional marriage was the only standard that was uniformly found acceptable. Male and female roles were proscribed. Until World War II, very few married women were employed outside the home. The husband was thought to be a man of stature because he was the provider who supported his wife and children. The woman was esteemed because she tended the home, nurtured the children, made the social arrangements, and kept the abode running smoothly. Her value was often belittled and her work demeaned as being "less than" the work of the wage earner.

Essentially, such a competitive hierarchy is based on the man being at the top, as the master of the house, and the woman being one step—or several steps—below. The man makes all the important decisions, or so it is made to appear. I heard one man brag, "I'm the king of our house, and my wife loves it that way." I've often wondered what she thought about that.

Peer Marriage: A Partnership of Equals

Peer marriage is an outgrowth of the new age of those baby boomers who insist on dispelling the old traditional gender roles and constraints. These couples endorse and strive to achieve the philosophy of couple advocacy and invested intimacy. Pepper Schwartz, Ph.D., in *Love Between Equals: How Peer Marriage Really Works* describes the integral aspects of equality in peer marriage—tenets that I affirm.[4]

- Both parties are responsible as experts in how to maintain the partnership.

- The identity of each party is appreciated for simply being, neither to be fused nor solely dependent on the other. Couple collaboration builds a stronger foundation.

- Mutual parenting is prescribed and is not the sole province of the woman.

- Peer couples are less secretive and emotionally defensive; they take pride in strengthening their negotiating skills.

- These mates expect equal participation in conversation-related decision making.

In other words, you can make yours a strong and lasting coupling if you are committed to equity, which embraces a deep and abiding friendship.

Five-to-One Ratio of Good Moments to Bad

After 20 years of research with 2,000 married couples, John Gottman, author of *Why Marriages Succeed or Fail . . . and How You Can Make Yours Last*, brings us exciting news. He has observed that if couples want a good marriage, there must be a "balance of positive and negative interactions between partners" that adheres to "a five-to-one ratio" of positive to negative moments: "A certain degree of negativity is crucial to a marriage. Without it surely a marriage will deteriorate over time. But when the negativity level gets too high, the marriage inevitably suffers."[5]

Gottman sees partners as thriving on a little negativity and a lot of positivity. He reports that his formula is reliable, whether yours is a *compatible, volatile, or imperturbable* relationship. I concur with Gottman that a limited degree of "dysfunction" or conflict does not destroy the marital union. In fact, discreet types of fighting styles can be the very dynamic that energizes the marital enterprise and stirs the creative juices of invested intimacy.

Gail's Resolve

Although Gail and Neil's marriage had been a traditional one, when Gail left she cast aside thoughts of ever returning to that encumbered kind of relationship. Liking her independence and living alone, she was cautious, truly apprehensive, of ever being trapped in an "absentee marriage," where her husband's career took precedence over the growth and enhancement of each partner and the relationship.

Gail was determined to stand her ground and needed the CS safety net to make certain Neil understood her position as being equal in stature and worth to any man.

CS: Couple Transformation in Process

Neil was quick to admit to Gail that he had been negligent. It wasn't just his crucial role as family provider that had weakened the marital ties, but it was also his long-standing fear of rejection that had seriously crippled their coupling.

In the third and last session, Neil said, "I never realized how much I pulled away just to avoid being hurt."

Gail also admitted why she had turned her attentions away from her husband. She said, "I've got to know I'm wanted and cared for on a daily basis, or what's the use of trying to make things work out?" And so the mates saw how they both had let a personal invest-ment in their union slip through their fingers.

By the time the couple had returned from their holiday, they had fallen in love all over again. Gail said, "Neil has changed so much in the last two months. When we were on vacation, he even began to ask for my opinion about some personnel problems he's responsible for at the plant. Whatever I told him hit the bull's-eye, and now he calls me his 'business consultant.' "

Smiling, Neil said, "Yes, I tell Gail she's my 'secret weapon.' You know I do believe I'm getting more comfortable with this invested intimacy stuff."

The couple nodded approvingly at one another as Gail said, "I never thought six months ago I'd be living in Costa Rica again."

Gone were their doubts. Two months later I received the fol-lowing Christmas greeting from Gail:

"Neil and I just wanted to let you know how much we appreciate all that you helped us accomplish. Without our CS, we would not be celebrating this wonderful season together. We are healthy and happy, and our marriage is better than it has been in a lot of years!"

Follow-Up: More Good News

The timing of my follow up call two years later was serendipitous I found Gail and Neil closing their Wisconsin home in preparation for moving to the West Coast. Neil was being transferred—his company had arranged for him to get his master's degree in aerodynamics.

Gail spoke enthusiastically about their CS. "The important thing is, it made us see that we had to leave the past behind us and move on from there . . . we are definitely happy. Our whole out-look on life is so different now."

Neil chuckled. "As for the CS, it was the congruence, a coming together of different events. Your helping us to be objective. . . . I woke up realizing here is a problem of intimacy I can't handle myself, and that had never happened to me before."

As for his marriage, Neil said, "It's going swimmingly for Gail and me. I can hardly imagine there was a life back there that existed that isn't there anymore."

Epilogue

As THIS BOOK draws to a close, let's say we have taken a heroic journey together. Perhaps in the beginning you felt trepidation not knowing what to expect, but you persevered with the eagerness to discover something new that might pull your marriage out of the doldrums and excite you, even tantalize you. Isn't that why we visit foreign lands—to take something back that will be of merit in the future?

At heart we are adventurers, seeking beyond the horizon of our shortsighted vision. We are challenged when we encounter possibilities that one second earlier we had not even conceptualized, much less had a chance to negate.

Before you go back to getting on with the business of living, I would ask you to return once more to the "wish list" presented at the beginning of Chapter 1. Look at where you were when your journey with me began. What were you thinking, feeling, and hoping for? What questions did you hope would be answered as we traveled together? Have you profited by identifying, reckoning with, and asking yourself the pressing questions that you hadn't dared ask before? And now, assess how far you have moved in the course of our journey.

As I look back at the first seedlings of this book—embryonic ideas and the earliest fragments of writings—I can see how far I have moved and how much I have learned in the production of this work. Nothing worthwhile is ever accomplished without determination, persistence, sweat, and tears. Call it hard work. But it is so worth the effort.

I hope you have been touched in body, mind, and soul in a way that leaves you more grounded, secure, and ultimately more decisive. Look at yourself and marvel at how you have changed.

In the final analysis, in respect to the "stay or go" question, what are we if we aren't all heart enlightened with a goodly sprinkling of practicality? May the answers you find give you peace of mind and the best to you in all your endeavors.

Author's Note

ALTHOUGH THIS book contains all the information you need to effect your own Controlled Separation agreement, you may wish to confer with a professional counselor or therapist as you struggle with the "stay or go" decision. You may ask friends, your family doctor, or your local clergy for the names of qualified professionals in your area; or you may want to contact one of the following organizations for a referral.

American Association for Marriage and
    Family Therapy (AAMFT)—Referral
1133 15th Street NW, Suite 300
Washington, DC 20005
Telephone: (202) 452-0109

Family Therapy Practice Academy (FTPA)
National Federation of Societies for
    Clinical Social Work (NFSCSW)
1200 Emerson Avenue
Teaneck, NJ 07666
Telephone: (201) 837-6342

The National Association of Social
    Work (NASW)
Clinical Register
750 First Street, NE, Suite 700
Washington, DC 20002-4241
Telephone: (202) 408-8600

Lee Raffel is available for consultation, lectures, and seminars. She can be reached at her website: www.leeraffel.com

Chapter Notes

Preface

1. Donald K. Granvold, "Structured Separation for Marital Treatment and Decision-Making," *Journal of Marital and Family Therapy* 9, no. 4 (1983): 403.

2. Marjorie Kawin Toomin, "Structured Separation for Couples in Conflict," *Family Process* 11 (1972): 299–310.

3. Bernard L. Greene, Ronald R. Lee, and Noel Lustig, "Transient Structured Distance as a Maneuver in Marital Therapy," *The Family Coordinator* 22, no. 1 (January 1973): 15–22.

4. Donald K. Granvold and Roxanne Tarrant, "Structured Marital Separation as a Marital Treatment Method," *Journal of Marital and Family Therapy* 9, no. 2 (1983): 189–97.

5. Granvold, "Structured Separation," 403–11.

6. Richard B. Stuart, *Helping Couples Change: A Social Learning Approach to Marital Therapy* (New York: Guilford Press, 1980), pp. 179–82.

7. David G. Rice, Ph.D., and Joy K. Rice, *Living Through Divorce: A Developmental Approach to Divorce Therapy* (New York: Guilford Press, 1986), pp. 155–58.

Chapter 1

1. U.S. National Center for Health Statistics, "Vital Statistics of the United States," Annual Report 1996–1997. Statistics are updated in "Monthly Vital Statistics Report" of the National Center for Health Statistics, a division of the Centers for Disease Control and Prevention.

Chapter 2

1. Diane Vaughan, *Uncoupling: How Relationships Come Apart* (New York: Vintage Books, Division of Random House, 1986), p. 188.

Chapter 4

1. Eric Berne, M.D., *What Do You Say After You Say Hello?* (Beverly Hills, CA: Grove Press, 1972), pp. 22–23.

2. Pepper Schwartz, Ph.D., *Love Between Equals: How Peer Marriage Really Works* (New York: The Free Press, 1994), p. 30.
3. Patricia Evans, *The Verbally Abusive Relationship: How to Recognize It and How to Respond* (Holbrook, MA: Bob Adams Publishers, 1992), p. 35.

Chapter 5

1. Augustus Y. Napier and Carl A. Whitaker, *The Family Crucible* (New York: Harper & Row, 1978), p. 225.

Chapter 6

1. Frank Fincham, Ph.D., "Relationship Problems: What Works?" *Psychological Health: Newsletter for the National Academy of Psychotherapy* 1, no. 1 (winter 1996): 4.
2. Hans Selye, *The Stress of Life* (New York: McGraw-Hill, 1976), pp. 171–78.
3. Jocelyn Olivier, "Stress and Somatic Solutions," *AHP Perspective* (November/December/January 1997–1998): 24.
4. Redford Williams, M.D., and Virginia Williams, Ph.D., *Anger Kills* (New York: HarperPerennial, 1994), pp. xii–xiv. The hardcover version was published in 1993.
5. T. H. Holmes and R. H. Rahe, "The Social Readjustment Rating Scale," *Journal of Psychosomatic Research* 11 (1967): 213–18.
6. Emily M. Brown, *Patterns of Infidelity and Their Treatment* (New York: Brunner/Mazel, 1991), p. 13.
7. Diane Vaughan, *Uncoupling: How Relationships Come Apart* (New York: Vintage Books, Division of Random House, 1986), pp. 186–209.

Chapter 7

1. Constance R. Ahrons, Ph.D., *The Good Divorce: Keeping Your Family Together When Your Marriage Comes Apart* (New York: HarperCollins, 1994), p. 109.
2. State Bar of Wisconsin, *Answering Your Legal Questions About Divorce* (pamphlet), 1993.

Chapter 8

1. Robert S. Weiss, *Marital Separation: Coping with the End of a Marriage and the Transition to Being Single Again* (New York: Basic Books, 1975), p. 11.
2. Ibid., pp. 39–40.

Chapter 9

1. M. B. Isaacs, B. Montalvo, and D. Abelsohn, *The Difficult Divorce* (New York: Basic Books, 1986), p. 7.

2. Andrew M. Greely, *Faithful Attraction: Discovering Intimacy, Love and Fidelity in American Marriage* (New York: A Tor Book, Tom Doherty Associates, 1991), p. 55.

3. Lynn Gigy and Joan B. Kelly, "Reasons for Divorce: Perspectives of Divorcing Women and Men," *Journal of Divorce and Remarriage* 18, no. 1/2 (1992): 169–87.

4. Miriam Arond and Samuel L. Pauker, M.D., *The First Year of Marriage: What to Expect, What to Accept, and What You Can Change for a Lasting Marriage* (New York: Warner Books, 1987), p. 215.

Chapter 10

1. Richard N. Mack, "Spouse Abuse—A Didactic Approach," in *Treating Couples: The Intersystem Model of the Marriage Council of Philadelphia*, ed. Gerald R. Weeks, Ph.D. (New York: Brunner/Mazel, 1989), pp. 191, 194.

2. Melody Beattie, *Codependent No More: How to Stop Controlling Others and Start Caring for Yourself* (New York: Harper & Row, 1987), pp. 33–34.

3. Michael Groetsch, *He Promised He'd Stop: Helping Women Find Safe Passage from Abusive Relationships* (Brookfield, WI: CPI Press, 1997), p. 130.

4. U.S. Bureau of Justice Special Report, "Violence Against Women: Estimates from the Redesigned Survey," August 1995.

5. Michael Paymar, *Violent No More* (Alameda, CA: Hunter House, 1993), p. 1.

6. U.S. Bureau of Justice statistics, "Selected Findings: Violence Between Intimates (NCT-149259)," November 1994, p. 1.

7. Barbara Hart, "Remarks to the Task Force on Child Abuse and Neglect," April 1992.

8. FBI Report, "Federal Bureau of Investigations, Crime in the United States: 1994," 1995, p. 17.

9. Patricia Evans, *The Verbally Abusive Relationship: How to Recognize It and How to Respond* (Holbrook, MA: Bob Adams Publishers, 1992), p. 131.

Chapter 11

1. "A Matter of Time: Risk and Opportunity in the Nonschool Hours" (Waldorf, MD: Carnegie Council on Adolescent Development).

2. Etienne Krug, Centers for Disease Control and Prevention study, February 1997.

3. Erik H. Erikson, *Childhood and Society*, 2d ed. (New York: W. W. Norton & Company, 1963), p. 95.

4. Craig Everett and Sandra Volgy Everett, *Healthy Divorce for Parents*

and Children: An Original, Clinically Proven Program for Working Through the Fourteen Stages of Separation, Divorce, and Remarriage (San Francisco: Jossey-Bass, 1994), pp. 51–55.

Chapter 13

1. Miriam Arond and Samuel L. Pauker, M.D., *The First Year of Marriage* (New York: Warner Books, 1987), p. 254.
2. Shirley P. Glass and Thomas L. Wright, Ph.D. "Clinical Implications of Research on Extramarital Involvement," in *Treatment of Sexual Problems in Individual and Couples Therapy*, ed. Robert A. Brown, Ph.D., and Joan Roberts Field, Ph.D. (New York: PMA Publishing, 1988), p. 301.
3. Annette Lawson, *Adultery: An Analysis of Love and Betrayal* (New York: Basic Books, 1988), p. 78.
4. Shirley P. Glass, Ph.D., and Thomas L. Wright, Ph.D., "Justifications for Extramarital Relationships: The Association Between Attitudes, Behaviors, and Gender," *The Journal of Sex Research* 29, no. 3 (August 1992): 361.
5. John Amodeo, Ph.D., *Love and Betrayal: Broken Trust in Intimate Relationships* (New York: Ballantine Books, 1994), p. 19.
6. Constance R. Ahrons, Ph.D., *The Good Divorce: Keeping Your Family Together When Your Marriage Comes Apart* (New York: HarperCollins, 1994), p. 101.
7. Emily M. Brown, *Patterns of Infidelity and Their Treatment* (New York: Brunner/Mazel, 1991), p. 19.

Chapter 14

1. Edward P. Monte, Ph.D., "The Relationship Life-Cycle," in *Treating Couples: The Intersystem Model of the Marriage Council of Philadelphia*, ed. Gerald R. Weeks, Ph.D. (New York: Brunner/Mazel, 1989), p. 302.
2. Ibid., pp. 287–316.

Chapter 15

1. Maureen Murdock, *The Heroine's Journey* (Boston and London: Shambhala Publications, 1990), pp. 87–88.
2. Terry Hunt, Ed.D., Karen Paine-Gernee, and Larry Rothstein, *Secrets to Tell, Secrets to Keep* (New York: Warner Books, 1994), p. 253.

Chapter 16

1. George R. Bach and Ronald M. Deutsch, *Stop! You're Driving Me Crazy* (New York: G. P. Putnam's Sons, 1980), pp. 272–73.

2. William J. Lederer and Don D. Jackson, M.D., *The Mirages of Marriage* (New York: W. W. Norton & Company, 1968), pp. 98–99.

Chapter 17

1. Jean Houston, *The Search for the Beloved: Journeys in Sacred Psychology* (Los Angeles and New York: Jeremy P. Tarcher, 1987), pp. 114–15.
2. Lewis B. Smedes, *Forgive and Forget: Healing the Hurts We Don't Deserve* (New York: Pocket Books, Division of Simon & Schuster, 1984), pp. 182–84.
3. Ibid., p. 184.

Chapter 18

1. Lee B. Raffel, M.S.W., "Active Waiting: Learning the Art of Patience," *Journal of Family Life* 4, no. 2 (1998): 49–50.

Chapter 19

1. Lois Gold, M.S.W., *Between Love and Hate: A Guide to Civilized Divorce* (New York: Plenum Press, 1992), p. 9.
2. U.S. National Center for Health Statistics, "Vital Statistics of the United States," Annual Report 1996–1997. Statistics are updated in "Monthly Vital Statistics Report" of the National Center for Health Statistics, a division of the Centers for Disease Control and Prevention.
3. Barry Paris, *Audrey Hepburn* (New York: G. P. Putnam's Sons, 1996), p. 47.
4. Michelle Weiner-Davis, *Divorce Busting* (New York: Summit Books, 1992), p. 230.
5. Constance R. Ahrons, Ph.D., *The Good Divorce: Keeping Your Family Together When Your Marriage Comes Apart* (New York: HarperCollins, 1994), pp. 1–2.
6. Gold, *Between Love and Hate*, pp. 247–77.
7. Jay Folberg and Ann Milne, eds., *Divorce Mediation: Theory and Practice* (New York and London: Guilford Press, 1988), p. 19.

Chapter 20

1. Kahlil Gibran, *The Prophet* (New York: Alfred A. Knopf, 1923), p. 16.
2. Thomas Moore, *Soul Mates: Honoring the Mysteries of Love and Relationship* (New York: HarperPerennial, 1994), p. 259.
3. Ibid.
4. Pepper Schwartz, Ph.D., *Love Between Equals: How Peer Marriage Really Works* (New York: The Free Press, 1994), pp. 183–84.
5. John Gottman, Ph.D., *Why Marriages Succeed or Fail . . . and How You Can Make Yours Last* (New York: Simon & Schuster, 1994), p. 230.

$\mathcal{S}$elected Bibliography

Ahrons, Constance R., Ph.D. *The Good Divorce: Keeping Your Family Together When Your Marriage Comes Apart.* New York: HarperCollins, 1994.

Arond, Miriam, and Samuel L. Pauker, M.D. *The First Year of Marriage: What to Expect, What to Accept, and What You Can Change for a Lasting Marriage.* New York: Warner Books, 1987.

Bach, George R., and Ronald M. Deutsch. *Stop! You're Driving Me Crazy.* New York: G. P. Putnam's Sons, 1980.

Beattie, Melody. *Codependent No More: How to Stop Controlling Others and Start Caring for Yourself.* New York: Harper & Row, 1987.

Berne, Eric, M.D. *What Do You Say After You Say Hello?* Beverly Hills, CA: Grove Press, 1972.

Erikson, Erik H. *Childhood and Society.* 2d ed. New York: W. W. Norton & Company, 1963.

Evans, Patricia. *The Verbally Abusive Relationship: How to Recognize It and How to Respond.* Holbrook, MA: Bob Adams Publishers, 1992.

Everett, Craig, and Sandra Volgy Everett. *Healthy Divorce.* San Francisco: Jossey-Bass, 1994.

Fincham, Frank, Ph.D. "Relationship Problems: What Works?" *Psychological Health: Newsletter for the National Academy of Psychotherapy* 1, no. 1 (winter 1996): 4.

Folberg, Jay, and Ann Milne, eds. *Divorce Mediation: Theory and Practice.* New York and London: Guilford Press, 1988.

Gibran, Kahlil. *The Prophet.* New York: Alfred A. Knopf, 1923.

Glass, Shirley P., and Thomas L. Wright, Ph.D. "Clinical Implications of Research on Extramarital Involvement." In *Treatment of Sexual Problems in Individual and Couples Therapy.* Edited by Robert A. Brown, Ph.D., and Joan Roberts Field, Ph.D. New York: PMA Publishing, 1988.

Glass, Shirley P., Ph.D., and Thomas L. Wright, Ph.D. "Justifications for Extramarital Relationships: The Association Between Attitudes, Behaviors, and Gender." *The Journal of Sex Research* 29, no. 3 (August 1992): 361.

Gold, Lois, M.S.W. *Between Love and Hate: A Guide to Civilized Divorce.* New York: Plenum Press, 1992.

Gottman, John, Ph.D. *Why Marriages Succeed or Fail . . . and How You Can Make Yours Last.* New York: Simon & Schuster, 1994.

Granvold, Donald K. "Structured Separation for Marital Treatment and Decision-Making." *Journal of Marital and Family Therapy* 9, no. 4 (1983): 403–11.

Granvold, Donald K., and Roxanne Tarrant. "Structured Marital Separation as a Marital Treatment Method." *Journal of Marital and Family Therapy* 9, no. 2 (1983): 181–98.

Greene, Bernard L., Ronald R. Lee, and Noel Lustig. "Transient Structured Distance as a Maneuver in Marital Therapy." *The Family Coordinator* 22, no. 1 (January 1973): 15–22.

Groetsch, Michael. *He Promised He'd Stop: Helping Women Find Safe Passage from Abusive Relationships.* Brookfield, WI: CPI Press, 1997.

Holmes, T. H., and R. H. Rahe. "The Social Readjustment Rating Scale." *Journal of Psychosomatic Research* 11 (1967): 213–18.

Houston, Jean. *The Search for the Beloved: Journeys in Sacred Psychology.* Los Angeles and New York: Jeremy P. Tarcher, 1987.

Hunt, Terry, Ed.D., Karen Paine-Gernee, and Larry Rothstein. *Secrets to Tell, Secrets to Keep.* New York: Warner Books, 1994.

Isaacs, M. B., B. Montalvo, and D. Abelsohn. *The Difficult Divorce.* New York: Basic Books, 1986.

Lawson, Annette. *Adultery: An Analysis of Love and Betrayal.* New York: Basic Books, 1988.

Lederer, William J., and Don D. Jackson, Ph.D. *The Mirages of Marriage.* New York: W. W. Norton & Company, 1968.

Mack, Richard N. "Spouse Abuse—A Didactic Approach." In *Treating Couples: The Intersystem Model of the Marriage Council of Philadelphia.* Edited by Gerald R. Weeks, Ph.D. New York: Brunner/Mazel, 1989.

Monte, Edward P., Ph.D. "The Relationship Life-Cycle." In *Treating Couples: The Intersystem Model of the Marriage Council of Philadelphia.* Edited by Gerald R. Weeks, Ph.D. New York: Brunner/Mazel, 1989.

Moore, Thomas. *Soul Mates: Honoring the Mysteries of Love and Relationship*. New York: HarperPerennial, 1994.

Murdock, Maureen. *The Heroine's Journey*. Boston and London: Shambhala Publications, 1990.

Olivier, Jocelyn. "Stress and Somatic Solutions." *AHP Perspective* (November/December/January 1997–1998).

Oursler, Will. *The Healing Power of Faith*. Glendale, CA: Westwood Publishing, 1989.

Paymar, Michael. *Violent No More*. Alameda, CA: Hunter House, 1993.

Rice, David G., Ph.D., and Joy K. Rice. *Living Through Divorce: A Developmental Approach to Divorce Therapy*. New York: Guilford Press, 1986.

Schwartz, Pepper, Ph.D. *Love Between Equals: How Peer Marriage Really Works*. New York: The Free Press, 1994.

Selye, Hans. *Stress Without Distress*. Philadelphia: J. B. Lippincott, 1974.

Smedes, Lewis B. *Forgive and Forget: Healing the Hurts We Don't Deserve*. New York: Pocket Books, Division of Simon & Schuster, 1984.

Stuart, Richard B. *Helping Couples Change: A Social Learning Approach to Marital Therapy*. New York: Guilford Press, 1980.

Toomin, Marjorie Kawin. "Structured Separation for Couples in Counseling: A Therapeutic Approach for Couples in Conflict." *Family Process* 11 (1972): 299–310.

Vaughan, Diane. *Uncoupling: How Relationships Come Apart*. New York: Vintage Books, Division of Random House, 1986.

Wallerstein, Judith, and Sandra Blakeslee. *The Good Marriage: How and Why Love Lasts*. Boston: Houghton Mifflin, 1994.

Weiner-Davis, Michelle. *Divorce Busting*. New York: Summit Books, 1992.

Weiss, Robert S. *Marital Separation: Coping with the End of a Marriage and the Transition to Being Single Again*. New York: Basic Books, 1975.

Williams, Redford, M.D., and Virginia Williams, Ph.D. *Anger Kills*. New York: HarperPerennial, 1993.

Recommended Readings

Marriage

Amodeo, John, Ph.D. *Love and Betrayal: Broken Trust in Intimate Relationships.* New York: Ballantine Books, 1994.

Arond, Miriam, and Samuel L. Pauker, M.D. *The First Year of Marriage: What to Expect, What to Accept, and What You Can Change for a Lasting Marriage.* New York: Warner Books, 1987.

Bach, George R., and Ronald M. Deutsch. *Stop! You're Driving Me Crazy.* New York: G. P. Putnam's Sons, 1980.

Bader, Ellyn, Ph.D., and Peter T. Pearson, Ph.D. *In Quest of the Mythical Mate.* New York: Brunner/Mazel, 1988.

Beattie, Melody. *Codependent No More: How to Stop Controlling Others and Start Caring for Yourself.* New York: Harper & Row, 1987.

Berne, Eric, M.D. *What Do You Say After You Say Hello?* Beverly Hills, CA: Grove Press, 1972.

Brown, Emily M. *Patterns of Infidelity and Their Treatment.* New York: Brunner/Mazel, 1991.

Carter, Steven, and Julia Sokol. *Lives Without Balance.* New York: Villard Books, 1992.

Evans, Patricia. *The Verbally Abusive Relationship: How to Recognize It and How to Respond.* Holbrook, MA: Bob Adams Publishers, 1992.

Gottman, John, Ph.D. *Why Marriages Succeed or Fail . . . and How You Can Make Yours Last.* New York: Simon & Schuster, 1994.

Hendrix, Harville, Ph.D. *Getting the Love You Want: A Guide for Couples.* New York: HarperPerennial, 1990.

Hudson, Patricia O'Hanlon, and William Hudson O'Hanlon. *Rewriting Love Stories.* New York: W. W. Norton & Company, 1991.

Keyes, Ken, Jr. *The Power of Unconditional Love: 21 Guidelines for Beginning, Improving, and Changing Your Most Meaningful Relationships.* Coos Bay, OR: Love Line Books, 1990.

Kirshenbaum, M. *Too Good to Leave, Too Bad to Stay.* New York: Dutton, 1996.

Lederer, William J., and Don D. Jackson, Ph.D. *The Mirages of Marriage.* New York: W. W. Norton & Company, 1968.

Medved, Diane. *The Case Against Divorce.* New York: Donald I. Fine, 1989.

Moore, Thomas. *Soul Mates: Honoring the Mysteries of Love and Relationship.* New York: HarperPerennial, 1994.

O'Hanlon, William. *Love Is a Verb.* New York: W. W. Norton & Company, 1995.

Schwartz, Pepper, Ph.D. *Love Between Equals: How Peer Marriage Really Works.* New York: The Free Press, 1994.

Sheehy, Gail. *Passages.* New York: Dutton, 1974.

Wallerstein, Judith, and Sandra Blakeslee. *The Good Marriage: How and Why Love Lasts.* Boston: Houghton Mifflin, 1994.

Weiner-Davis, Michelle. *Divorce Busting.* New York: Summit Books, 1992.

Williams, Redford, M.D., and Virginia Williams, Ph.D. *Anger Kills.* New York: HarperPerennial, 1993.

Divorce

Ahrons, Constance R., Ph.D. *The Good Divorce: Keeping Your Family Together When Your Marriage Comes Apart.* New York: HarperCollins, 1994.

Amodeo, John, Ph.D. *Love and Betrayal: Broken Trust in Intimate Relationships.* New York: Ballantine Books, 1994.

Belli, Melvin, and Mel Krantzler. *Divorcing.* New York: St. Martin's Press, 1988.

Bennett, M. *Sudden Endings: Wife Rejection in Happy Marriages.* New York: William Morrow & Company, 1991.

Everett, Craig, and Sandra Volgy Everett. *Healthy Divorce for Parents and Children: An Original, Clinically Proven Program for Working Through the 14 Stages of Separation, Divorce, and Remarriage.* San Francisco: Jossey-Bass, 1994.

Fassel, Diane. *Growing Up Divorced: A Road to Healing for Adult Children of Divorce*. New York: Simon & Schuster, 1991.

Gardner, Richard. *The Boys and Girls Book About Divorce*. New York: Bantam Books, 1970.

Gardner, Richard. *The Parents Book About Divorce*. New York: Bantam Books, 1979.

Gold, Lois, M.S.W. *Between Love and Hate: A Guide to Civilized Divorce*. New York: Plenum Press, 1992.

Grollman, Earl. *Talking About Divorce and Separation*. Boston: Beacon Press, 1975.

LeShan, Eda. *What's Going to Happen to Me? When Parents Separate or Divorce*. New York: Aladdin Books, 1986.

Milne, Ann, and Jay Folberg. *Divorce Mediation*. New York: Guilford Press, 1988.

Ricci, Isolina. *Mom's House, Dad's House: Making Shared Custody Work*. New York: Macmillan, 1981.

Vaughan, Diane. *Uncoupling: How Relationships Come Apart*. New York: Vintage Books, Division of Random House, 1986.

Wallerstein, Judith, and Sandra Blakeslee. *Second Chances: Men, Women, and Children a Decade After Divorce*. New York: Ticknor & Fields, 1989.

Weiss, Robert S. *Marital Separation: Coping with the End of a Marriage and the Transition to Being Single Again*. New York: Basic Books, 1975.

Index